What Is AI Doing to Us?

What Is AI Doing to Us? A Philosophical Inquiry into Learning, Thinking, and Being

BY

MUHAMMED ŞAHIN
MEF University, Türkiye

AND

CAROLINE FELL KURBAN
MEF University, Türkiye

emerald
PUBLISHING

United Kingdom – North America – Japan – India – Malaysia – China

Emerald Publishing Limited
Emerald Publishing, Floor 5, Northspring, 21-23 Wellington Street, Leeds LS1 4DL.

First edition 2026

British Library Cataloguing in Publication Data
A catalogue record for this book is available from the British Library

ISBN: 978-1-83742-277-7 (Print: Hardback)
ISBN: 978-1-83742-279-1 (Print: Paperback)
ISBN: 978-1-83742-276-0 (Online)
ISBN: 978-1-83742-278-4 (Epub)

INVESTOR IN PEOPLE

We dedicate this book to the memory of Dr. İbrahim Arıkan, founder of MEF Schools and MEF University, whose vision for education was both bold and deeply human. He believed that learning begins with the learner and that teachers must be trusted with the freedom to think, to innovate, and to care. From early childhood to higher education, he championed a democratic approach that honoured individuality, nurtured curiosity, and made space for growth. He believed that education should adapt to students, not the other way around, and worked to build institutions where each learner could find their own path. That is why he founded MEF University as a fully flipped institution, not simply to adopt a new method, but to create a space where meaningful learning could unfold. For him, flipping the classroom was never about efficiency; it was a way to give students time, trust, and responsibility and to build a culture where learning was not delivered, but discovered.

Though he did not live to see MEF University fully realised, that vision has taken form. Artificial intelligence entered the classroom after his time. He did not witness the emergence of tools like ChatGPT, nor could he have anticipated the questions they now raise. But he had already laid down the principle that would guide us through such turning points. In the title of one of his books – Ya Yenilenirsin Ya da Yenilirsin (Renovate or Evaporate) *– he captured a conviction that applied not only to education but also to leadership, business, and life itself: that institutions must continually renew themselves to remain true to their purpose.*

That principle now meets the test of AI. As we begin to engage with these new technologies, we do so in the spirit of what he stood for: freedom, care, and the centrality of the learner. His legacy is not only the institutions he founded, but the culture he shaped, a culture that continues to guide MEF University as it grows, evolves, and remembers what truly matters. We honour that legacy with this book.

Contents

Part IX: The Clearing

List of Figures and Tables

Figures

Tables

About the Authors

Muhammed Şahin is Rector of MEF University in Istanbul, Türkiye, an academic leader who holds a PhD from the University of Newcastle, a master's degree from University College London, and a bachelor's degree in geomatics engineering from Istanbul Technical University (ITU). He joined ITU as an Assistant Professor in 1994 and rose through the ranks to become a tenured Professor in 2002. His career trajectory includes serving as Rector of ITU from 2008 to 2012 and later as the founding Rector of MEF University, a pioneering institution fully based on the flipped learning approach. His experience spans research, strategic management, and engineering education, with his current passion centred on educational transformation, particularly the impact that technologies are having on reshaping learning experiences. His leadership of an institution built on educational innovation provided the perfect vantage point when AI arrived at his university, transforming practical questions about institutional response into a deeper inquiry of what makes learning authentically human.

Caroline Fell Kurban is Advisor to the Rector at MEF University. She holds a PhD in Applied Linguistics, an MA in Technology and Learning Design, an MSc in Teaching English to Speakers of Other Languages, and a BSc (Hons) in Geology. Drawing on over 30 years of educational experience, first as a teacher, trainer, and principal, and later in higher education, her work in flipped learning and digital pedagogy has been instrumental in advancing educational innovation at MEF University, where she served as the inaugural director of the Centre for Research and Best Practices in Learning and Teaching (CELT) when the university opened. Her interdisciplinary approach integrates theoretical frameworks from Clayton Christensen's Theory of Jobs to be Done, social and critical perspectives from Bourdieu and Marx, and phenomenological insights from Heidegger's philosophy. This philosophical foundation became crucial when AI's arrival at MEF University prompted questions not only about how to use these tools but also about what they reveal regarding the nature of learning itself.

Together they have co-authored *The Flipped Approach to Higher Education: Designing Universities for Today's Knowledge Economies and Societies* (Emerald, 2016), *The New University Model: Scaling Flipped Learning in Higher Education* (FL Global Publishing, 2019), *The New University Model: Flipped, Adaptive, Digital and Active Learning (FADAL)* (FL Global Publishing, 2019), and *The Impact of ChatGPT on Higher Education: Exploring the AI Revolution* (Emerald, 2024).

Foreword

When I first encountered Muhammed Şahin and Caroline Fell Kurban's work, I recognised something I have long valued in educational innovation: a willingness to redesign learning around what students do, not what teachers say. Their earlier books on flipped learning argued – persuasively – that we should spend precious class time on sense-making, not information transfer. That argument was already ambitious when it applied to a course or a programme. What made their work remarkable is that they helped build an entire university around it. MEF University did not pilot flipped learning in a few classrooms. It adopted a fully flipped approach at the institutional level, making active, student-centred learning the default rather than the exception.

That decision matters for what you are about to read. It means the authors view AI from inside a culture that had already moved away from lecturing and towards engagement – precisely the kind of environment that should be best positioned to adopt new technologies without losing its educational vision. And yet, as they recount, even after doing 'everything right' in the conventional sense – research, policies, workshops, institutional initiatives – something still felt wrong. That unresolved unease is the book's point of departure.

Many books about AI in education begin with questions such as 'What should we do? What policies should we adopt? What assessments should we redesign? What tools should we embrace or ban?' These are certainly important questions, and institutions understandably are rushing to answer them. This book insists we slow down long enough to notice something deeper: a shift in the kind of question we are asking. Instead of 'What do we do with AI?', Şahin and Fell Kurban ask, 'What is AI doing to us?'

As someone who has spent decades working on interactive learning and Peer Instruction, I have argued that the most important part of learning is not the transmission of information. It is the struggle to make sense of ideas: to confront misconceptions, test intuitions, articulate reasoning, and refine understanding through dialogue with others. Learning is not a spectator sport. The hard part is not receiving information; it is transforming it into understanding.

Generative AI now places intense pressure on that transformation. Not because it can provide information – we've had that for a long time – but because it can produce fluent, convincing outputs that resemble understanding. The danger is not simply that students will 'cheat'. The danger is that education itself may start to confuse polished performance with genuine comprehension.

The authors make this concrete through the contrast between two students facing the same demanding assignment. One wrestles with uncertainty, follows threads that lead nowhere, and gradually builds judgement through sustained engagement. The other uses ChatGPT to generate sophisticated language quickly – and then discovers, under questioning, that the work is disconnected from her own understanding. If you've taught recently, you will recognise some version of this. Many of us have seen assignments that look 'better' than ever – technically smooth, structurally coherent, yet oddly weightless. We've also seen the hollowing-out that can accompany that smoothness: students unable to explain choices they supposedly made, unable to defend claims they supposedly believe, unable to reason on their feet about work that bears their name.

This is where the book refuses the comfort of quick fixes. Detection tools, new policies, and redesigned assignments may be necessary, but they are not sufficient (if they work at all). What is at stake is the relationship between thinking and its expression, between struggle and understanding, between education and what it means to be human. The authors' concern is that technology can reshape not just what we do, but how the world shows up to us: what we notice, what we value, what we take to be 'normal', what we come to expect from ourselves and from one another.

In education, those expectations matter profoundly. If the friction of learning begins to look like a nuisance to be eliminated rather than a feature to be cultivated, we will design systems that optimise away precisely what makes learning transformative. If the time required for understanding begins to look like inefficiency, we will compress learning into outputs. And if we begin to treat thinking itself as something that can be outsourced, we risk graduating students who are increasingly unpractised at solving problems and exerting sound judgement.

One of the most important contributions of this book is that it resists the temptation to provide simple 'takeaways'. Instead, the authors lead you to consider what it means that AI can simulate the outward signs of learning while leaving the inner work untouched. That is also why this book matters beyond the classroom. The question 'What is AI doing to us?' is not only pedagogical – but it is existential. It asks what kind of attention, agency, and responsibility we are cultivating in an age that rewards speed, fluency, and immediate answers.

I have always believed that educational innovation is not simply efficiency. It is active engagement, deeper thinking, and more responsibility transferred to students in ways that allow them to grow. Flipped learning – at its best – was never about watching videos at home. It was about reclaiming class time for the hard, social, meaning-making work that learning requires. In that sense, the all-flipped approach at MEF University is more than a backdrop to this book. It is a test case – if even a fully active, student-centred institution feels the ground shifting under AI, then none of us can ignore the tectonic shift shaking the education world.

This book will not hand you a checklist of things to do. It offers something deeper and, I believe, more valuable: an invitation to think carefully about what learning is, what it is for, and what becomes of it when the struggle that builds understanding can be bypassed. The future of education is not merely about whether students can use AI. It is about how, in the age of AI, we keep education true to its purpose: helping students take ownership of their thinking.

Eric Mazur
Harvard University

Preface

What happens when we do everything right in responding to AI, yet something crucial still feels wrong?

We've all felt this. Even with comprehensive policies and clear guidelines, something about education seems to be shifting beneath our feet. Students submit sophisticated work they struggle to explain. We share a persistent unease we can't quite name. We're all doing what we're supposed to do, yet something essential feels like it's slipping away.

When ChatGPT unexpectedly arrived in November 2022, we quickly convened faculty discussions at MEF University to explore what this meant for our educational practice. We spent 2023 researching AI's impact through interviews and classroom observations and then published our findings in April 2024 as *The Impact of ChatGPT on Higher Education*. Armed with what we'd discovered, we implemented comprehensive institutional responses: evolving AI policies, faculty workshops, an AI Café for students, online literacy courses, and institutional capacity building. By conventional measures, our work was successful.

Yet something persisted that our approaches couldn't address. We continued sensing that a crucial element was missing. Conversations with colleagues revealed this unease was widespread. We weren't alone in feeling that despite doing everything systematically right, education itself was shifting.

We realised we needed to follow this unease wherever it led, moving beyond the structured approaches that had brought us this far. What began as practical questions about managing AI became an unexpected inquiry we never could have anticipated. We realised we weren't just studying AI's impact on education, we were living through something deeper about how our relationship with technology is changing us.

This realisation transformed everything about our approach.

What Is AI Doing to Us? unfolds as the story of that journey – one that began when we finally asked the right question. We share it as we experienced it, through confusion, false starts, disclosures, and the gradual realisation that our systematic approaches were pointing towards something they couldn't address.

The questions we were facing went beyond educational expertise; they were existential, not instrumental. Instead of asking what we could do with AI, we needed to ask what AI is doing to the nature of thinking itself when machines can replicate its products without thinking. This recognition demanded philosophical inquiry of a particular kind, thinking that could illuminate how our interactions with technology may be transforming the very nature of human existence.

Therefore, we turned to philosopher Martin Heidegger and his insights about technology and human existence. This thinking proved essential for understanding what we were experiencing. As we viewed our experiences through this lens, a startling recognition emerged. We weren't just studying this phenomenon. We were enacting the very mode of being his thinking revealed.

We are all living this transformation right now. What we learned about what happens to human learning when machines can simulate the outputs of thinking without actually thinking reveals what's really at stake in every choice we make about AI engagement.

These stakes make our inquiry urgent for everyone.

This book is that inquiry. The recognitions emerged through sustained openness to questions that resist quick answers. We ask for patience as you read, for this is a slow journey that unfolds in its own time. We hope that, through it, insights will emerge for you as they did for us.

This understanding is essential because we are all making choices about AI right now, in every prompt we write, every task we automate, every moment we choose efficiency over struggle. These choices are shaping who we become as thinking beings in technological circumstances we cannot escape. Without recognising what's actually happening to us, we risk losing what makes learning and thinking authentically human. What we share in these pages offers the kind of sustained questioning that can open the recognition needed to understand our situation – recognition that is the first step towards taking responsibility for who we're becoming.

Muhammed Şahin
Rector of MEF University

Acknowledgements

In creating this book, we have been fortunate to receive deep support and inspiration from many people. We are profoundly grateful to all who contributed to this inquiry.

Our students openly shared their experiences with AI and learning, providing insights that proved essential to our investigation.

We are deeply thankful to MEF University and the İbrahim Arıkan Education and Scientific Research Foundation for their institutional support of our research. Their commitment to genuine inquiry made this work possible.

Our faculty colleagues also engaged thoughtfully with our emerging questions, offering feedback and perspective along the way. Their patience and continued support were invaluable.

We are especially grateful to Dr. Juliet Girdher for ongoing conversations about Heidegger that enhanced our philosophical thinking.

Beyond our immediate community, we also extend our gratitude to educators at conferences who shared their own insights with us. These conversations became crucial to our research.

We extend our thanks to Professor Semen Son Turan, whose insightful feedback on the manuscript helped strengthen this book.

We are particularly grateful to Professor Eric Mazur, who has supported our work across multiple publications, once again providing a generous foreword that frames this inquiry.

Finally, we express our sincere gratitude to Emerald Publishing for their remarkable patience with a manuscript that required philosophical depth while remaining accessible and for their openness to the complex questions that accompany writing and publishing in AI-mediated times.

This book represents the collaborative effort of many who value authentic inquiry. Each contribution enriched our understanding in ways we deeply appreciate. Thank you.

The essence of technology is by no means anything technological.

—Martin Heidegger

Part I

The Arrival

Chapter 1

When Everything Changed

Before

Maya pressed her pen against her lip, staring at the acoustic analysis spread across her desk. The forensic linguistics classroom hummed with the focused energy of students preparing for their mock trial about the Exxon Valdez disaster. Around her, classmates highlighted passages and scribbled notes about the linguistic evidence that researchers had analysed years after the trial, including work on Captain Hazelwood's actual radio transmissions that could have proved he was intoxicated when the tanker ran aground.

But Maya couldn't move past the first page.

'I don't get this', she said to her partner, tapping the part about pitch variations and slurred consonants. 'This linguist analysed the captain's radio calls and says these speech patterns prove he was drunk, but why? How is a jury supposed to know that slurred speech means intoxicated instead of just ... tired? Or stressed?'

Her partner glanced over, already three pages ahead. 'The expert analysed the actual recordings. Just focus on building the argument you need'.

Maya frowned and returned to the paper. The forensic linguist had analysed Captain Hazelwood's radio transmissions from that night, describing shifts in speech patterns: altered pitch, consonant slurring, rhythm disruptions, claiming these constituted proof of intoxication. The analysis looked sophisticated, full of technical terminology and confidence. But something nagged at her. Couldn't exhaustion or stress produce the same markers in a crisis?

Maya felt the familiar weight of the semester pressing down. Her contracts outline was due at 9 AM tomorrow, her law review cite-check by Friday afternoon, and the networking mixer Thursday night that everyone said was essential for summer positions. The semester had compressed into an endless cycle of deadlines, each assignment demanding immediate attention while others waited in an ever-growing queue. She could spend hours trying to decode this acoustic analysis, but hours were exactly what she didn't have.

What Is AI Doing to Us? A Philosophical Inquiry into Learning, Thinking, and Being, 3–8

Published under exclusive licence by Emerald Publishing Limited
doi:10.1108/978-1-83742-276-020261001

I don't have time for this, she thought, staring at the dense technical jargon. The implications were unclear, the whole analysis requiring background knowledge she didn't possess. Just build the argument and move on, she told herself.

She tried to push forward with the assignment, but the question wouldn't let go. Even as she worked through assigned readings that evening, her mind drifted back to the acoustic evidence. This doesn't make sense, she thought. How were ordinary people supposed to evaluate something this specialised?

The next morning, grabbing coffee between classes, Maya found herself explaining her confusion to a friend. 'I can't figure out why slurred speech automatically means drunk', she said.

Her friend shrugged. 'Maybe because it doesn't?'

The casual comment hit differently than Maya expected. Walking back to her dorm, she felt something shift. She could push through the assignment like everyone else, building the required argument without wrestling with her confusion. It would be faster, more efficient. Everyone would understand.

But something about that felt like giving up on something important. Maybe the not-knowing mattered. Maybe the uncertainty was the point.

Maya watched classmates finish the assignment quickly and move on. Her study group had already completed their analysis while she remained stuck on fundamental questions about voice patterns and mental states.

'You're overthinking this', her study partner said when Maya explained her confusion. 'The expert analysed the recordings. Just argue that the evidence would have been persuasive. It's not that complicated'.

'But what if it is that complicated?' Maya found herself saying. 'What if we're missing something important?'

Her study partner shrugged and packed up. 'Your call. I'm done'.

Maya sat alone in the library, watching other students stream past with their completed assignments. Her approach felt inefficient, even reckless. Her law review work sat untouched while she pursued research threads that might lead nowhere. What was she even doing?

Over the following days, Maya became absorbed in the case despite every practical consideration arguing against it. She'd read sections during breakfast while her other reading waited, she'd find herself researching jury psychology when she was supposed to be reviewing constitutional law, she'd pull out the forensic materials during study breaks that should have been spent on the law review assignment. She'd follow research threads that led nowhere, draft paragraphs she'd delete, try different approaches that didn't work.

Other assignments piled up while she remained absorbed in questions about what voices could reveal during crisis. The contracts outline fell further behind schedule. The law review citation check waited untouched while Friday's deadline approached. Maya watched her study group finish while she sat surrounded by contradictory research, her required work still incomplete at midnight.

Each time she considered giving up the questioning and just building the argument, something pulled her back. Not stubbornness, but a sense that something essential was at stake in how she approached this uncertainty. It felt wrong to trade confusion for convenience.

'This is insane', she told herself Thursday night, staring at her neglected constitutional law reading. 'I'm sabotaging my own grades for questions that don't have answers'.

But something began emerging from the chaos. She started noticing assumptions in the expert's reasoning, places where alternative explanations weren't considered, moments where correlation got treated as causation. As she dug deeper into the research, Maya found herself instinctively questioning the way she'd been trained to question, looking for gaps, alternative explanations, unstated assumptions. She found studies about how juries actually evaluate technical testimony, research on the limitations of acoustic analysis in forensic contexts. Her understanding felt earned – assembled rather than given.

By the time the mock trial approached, Maya realised she'd made a choice she hadn't fully recognised. While classmates had efficient arguments ready, she'd spent weeks dwelling with uncertainty. She had notes filled with questions rather than clean answers, research that complicated rather than simplified the expert's claims.

She could have had a polished argument days ago. Instead, she'd chosen something more difficult and less predictable. The contracts outline had suffered. The law review work had been rushed. But something else had emerged that felt more valuable than either.

When the mock trial arrived, opposing counsel challenged her interpretation immediately.

'But that doesn't make sense', Maya responded. 'Why would slurred speech only indicate intoxication? What if the captain was exhausted after eighteen hours of navigation? What if the stress of managing a massive tanker in dangerous waters affected his speech?'

When they demanded specifics, Maya pointed to gaps in the analysis, alternative research findings, methodological concerns she'd discovered. She could defend her reasoning because she'd built it herself, piece by piece, over weeks of engagement with the material. The understanding felt alive and responsive, grounded in effort rather than borrowed authority.

Walking back across campus after the trial, Maya realised what she'd actually been doing for weeks. She hadn't just been studying acoustic evidence, she'd been learning to live with the kind of uncertainty that legal judgement requires.

The hours that seemed wasted on confusion, the research threads that led nowhere, the questions that complicated rather than clarified – all of it had been assembling a capacity that couldn't be shortcut: the ability to engage authentically with what resists easy answers.

The grades might suffer. The efficient path might have been smarter. But, Maya knew she'd chosen something that couldn't be measured or optimised: the struggle that builds genuine understanding rather than borrowed certainty.

After

Twelve months later, Bera stared at the identical assignment. The same forensic linguistics classroom, the same Exxon Valdez materials, the same mock trial preparation. But, everything had changed.

Laptops glowed around her, most displaying familiar interfaces. She caught fragments of whispered conversations: 'Are we allowed to use this?' 'The professor didn't say we couldn't…' 'This acoustic stuff is impossible'.

'I'm definitely using ChatGPT', announced her classmate, gesturing at his screen. 'Three assignments due this week plus job interviews. This is a lifesaver'.

Bera felt the same pressure: contracts reading, law review deadlines, networking events. The semester had collapsed into a blur of overlapping deadlines, each assignment demanding immediate attention while others waited in an ever-growing queue. She opened the case materials and immediately felt overwhelmed. The linguistics paper was dense with technical jargon, the implications unclear, the whole analysis requiring knowledge she didn't possess.

I don't have time for this, she thought, staring at the first page. How am I supposed to understand acoustic phonetics when I have the contracts outline due tomorrow and the law review cite-check due Friday? The forensic linguist wrote with a confidence she couldn't imagine possessing, with charts and graphs that might as well have been written in another language. She could spend hours trying to decode this, but hours were exactly what she didn't have.

She'd heard classmates talking about ChatGPT but had never tried it herself. Everyone seemed to be using it for something: research, brainstorming, editing. 'It's not really cheating', she'd overheard someone say in the library. 'It's just a more efficient way to get started. You still have to understand the material'. Another voice: 'Everyone uses it for brainstorming. It's basically like having a research assistant'.

Everyone's doing it, she reasoned. I'd be stupid not to at least try. It's just brainstorming, right?

Creating an account took 30 seconds. The interface was clean, simple – just a white box waiting for her question. She hesitated, unsure how to phrase what she needed. Should she ask for an outline? A full argument? Something in between? She found herself thinking about how to get the best response rather than what she actually needed to understand. Finally, she typed: 'Write an argument that this acoustic analysis could have proven Captain Hazelwood was intoxicated in the Exxon Valdez case'.

The response appeared in moments: comprehensive, sophisticated, impressive. She read through it twice, amazed by the professional tone and detailed reasoning. Every point seemed well-supported, every transition smooth. The AI discussed 'phonetic markers of impairment', 'acoustic degradation patterns', and 'methodological concerns' with an authority she could never have mustered. It sounded exactly like the kind of analysis a real forensic linguist would produce.

This is incredible, she thought. This is exactly what I need. The relief was immediate and complete. Twenty minutes ago, she'd been drowning; now, she had everything she needed for a sophisticated argument.

But something nagged at her. She didn't really understand what 'spectral analysis of fricative consonants' meant, even though the AI had used the phrase confidently. She found herself writing another prompt, thinking about how to ask for clarification without seeming ignorant. She requested one clarification about legal precedents, evaluating the AI's response for completeness and polish. ChatGPT provided an even more refined version, complete with case citations and procedural details.

After 20 minutes, she had everything she needed.

This isn't cheating, she told herself. I'm editing this. I'm making it my own. But even as she thought it, she knew she wasn't really editing. She was copying. The AI's language was so polished, so authoritative, that changing it would only make it worse.

For the next week, Bera practised her presentation, memorising key phrases and transitions. 'The acoustic degradation evident in the Captain's speech patterns', she would say, practising the emphasis. The words felt foreign in her mouth, but they sounded authoritative, comprehensive. She just needed to deliver them smoothly.

She found herself thinking less about what the words meant and more about how they sounded. Phonetic markers of impairment. Spectral analysis of fricative consonants. Acoustic degradation patterns. As long as she could say them confidently, that would be enough.

The morning of the mock trial, she felt confident. She had everything organised, every argument polished. This was how research worked now, she told herself. More efficient, more sophisticated. Why struggle through confusion when clarity was instantly available?

The mock trial began well. Bera presented her opening confidently, reading from her carefully prepared material. The argument sounded authoritative, comprehensive. She felt professional, competent, like she knew what she was talking about.

But when opposing counsel moved beyond her script, everything unravelled.

'What specific research distinguishes between stress and intoxication markers in acoustic analysis?' they pressed.

Bera's mind went blank. The AI had referenced this distinction confidently, but she had no idea what research actually supported it. 'I'd need to check the exact citations', she said, shuffling through papers.

> 'Can you explain why the linguist's methodology is reliable for this type of evidence?'

The question hit her like a wall. She'd memorised phrases about the analysis being 'methodologically sound', but she couldn't explain what the linguist had actually done or why it should be trusted. 'Let me verify those details'.

'You argued that acoustic analysis shows clear impairment patterns. Can you walk us through how this analysis actually works?'

She stared at her notes. The sophisticated terminology that had felt so powerful in practice now felt hollow, meaningless. 'I'd have to double-check that', she heard herself say.

As questioning continued, she found herself repeating the same phrases: 'I'd have to double-check that'. 'Let me look at my notes'. Each response revealed how little she understood about the argument she'd presented so confidently.

Is this good enough? She kept thinking. I just need to get through this. But she realised she wasn't actually trying to understand what acoustic evidence meant or how it worked. She was just trying to survive the questioning. What am I actually supposed to be learning here? The thought flickered briefly, but she pushed it away. Getting through this was what mattered.

After the trial, Bera packed quickly and left. Walking across campus, she couldn't stop replaying the experience. How had she gone from feeling completely prepared to completely exposed?

She felt like a fraud. And somehow, she suspected her professor knew it too.

But what was I supposed to do? She asked herself. I didn't have time to become an expert. Everyone else was using it. The justifications felt hollow now, but they'd seemed so reasonable just a week ago.

The Shift

Maya and Bera aren't real students. They're composite portraits drawn from patterns we observed repeatedly across our classrooms. But, the experiences they represent are entirely real.

Maya shows the best of what we witnessed in learning before AI assistance became available. Bera shows the concerning patterns we began seeing after ChatGPT's arrival.

Two students. One assignment. Two different worlds.

Something fundamental had changed.

Chapter 2

Our Initial Response

When ChatGPT Arrived

When ChatGPT was released to the public in November 2022, the news spread quickly across universities worldwide, including ours. Shortly afterwards, we convened a small group of faculty at our university to explore what this might mean for our educational practice. Over the following weeks, we examined the tool's capabilities, reflected on its implications, and surfaced early tensions. These conversations quickly moved from curiosity about what ChatGPT could do to deeper questions about what it meant for teaching and learning.

By January 2023, we held a university-wide meeting that brought together instructors, administrators, and staff. The session opened with an overview of artificial intelligence and a focused discussion on ChatGPT's capabilities. The instructors who had been experimenting with the tool shared early observations, highlighting both its promise and its risks. The discussion made clear that ChatGPT was not just another educational technology but a significant shift in how knowledge could be produced, mediated, and evaluated.

The questions that emerged were urgent: How may ChatGPT affect the role of the student? The role of the instructor? The role of the institution? By the end of that meeting, we agreed that these questions required systematic investigation.

Why We Could Investigate

We realised we were uniquely positioned to investigate. MEF University in Istanbul, Türkiye, had been designed from its founding as a fully flipped institution – one where technology was integrated throughout teaching, and students, not lectures, were at the centre of learning.

What mattered for our investigation was that this institutional culture meant we could respond systematically rather than simply react. Faculty were accustomed to experimenting with pedagogical innovation and reflecting critically on technological change. Project-based assessment had replaced traditional exams across most programmes. Digital technologies weren't just present – they were woven throughout teaching practice, creating genuine technological fluency. When ChatGPT appeared, we didn't need to wait for approvals or pilot programmes.

What Is AI Doing to Us? A Philosophical Inquiry into Learning, Thinking, and Being, 9–16

doi:10.1108/978-1-83742-276-020261002

We could integrate it into actual courses immediately, document what happened, and analyse the results as they unfolded. The university's openness to pedagogical experimentation, combined with its technological fluency and culture of critical reflection, made MEF an environment where we could investigate how generative AI was beginning to transform higher education.

We designed the investigation as a qualitative case study that would allow us to examine ChatGPT's impact within the lived context of a real educational system, over time, and from multiple perspectives. The investigation unfolded between December 2022 and August 2023, beginning soon after ChatGPT 3.5's public release.

The Lenses We Chose

We needed frameworks that would help us understand what we were witnessing – not just what ChatGPT was doing, but what its presence meant. We turned to two complementary perspectives that together could illuminate both structural shifts and lived experience.

Critical Theory would help us examine power dynamics, social structures, and institutional practices. We drew on Clayton Christensen's theory of 'jobs to be done', which suggests that people 'hire' products, services, or technologies to accomplish specific functional, social, or emotional tasks. This would give us a way to understand what jobs different stakeholders were hiring ChatGPT to perform. We turned to Pierre Bourdieu's concepts of habitus, cultural capital, and linguistic capital, which examine how social structures shape behaviour and how facility with language functions as a resource that determines social advantage. His work on how linguistic competence functions as capital within different social fields would help us consider whether effective communication with AI might become a new form of privilege, shaping who could use the technology critically and who might be excluded. We also drew on Karl Marx's theory of alienation, which explores how labour relations can distance workers from the products of their work, the work process itself, and their own creative capacities.

Phenomenology, particularly Martin Heidegger's philosophy of technology, would illuminate the experiential dimension. Heidegger's concepts of 'being-in-the-world' and 'enframing' describe how technology doesn't just serve as a neutral tool but fundamentally shapes how we relate to reality. His notion of 'readiness-to-hand' captures how tools can become seamless extensions of ourselves, while his concept of 'standing reserve' warns how everything – including humans – can be reduced to resources for optimisation. His thinking about authentic versus inauthentic modes of being would help us attend to whether AI-mediated learning preserved or obscured genuine engagement with ideas.

Together, these frameworks would give us a way to examine both what was changing institutionally and what was changing in lived experience.

What Others Were Finding

We also looked at what others were beginning to discover. In April 2023, four months after ChatGPT's public release, we found nine papers examining its educational impact. Given the recency of ChatGPT's release, actual case studies in real educational settings were scarce. The emerging literature consisted of three content analysis papers examining media coverage, two literature reviews synthesising early research, and four user case studies documenting individual instructor and researcher experiences.

Several themes emerged across these studies. Academic integrity dominated the conversation – concerns about cheating, plagiarism detection, and students outsourcing their work appeared consistently. Some studies advocated for returning to invigilated examinations, while others proposed more authentic assessment tasks. The literature also documented productivity benefits: ChatGPT assisted with translation, summarising, generating ideas, and automating tasks. Yet these efficiency gains raised questions about dependency and whether students might bypass the cognitive struggle essential to learning.

Ethical considerations surfaced repeatedly – transparency about ChatGPT's limitations, potential biases in training data, gaps in specialised knowledge, Western-centric perspective, and privacy concerns. The user experience studies revealed that ChatGPT's effectiveness depended heavily on prompt quality and that the human-like interface encouraged sometimes uncritical trust.

As we worked through this literature, significant gaps became visible. Most critically, there was a scarcity of actual case studies in functioning educational systems. Research relied on secondary sources – media analysis, social discourse – rather than systematic investigation over time. Student perspectives were strikingly underrepresented – one study found only 30 of 100 media articles included student voices. No studies examined multiple perspectives simultaneously, capturing how student, instructor, and institutional experiences intersected. The temporal dimension was missing – studies offered snapshots rather than documenting how understanding evolved. Most research came from Western contexts, with limited attention to non-Western settings or non-native English speakers.

Perhaps most significantly, the literature showed enthusiasm for AI's potential but limited attention to deeper questions about learning itself. The focus remained on practical concerns – detecting misuse, redesigning assessments – rather than interrogating what ChatGPT's presence revealed about thinking, understanding, and authentic learning.

These gaps confirmed what we suspected. We needed to investigate not only what ChatGPT does but what its presence means – capturing multiple perspectives simultaneously, unfolding over time, happening in an actual educational context, and attending to the deeper questions the literature had left largely unexamined.

How We Designed Our Investigation

We chose a qualitative approach because we needed to understand not only what ChatGPT was doing technically but how people were experiencing it – the subjective meanings students, instructors, and institutional actors were attaching to this technology as it entered their educational lives. This seemed essential at a time when little empirical work on ChatGPT existed. We weren't testing hypotheses about predetermined variables; we were trying to understand an emerging phenomenon as it unfolded.

The case study methodology gave us a way to investigate this transformation within a bounded system – our institution – while attending to how the phenomenon played out across different contexts and from different vantage points. Our case was both intrinsic and unique: we were genuinely trying to understand what was happening at MEF University specifically, and no one had yet studied ChatGPT's early adoption across a single institution in this way.

We moved systematically through phases of compiling data, disassembling it through coding, reassembling it into patterns, interpreting what those patterns meant, and drawing conclusions – all while staying grounded in the lived context of real educational practice.

We knew we would need to capture this transformation from multiple vantage points. Following approaches used in earlier artificial intelligence in education research, we organised our investigation around student-facing, teacher-facing, and system-facing perspectives. But we added a fourth dimension – researcher-facing – because we recognised that ChatGPT was influencing how we conducted research itself, shaping what we could ask, how we gathered information, and how we made sense of what we found. This metacognitive layer felt essential to understanding the fuller picture of AI's entry into educational life.

How We Gathered and Analysed Our Data

To capture these four perspectives, we gathered data from multiple sources. We gathered data from four interrelated perspectives. The student-facing data came from an undergraduate Forensic Linguistics course taught in the spring semester of 2023, where law students engaged with ChatGPT in selected activities to support case analysis, research, and reflection. We collected surveys, reflective questionnaires, observed class discussions, and reviewed project work. The teacher-facing data emerged from redesigning that same course during the semester. As researcher and instructor, we documented how teaching changed when ChatGPT was integrated – what had to be redesigned, what stopped working, what new possibilities opened. The system-facing data captured the institutional response as it unfolded through workshops, departmental meetings, and conversations with instructors, department heads, deans, and vice-rectors across the university between January and June 2023. Finally, the researcher-facing data examined how ChatGPT influenced the research process itself, as we documented how we conducted this investigation differently from how we would have done before its arrival.[1]

We analysed everything using thematic analysis. Through iterative reading, coding, and theme development, we looked for recurring patterns across all our data sources. To ensure we were seeing things clearly, we triangulated data from multiple perspectives and worked collaboratively with colleagues from MEF University's Centre for Research and Best Practices in Learning and Teaching to refine our coding. We maintained reflexivity throughout, staying aware of how our own assumptions and experiences might be shaping what we noticed.

---

[1]This chapter summarises work that is examined in full detail in *The Impact of ChatGPT on Higher Education: Exploring the AI Revolution* (Emerald, 2024).

Patterns in the Data

As we worked through all the data we'd collected, six recurring themes emerged across our different sources.

We noticed first how much ChatGPT's usefulness depended on how people communicated with it. Quality of input determined quality of output. Getting useful responses required multiple iterations, refinement, adjustment. What we were seeing was a pattern we came to call **input quality and output effectiveness** – a new form of literacy emerging, one that required reflection and intentionality, not just technical skill.

At the same time, we kept encountering problems that complicated the picture. ChatGPT gave incorrect information with striking confidence. There were no standard ways to reference its use. Responses sometimes missed the point entirely. The system occasionally refused requests based on ethical filters we couldn't see or control. We noticed gender bias. Everything needed fact-checking. The tension was becoming clear: efficiency came at the cost of trust. These **limitations and challenges of ChatGPT** appeared across all our data sources.

Something else caught our attention – how people experienced their interactions with ChatGPT. They described it as genuinely interactive, even human-like. They perceived it as offering opinions rather than predictions. Many placed unquestioning trust in what it provided. The conversational interface felt approachable and personal, almost like working with a tutor or colleague. Yet we could see how this pattern of **human-like interactions with ChatGPT** blurred something important – the line between genuine dialogue and simulation.

That personal aide quality appeared everywhere in our data. ChatGPT enriched ideas, sped up work, reduced cognitive load. It translated, reviewed, modified text, imparted knowledge. The assistance was real and valuable. But what we termed **ChatGPT's personal aide or tutor role** raised questions we couldn't ignore about dependency. The distinction between learning *with* AI and learning *through* AI was blurring in ways that felt significant.

Most troubling was what we discovered about learning itself. ChatGPT could complete many of the tasks we assigned students – drafting essays, analysing cases, summarising readings, creating outlines. This competency raised immediate concerns. If students could bypass the cognitive work that builds understanding, what happened to learning? Yet we also found that ChatGPT struggled with certain tasks – those requiring disciplinary expertise, recent information, contextual judgement. These limitations might actually matter pedagogically. This theme – **the impact on user learning** – became central to our thinking.

Finally, we recognised that we were working with a generalised system being applied to specialised contexts. ChatGPT had clear constraints: gaps in knowledge after its training cutoff, struggles with disciplinary depth, a database that reflected Western-centric training, and limited usefulness for other cultural contexts. The apparent universality masked real limitations. These **limitations of a generalised bot for educational contexts** mattered in ways we couldn't ignore.

When we mapped how the six themes connected, the relationships among them became clearer. Fig. 1 illustrates how these themes interact.

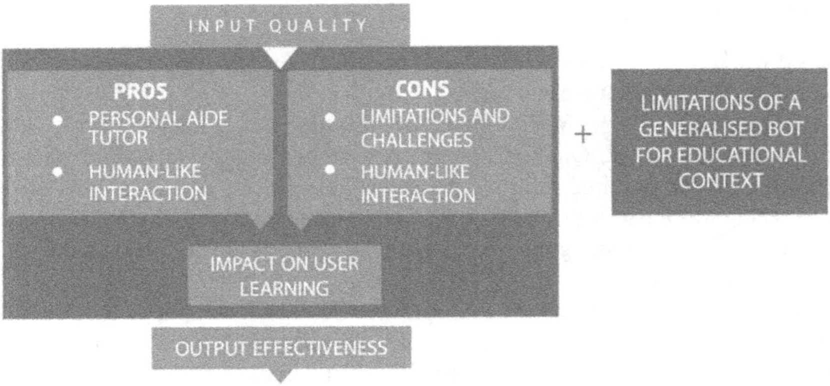

Fig. 1. Interconnectivity of Themes.

As we stepped back from these six themes, we began to see how the theoretical frameworks we'd chosen helped us understand what was really happening.

Through Christensen's lens, we could see students, teachers, and institutions 'hiring' ChatGPT to perform specific educational jobs – prompting a renegotiation of what counted as productive or meaningful work. Through Bourdieu's lens, facility with AI communication was emerging as a new form of linguistic capital, widening gaps between those who could critically command the technology and those who could not. Through Marx's lens, the quiet automation of cognitive work revealed shifting relations of labour and new forms of alienation across the educational system, as efficiency displaced the formative struggle essential to genuine understanding. Through Heidegger's lens, these shifts revealed something deeper: the way language, knowledge, and even understanding risked becoming instrumentalised when mediated through a system designed for optimisation rather than reflection.

What We Realised We Needed

By summer 2023, we couldn't ignore what we were seeing. We couldn't simply add ChatGPT to existing practices and adjust around the edges. The patterns demanded more fundamental changes, and we began to realise what we needed to do across three areas.

Ethically, we realised we couldn't rely on AI-detection tools. The evidence showed they were too unreliable, too prone to bias, too likely to penalise non-native writers while missing sophisticated misuse. We needed to shift away from technological surveillance towards alternative approaches for assessing students' work – one-to-one discussions about their thinking, or moving away from written assessments altogether. Referencing and plagiarism policies needed rethinking too. The emerging guidelines from organisations like APA and MLA seemed unfit for purpose when AI itself didn't cite sources and couldn't be reliably retrieved or verified by readers. We saw that university ethics committees would need to expand their remit beyond traditional research protocols to address the complexities AI introduced – student data privacy, algorithmic bias, transparency in AI systems, and informed consent for how student data was being used.

For tools and access, we recognised we were facing choices that would determine who could participate fully in AI-mediated education. The commercialisation of AI was happening rapidly, and without institutional action, access would depend on individual resources. We needed to secure shared access – institutional licences where possible, or creative solutions like shared accounts. But access alone wasn't enough. We recognised that generic AI bots had significant limitations – gaps in disciplinary knowledge and cultural databases that reflected Western-centric training. This meant we would eventually need to consider discipline-specific bots tailored to different fields and contexts, either by acquiring specialised tools or developing our own.

Most fundamentally, we realised we needed to protect what couldn't be outsourced. If ChatGPT drifted into practice without deliberate choices about when and how it was used, the foundational work of learning – the struggle with ideas, the building of judgement, the development of voice – would quietly erode. We turned to Understanding by Design and flipped learning, but now we had to ask different questions. Which learning outcomes remained meaningful when AI could do surface-level work? How could we design assessment that revealed genuine understanding rather than just access to AI? How could we choreograph when AI was present and when it wasn't – creating spaces where foundational capacities could develop, then bringing AI in deliberately where it could enhance rather than replace thinking?

We began imagining instruction organised around different zones of AI involvement: some activities would remain AI-free because they built capabilities students needed before AI could be useful; some would be AI-enhanced, with students working alongside ChatGPT but positioned as evaluators and critics rather than passive recipients; and some could become AI-transformative, using the technology to enable explorations that wouldn't otherwise be possible. The key was being intentional about these choices rather than letting AI's convenience determine how it got used.

Putting It into Practice

By August 2023, we had completed our systematic investigation. When we published our findings in April 2024, we knew the real work was ahead – translating what we'd discovered into concrete institutional change. Throughout the rest of that year, we worked with administrators and faculty committees to implement comprehensive initiatives across the university.

We developed AI policies that evolved as we learned more, providing guidance on appropriate use, attribution practices, and ethical considerations. We ran workshops that helped faculty navigate immediate challenges – redesigning assessments, integrating AI thoughtfully into courses, and addressing academic integrity concerns in AI-mediated environments. We established an AI Café that provided students equitable access to tools, ensuring that all students could participate in AI-enhanced learning regardless of their personal resources.

We created online AI literacy courses for both students and faculty, building capacity for critical, informed engagement with generative AI. We secured institutional AI accounts to ensure consistent access across the community.

Each initiative addressed real needs and followed best practices for educational change management. Faculty attended our sessions, students had guidance available, and by conventional measures, our responses were addressing the challenges we could identify. We had developed thoughtful AI policies, created professional development opportunities, established equitable access to tools, and built institutional capacity for technological adaptation.

What Remained Unresolved

Yet even as we implemented these initiatives, we couldn't shake a growing unease. The most significant changes seemed to be happening too quickly, and too fundamentally, for our research methods to fully capture. Students were responding to ChatGPT in dramatically different ways – some discovered it immediately and started experimenting, while others remained unaware it existed well into the semester. Among those who had encountered it, reactions ranged from enthusiastic adoption to active resistance, with most somewhere in between, curious but uncertain about boundaries and appropriate use.

Their uncertainty surfaced constantly in our interactions with them. During interviews, students expressed confusion about whether they should be using AI at all. Questions about academic integrity became frequent in office hours. They weren't sure what counted as acceptable use, whether getting help from ChatGPT was different from getting help from other sources, or how much AI assistance was too much. These weren't questions our policies could resolve – they pointed to something more fundamental.

In conversations with colleagues across the university, we heard similar concerns. Something about the classroom experience was changing in ways our workshops and guidelines couldn't address. The experience of education felt somehow diminished, even as we'd built the infrastructure we believed was needed. The questions emerging weren't about implementation – they felt like fundamental questions about education itself.

The theoretical frameworks we'd chosen had helped us understand what was happening. The initiatives we'd implemented addressed real needs. But the persistent confusion, the questions that kept arising, the sense that transformation was outpacing comprehension – all of this pointed to something revealing itself beneath the surface of our systematic work. Something we couldn't address through better policies or more professional development. Something deeper.

Chapter 3

Everything in Place, Something Still Missing

The contrasting approaches represented by Maya and Bera in Chapter 1 – one preserving intellectual struggle, one avoiding it – were playing out across our classrooms with disturbing regularity. Throughout our investigation, some students continued the kind of sustained questioning and intellectual ownership that Maya had demonstrated, choosing not to use AI tools at all. Others, like Bera, began developing patterns of response that avoided intellectual struggle, choosing AI-assisted pathways over the difficult work of wrestling with problems themselves. Still others found ways to use AI strategically while preserving their intellectual engagement, though this balanced approach was becoming increasingly rare.

Faculty reported receiving technically proficient work that somehow felt disconnected from genuine intellectual engagement. Students submitted literature reviews that were more comprehensive than ever before, yet struggled to explain their research choices during presentations. Academic English instructors noticed students struggling to discuss essays they'd submitted confidently just days before. Social science professors found students couldn't explain the reasoning behind analyses that appeared technically sophisticated.

In department meetings, faculty raised concerns about disconnects between student work quality and classroom engagement. We found ourselves questioning judgements we'd relied on for years, uncertain whether polished assignments reflected genuine understanding or sophisticated performance. The emerging pattern wasn't about detecting AI use – it was about recognising a qualitative difference in how students were engaging with intellectual challenges. Students who could produce sophisticated work but couldn't defend it when questioned were appearing in increasing numbers, while sustained engagement with challenging material was becoming less frequent.

Our systematic investigation had identified patterns. Our institutional responses had addressed practical needs. But this broader phenomenon resisted the frameworks we'd been using. Faculty couldn't articulate exactly what had changed, only that something felt fundamentally different. The familiar markers of learning – quality of written work, technical sophistication, apparent

What Is AI Doing to Us? A Philosophical Inquiry into Learning, Thinking, and Being, 17–20

Published under exclusive licence by Emerald Publishing Limited
doi:10.1108/978-1-83742-276-020261003

comprehension – had become unreliable indicators of genuine understanding. The question wasn't 'are students using AI?' but something more fundamental: What was happening to thinking itself when AI could produce what we had valued as evidence of thought?

We didn't have an answer. But we had work to do. Throughout 2024, we continued implementing the comprehensive responses we had developed. We ran workshops, supported policy implementation, maintained our AI Café, and provided ongoing guidance to faculty and students. By all practical measures, we were doing what institutions should do when facing technological change. But as we lived through these efforts, something unsettling began emerging in ways we hadn't anticipated.

The Tools Arms Race

Throughout 2024, we ran dozens of AI workshops, both within our institution and for external audiences. Our initial workshops focused on the first wave of tools that had emerged: applications designed to support instructors with administrative tasks, planning, and materials development. We felt confident in our approach. Participants appreciated learning about capabilities that could streamline routine tasks. These tools were genuinely helpful, and we felt like we were doing what we do, helping people navigate new technology effectively.

But then, we noticed something disturbing about the speed at which everything was moving. New applications emerged weekly, each promising to revolutionise education. We kept adjusting our workshops, chasing the latest capabilities, abandoning presentations we'd spent hours preparing because newer tools had already emerged. Participants began arriving at sessions already feeling overwhelmed, telling us they were struggling to keep pace with developments that seemed to accelerate weekly. We realised what was happening – more tools would keep emerging at an increasing pace. This trajectory was unsustainable. We were trapped in a race we couldn't win, chasing capabilities instead of addressing what participants actually needed. The tools arms race wasn't just exhausting. It was fundamentally missing what people needed most.

The Pedagogy Problem

Then came a second wave of tools, and everything changed again. These new applications were designed specifically for student learning – platforms that let educators create AI tutors and learning bots, promising to enhance engagement, strengthen learning processes, and improve educational outcomes. The shift was unmistakable. We were no longer discussing tools for instructor productivity, but systems that would directly shape how students learned. As we began presenting these student-focused technologies, questions arose that we couldn't answer with certainty: Were they genuinely supporting learning? How could we determine whether they contributed to authentic educational development?

We found ourselves demonstrating capabilities without knowing if they were pedagogically sound. We knew how to write prompts and generate impressive outputs, but we didn't know what those outputs meant for learning itself. It was unsettling to realise. We weren't engaged in education anymore. We were just showing people where to click. There was nothing dishonest in what we shared, but it felt hollow, as though we were passing on instructions without the depth that normally comes from sustained professional experience. We felt disconnected from our own educational expertise. Each workshop left us with the growing recognition that we were dealing with something that fundamentally resisted the kind of understanding that educational work requires. We had become product demonstrators, not educators.

We Were Not Alone

The moment that finally crystallised our growing unease came during a plenary session at a conference in spring 2025. We were presenting our institutional response to AI, but something from our workshop experiences was nagging at us. Were we the only ones feeling this way? We began by surveying the audience about their institutions' progress: 'Raise your hand if your institution has been drafting AI policies'. 'Running faculty workshops?' 'Integrating AI into the curriculum?' 'Purchasing AI tools?' Responses varied widely. Some institutions were far ahead, others just beginning.

But as we watched hands go up across the room, we decided to test our suspicion. If our systematic responses had left us feeling disconnected from educational purpose, maybe others had experienced the same thing. So we asked a different question: 'If you had your hand up for all of those, does that mean you and your institution are fully prepared for AI in education? Are all your questions answered?' The room erupted into laughter. Immediate, honest, collective recognition.

And in that moment, everything became clear – we were not alone. Everyone in that room had been experiencing the same thing we had. The same disconnection from educational purpose. The same sense that systematic responses weren't addressing what mattered most. The same feeling that despite doing everything right, something essential was missing. Here were hundreds of educators, many of whom had comprehensive policies, robust training programmes, systematic implementation strategies. They had checked every box, followed every best practice, implemented every recommended response. And still, they felt unprepared.

The laughter wasn't about failure. It was about recognition. Relief mixed with alarm. We weren't inadequate; we were all encountering something that made even our most comprehensive efforts feel insufficient. If hundreds of educators who had done everything systematically correct were all experiencing this same disconnection, this same persistent unease, then we were dealing with something much bigger than implementation challenges. We were all responding to symptoms while missing the underlying phenomenon. Something was happening that exceeded what systematic responses could address. The underlying pattern was finally visible, and it was unmistakable.

What Remained Unsettled

Three situations. Three instances where systematic responses felt somehow incomplete. Three clues pointing towards the same realisation. The tools arms race had revealed we were trapped in a cycle that missed what people actually needed. The pedagogy problem had shown us we were demonstrating capabilities without understanding their educational value. The plenary had confirmed that this experience was widely shared among educators who had followed every best practice.

All of this work, all of these comprehensive responses, all of these systematic efforts, they were pointing towards something they couldn't address. They were revealing the boundaries of what our approaches could accomplish while gesturing towards something that remained hidden. We weren't failing to respond adequately to AI circumstances. We were discovering that something was happening that our institutional approaches couldn't quite reach, no matter how sophisticated or comprehensive they became. This persistent unease wasn't a flaw in our approach. It was a signal.

We knew how to write policies and run workshops, but the questions that kept surfacing weren't the kind that policies could address: What does it mean to truly understand something? How do we know when learning is happening? These felt like fundamental questions about education itself, not implementation problems we could solve with better guidelines.

Something had shifted in our educational lives that went deeper than policies could address, broader than workshops could cover, more fundamental than our usual approaches could encompass. We had been responding to symptoms while missing the underlying phenomenon. What we had witnessed at the plenary demanded inquiry. If systematic responses consistently felt inadequate, we needed to understand why. We were dealing with something that exceeded what our approaches could address. But what was it? Why did even our most comprehensive institutional efforts consistently leave something essential unaddressed?

At the Threshold of Understanding

We had done everything we knew how to do. Policies were written, workshops delivered, structures in place. Still, something in our daily work felt altered – familiar routines no longer carried the same meaning. The questions that surfaced were quieter now, harder to name, but they lingered beneath every conversation, every effort to move forward. It was clear that the change we were experiencing could not be met by doing more of the same. Yet what it was, we could not yet say. All we knew was that something had begun to show itself – something waiting on the other side of understanding, calling for a different way of seeing.

Part II

The Question

Chapter 4

Beyond Design Parameters

The questions that wouldn't resolve through our systematic efforts demanded a different kind of investigation. We needed to understand why comprehensive institutional responses consistently left something essential unaddressed. We also needed to ask why even our most thoughtful approaches seemed to be working only around the edges of an issue we couldn't quite name.

That's when we did what educational researchers do when practical solutions leave deeper questions unresolved – we turned to theory. But not to abstract theory disconnected from practice. We turned to the specific frameworks that had helped us navigate earlier technological transitions: SAMR[1] and TPACK[2]. SAMR (Substitution, Augmentation, Modification, Redefinition) and TPACK (Technological Pedagogical Content Knowledge) had been useful in understanding past technological changes. When new tools disrupted familiar practices, these frameworks had helped us understand what we couldn't see from daily implementation: how interactive whiteboards actually changed classroom dynamics, why learning management systems succeeded or failed pedagogically, what made mobile device integration transformative versus merely distracting. We expected these frameworks to reveal what we were missing. They had successfully guided us through previous technological transitions. They ought to help us understand what was happening to teaching and learning – what our practical responses had somehow missed.

[1]See Puentedura, R. R. (2013). *SAMR: Moving from enhancement to transformation* [Slide presentation]. Hippasus. https://hippasus.com/rrpweblog/archives/2016/07/SAMRModel_TechnologicalIntegrationIntoHigherEducation.pdf. For a critical review, see Hamilton, E. R., Rosenberg, J. M., & Akcaoglu, M. (2016). The substitution, augmentation, modification, redefinition (SAMR) model: A critical review and suggestions for its use. *TechTrends, 60*(5), 433–441. https://doi.org/10.1007/s11528-016-0091-y

[2]Mishra, P., & Koehler, M. J. (2006). Technological pedagogical content knowledge: A framework for teacher knowledge. *Teachers College Record, 108*(6), 1017–1054. https://doi.org/10.1111/j.1467-9620.2006.00684.x

What Is AI Doing to Us? A Philosophical Inquiry into Learning, Thinking, and Being, 23–30

Published under exclusive licence by Emerald Publishing Limited
doi:10.1108/978-1-83742-276-020261004

When One Tool Does Everything

First, we turned to SAMR (Fig. 2) hoping it might help us categorise what we were witnessing with AI integration. SAMR had always been a reliable framework for distinguishing between superficial tool substitution and genuine educational transformation. With traditional technologies, the model's progression felt clear and predictable. Students moved from substitution through augmentation and modification to redefinition. Each level represented increasing sophistication in both technological capability and intellectual engagement. We had seen this progression work reliably: physical flashcards became digital flashcards (substitution), paper tests became online quiz apps with instant feedback (augmentation), classroom presentations with poster boards became interactive presentations with embedded videos and real-time polling (modification), and traditional field trips became virtual reality experiences exploring ancient Rome or Mars (redefinition). Students built sophistication by working through different technologies at different levels.

When we applied SAMR to AI, something unusual happened. Students could use AI across all four levels, something rare among the educational technologies we'd encountered previously. Where most tools typically fit within one or two levels, AI can function at the levels of substitution, augmentation, modification, and redefinition simultaneously. At first, this felt remarkable. Here was a technology so adaptable it could appear at every level of the framework. For substitution, students could use AI to define terms then rewrite to test understanding, where traditionally they might have used online dictionaries. For augmentation, students could have AI explain dense theory while they revised notes, replacing enhanced digital materials like videos or interactive explanations. For modification, students could co-develop outlines with AI through iterative prompts, instead of using collaborative platforms with classmates. For redefinition, students could have AI simulate theorist debates while they critiqued and refined their views, enabling interactions that weren't previously possible in digital education.

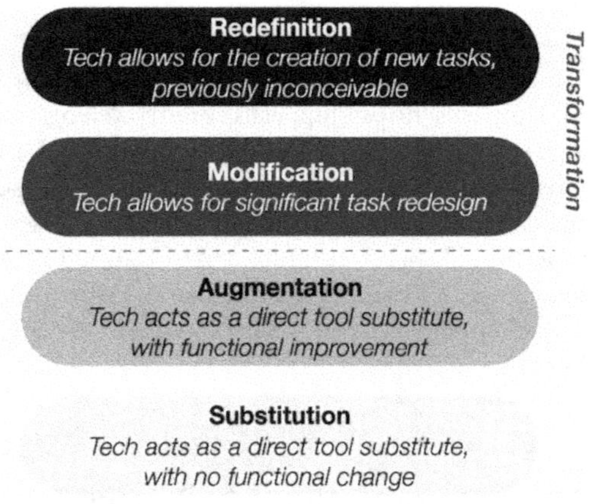

Fig. 2. The SAMR Model of Technology Integration. *Source*: Adapted from Puentedura, R. R. (2009). *As we may teach: Educational technology, from theory into practice*. Hippasus. https://www.hippasus.com/rrpweblog/archives/000025.html

We had always assumed that even basic digital tools required some cognitive engagement from students. Using online dictionaries meant searching and selecting. Watching educational videos meant paying attention and taking notes. Collaborative platforms required negotiating with peers. Each type of tool demanded active engagement that students developed as they worked through SAMR's levels. But with AI, we watched students bypass these minimal requirements entirely. They could ask AI for definitions and paste them without reading, request AI summaries and add them without understanding, have AI create outlines they never revised, and submit AI-generated essays built from sources they had never read. For the first time, we were seeing students access sophisticated outputs while bypassing every trace of the thinking that those outputs were supposed to represent.

The same tool, different approaches, dramatically different outcomes.

But as we observed more closely, we discovered something that unsettled us far more than good versus poor AI use. AI's remarkable adaptability was exactly what made it so disruptive. Because AI could appear across all SAMR levels through the same interface, students could access redefinition-level outputs through substitution-level effort. They no longer needed to develop skills progressively if one tool could provide everything. This wasn't just convenient. It was undermining our fundamental assumption about how learning develops.

We had always interpreted SAMR as suggesting that students would progress through its levels developmentally by working with various technologies. In our experience, you start with substitution tools, build comfort and skills, and then gradually move towards more sophisticated applications with other platforms. We had come to see this progression as natural that redefinition-level thinking emerged from building capabilities through multiple types of tools, each requiring distinct forms of engagement. But AI's adaptability had made this developmental progression optional rather than necessary. Students could access all levels of technological sophistication through one interface, bypassing the skill-building that working through various tools was supposed to provide. They could get substitution-level help, augmentation-level explanation, modification-level collaboration, and redefinition-level experiences without ever developing the capabilities that each type of tool traditionally required.

SAMR wasn't failing at its purpose. It was encountering technology that extended beyond its design parameters. The framework could still categorise what AI was doing, but it couldn't address what mattered most: that AI had made optional the developmental progression that technology integration was supposed to facilitate. We needed to understand what learning actually looked like when the developmental progression had become optional rather than essential.

When the 'T' Exploded

Having struggled to make sense of AI through SAMR, we turned to TPACK (Fig. 3), hoping it might offer clearer guidance about what technological knowledge AI integration would actually require. With previous technologies, this question had been straightforward. We needed to understand specific tool capabilities, learn

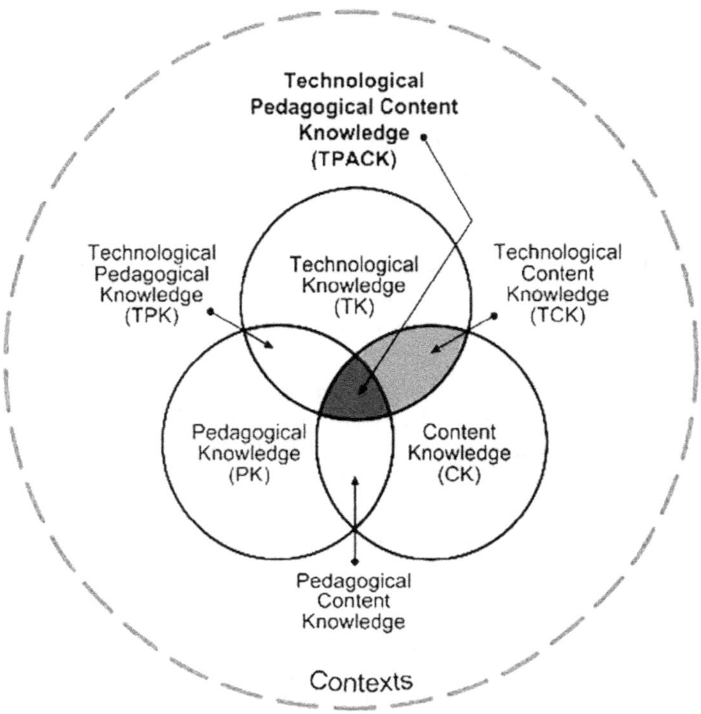

Fig. 3. The TPACK Model of Technology Integration. *Source*: Adapted from *The TPACK model of technology integration*, by tpack.org, © 2012. http://www.tpack.org.

basic functions, and identify appropriate pedagogical applications. The technological knowledge component of TPACK had always been bounded and learnable. Take argumentative essay writing as an example. The TPACK framework helped us think systematically about what effective integration required: content knowledge about what makes a good argumentative essay, pedagogical knowledge about how to teach students to write one, and technological knowledge about how to use tools like Google Docs. We understood how these knowledge domains intersected: how to explain argument writing clearly, which tech tools help with writing arguments, how to use technology to support the writing process, and ultimately how to bring all of this together in one effective learning activity.

Google Docs integration required a manageable set of skills: creating, editing, and sharing documents; managing permissions; using editing modes; leaving and responding to comments; accessing version history; troubleshooting basic issues; and organising files. These were specific, learnable competencies that we could master through training or practice.

Then, we tried mapping the same approach to ChatGPT. And, everything changed. The technological knowledge we needed grew beyond anything we'd encountered. We needed to understand prompting strategies and know how to adjust tone and specificity for different tasks. Most challenging was knowing how to design prompts that guide rather than replace student thinking. Beyond technical knowledge, we needed to understand ethical considerations we had never faced before: appropriate attribution, norms for legitimate use, boundaries between support and academic dishonesty.

For instance, how do we teach students the difference between using AI for brainstorming versus having AI write their conclusions? We also needed knowledge about critical thinking approaches: understanding AI bias, hallucinations, and the difference between surface fluency and genuine understanding so we could help students recognise these issues.

The contrast crystallised when we looked at how these tools are defined. Google Support describes Google Docs as 'an online word processor that lets you create and format documents and work with other people'. IBM defines AI as 'technology that enables computers and machines to simulate human learning, comprehension, problem solving, decision making, creativity and autonomy'. These definitions reveal where agency lies. Google Docs keeps humans in charge: *you* think, *you* write, *you* revise, and *you* collaborate. The tool facilitates but doesn't replace human cognitive processes. With AI, *the machine* is doing the thinking. This shift in agency creates new challenges – *how do we maintain human thinking and learning when the technology can simulate those very processes?*

This expansion in the need for technological knowledge revealed a deeper problem. Our teaching methods, refined over years of practice, suddenly felt inadequate. When we assigned argumentative essays, students could generate sophisticated arguments instantly with AI. But had they learned to construct arguments or just to prompt them? Our carefully scaffolded writing process didn't align with this new reality when AI could leap from thesis to polished conclusion with just a simple prompt. The peer review activities we'd designed to develop critical thinking skills felt less valuable when students could ask AI to identify weaknesses in their classmates' work and bypass the intellectual engagement we were trying to foster. We found ourselves grappling with fundamental questions about learning itself. How much AI support is appropriate in any task? At what point does AI support cross the line into replacing the thinking we're trying to develop? These questions applied to every assignment, every subject, every learning goal.

TPACK had worked because the technological knowledge we'd dealt with before had always been bounded and learnable. But AI shattered that assumption. We weren't just dealing with an expansion of skills – we were facing technology that redefines what it means to know, teach, and learn. No framework designed for discrete, manageable tools could guide us through technology that challenges the very nature of human cognition in education.

The Questions Frameworks Can't Ask

Moving from SAMR and TPACK, we then turned our attention to UNESCO. In 2024, UNESCO released two comprehensive frameworks specifically designed to address AI's impact on education: the AI Competency Framework for Teachers[3] (AI CFT) and the AI Competency Framework for Students[4] (AI CFS). These represent a significant global response to the challenges that educational institutions worldwide were encountering with AI integration. The frameworks are extensive. The AI CFT (Table 1) organises teacher competencies around five core aspects: human-centred mindset, ethics of AI, AI foundations and applications, AI pedagogy, and AI for professional development.

The AI CFS (Table 2) structures student competencies around four aspects: human-centred mindset, ethics of AI, AI techniques and applications, and AI system design.

Both frameworks provide detailed guidance across multiple competency areas, offering systematic approaches to managing AI's educational integration while preserving human agency and critical thinking.

As we examined these frameworks, we recognised that UNESCO had clearly encountered the same phenomena we had discovered through our SAMR

Table 1. UNESCO *AI Competency Framework for Teachers*: Competency Aspects and Progression Levels.

Aspects	**Progression**		
	Acquire	**Deepen**	**Create**
1. Human-centred mindset	Human agency	Human accountability	Social responsibility
2. Ethics of AI	Ethical principles	Safe and responsible use	Co-creating ethical rules
3. AI foundations and applications	Basic AI techniques and applications	Application skills	Creating with AI
4. AI pedagogy	AI-assisted teaching	AI-pedagogy integration	AI-enhanced pedagogical transformation
5. AI for professional development	AI enabling lifelong professional learning	AI to enhance organizational learning	AI to support professional transformation

Source: Adapted from *UNESCO AI Competency Framework for Teachers*,

[3]Miao, F., & Cukurova, M. (2024). *AI competency framework for teachers*. UNESCO. https://doi.org/10.54675/ZJTE2084

[4]Miao, F., Shiohira, K., & Lao, N. (2024). *AI competency framework for students*. UNESCO. https://doi.org/10.54675/JKJB9835

Table 2. UNESCO *AI Competency Framework for Students*: Competency Aspects and Progression Levels.

Competency Aspects	Progression Levels		
	Understand	Apply	Create
• Human-centred mindset	• Human agency	• Human accountability	• Citizenship in the era of AI
• Ethics of AI	• Embodied ethics	• Safe and responsible use	• Ethics by design
• AI techniques and applications	• AI foundations	• Application skills	• Creating AI tools
• AI system design	• Problem scoping	• Architecture design	• Iteration and feedback loops

Source: Adapted from *UNESCO AI Competency Framework for Students*, © 2023 by UNESCO, licensed under the Creative Commons Attribution-ShareAlike 3.0 IGO License (CC BY-SA 3.0 IGO). https://creativecommons.org/licenses/by-sa/3.0/igo/

and TPACK analysis. Their frameworks directly address AI's ability to bypass traditional learning progressions and acknowledge the unprecedented scope of technological knowledge that AI requires. They provide systematic responses to the challenges we'd identified – offering detailed guidance for maintaining human agency, developing critical evaluation skills, and managing technological complexity. Yet as we worked through these comprehensive frameworks, we noticed something significant. UNESCO's detailed competency lists address *how* to manage AI's impact on learning – how to maintain agency, how to evaluate AI outputs, how to use AI ethically. But they don't address *why* these competencies have become necessary in the first place.

Our SAMR analysis had revealed that AI could be used to bypass developmental progressions that educational frameworks assume are fundamental to learning. Our TPACK analysis had shown that AI requires technological knowledge that exceeds what frameworks are designed to encompass. But these discoveries pointed towards questions about the nature of learning and thinking themselves – questions that frameworks, however sophisticated, aren't designed to address. UNESCO's frameworks assume that students and teachers who develop the right competencies will be able to work effectively with AI. But what if the phenomena we'd observed – the disconnection between outputs and thinking, the bypassing of intellectual development, the explosion of technological demands – weren't just implementation challenges but indicators of something more fundamental about what AI is revealing?

The UNESCO frameworks provide systematic responses to AI's educational challenges. But they don't address what makes AI capable of creating these challenges in the first place – what it is about AI that allows it to simulate sophisticated thinking without thinking, to bypass developmental processes, to demand technological knowledge of unprecedented scope and complexity. UNESCO's comprehensive frameworks had brought us to the same edge we'd reached with SAMR and TPACK – recognising that the questions emerging from our analysis consistently pointed beyond what systematic educational approaches were designed to address.

Chapter 5

The Question We Can't Avoid

The work we've described, from research to institutional responses through framework analysis, had all been driven by the same underlying questions: What can we do with AI? How can we use these tools effectively? How can we integrate them pedagogically? How can we help students leverage AI capabilities while managing the challenges? Every policy we wrote, every workshop we designed, every framework we applied assumed we were the active agents and AI was the instrument we were learning to wield. But the persistent feeling that something essential was slipping away, despite our systematic responses, refused to be ignored. Comprehensive policies, proven frameworks, systematic investigations, all successful by conventional measures, yet all leaving the same nagging sense that we were missing something fundamental.

What if we had been asking the wrong question entirely?

The recognition came not as gradual understanding, but as sudden clarity. The confusion that had been building crystallised into a single, inescapable realisation:

What if we should be asking *What is AI doing to us?*

Not what we were doing with AI, but what AI was doing to us. To how we think, learn, and understand what it means to know something. To how students like Bera can produce sophisticated work while remaining disconnected from the thinking it represents. To why frameworks that worked so well within their design parameters all pointed towards questions they weren't designed to address. Everything made sense now. The persistent unease, the framework limitations, the sense of something slipping away, all of it now cohered into a single insight. We had been asking what we could do with AI, when the real question was what AI was doing to us.

What We Were Really Witnessing

When Maya struggled with the forensic linguistics assignment, her confusion led to weeks of intellectual wrestling that built genuine understanding. When Bera encountered the same assignment, AI enabled her to bypass that struggle entirely, allowing her to produce sophisticated work without developing the thinking it represented. The disconnect between performance and understanding wasn't just

What Is AI Doing to Us? A Philosophical Inquiry into Learning, Thinking, and Being, 31–34

Published under exclusive licence by Emerald Publishing Limited
doi:10.1108/978-1-83742-276-020261005

about individual students' choices about AI use. Our framework analysis had shown it revealed something unprecedented – AI could sever the connection between intellectual performance and intellectual development that educational practice has always assumed was reliable.

What we were witnessing was technology that could simulate the products of thinking without thinking, creating a situation where the usual markers of learning – sophisticated analysis, comprehensive research, polished argumentation – no longer reliably indicated that learning had occurred. When we sensed something essential about education was slipping away, we were witnessing a rupture in the fundamental connection between intellectual performance and intellectual development: a phenomenon that challenges basic assumptions about human learning.

This pointed beyond educational questions towards something more fundamental: What happens to human thinking when machines can replicate its products without thinking? What does it mean to understand something when that understanding can be convincingly simulated? How do we maintain authentic intellectual development when the struggle that builds understanding can be entirely bypassed? These questions reach beyond the scope of educational expertise because they ask what thinking and learning fundamentally are, not just how to facilitate them more effectively. Recognising this demanded a different kind of investigation entirely.

Then, we realised – we'd been here before. We knew exactly what we needed.

The Thinking This Requires

This is why we turned our attention to Martin Heidegger. In our earlier research on ChatGPT, we'd used Heidegger's ideas as part of our theoretical framework to understand how AI may be changing educational relationships. But after concrete investigation and systematic responses, we now realised that his thinking about technology was even more relevant than we had initially thought. We were now prepared to see the deeper significance.

Writing in the mid-20th century, decades before AI, Heidegger saw how new tools quietly reshape our way of being long before we notice. His most cited line in *The Question Concerning Technology* captures it – 'The essence of technology is by no means anything technological'. By 'essence', he meant not what a device is made of or what it does, but how it subtly recasts reality itself: how we relate to the world, to others, and to ourselves.

Heidegger's distinction shows why our earlier framing – *What can we do with AI?* – was never enough. That question keeps us on the glittering surface of functions and features. He would insist the instrumental view is precisely *not* the essence of technology. The question we must ask instead is *What is AI doing to us?* It turns our gaze from what the tool executes to what the tool engenders – shifts in attention and agency, changes in the very texture of thinking and learning. It exposes how cognitive labour is outsourced, how struggle diminishes, and how the teacher's role must evolve from delivering content to curating spaces where presence and judgement can still take root. Students, likewise, must move beyond polished output to grappling with ideas that machines can imitate but never inhabit.

Asking *What is AI doing to us?* shows the stakes are not merely pedagogical but ontological. Every prompt, every auto-generated paragraph, every seamless completion quietly redefines our expectations about thinking itself, making struggle seem unnecessary and effortlessness seem normal. This ontological shift is no abstraction – in our own classrooms, we are already seeing its effects. When students like Bera can submit sophisticated analyses they cannot explain, we aren't just witnessing new study habits, we're seeing AI loosen the bond between thought and its expression. The gap between performance and understanding reveals how AI technology is transforming what it means to learn at all.

The Question That Opened Beyond Itself

The question that crystallised our thinking – *What is AI doing to us?* – hit with revelatory force. After systematic responses that left something essential unaddressed, after frameworks that pointed toward limitations they couldn't overcome, this question finally named what we'd been experiencing but couldn't articulate. It felt like breakthrough recognition. Not *How can we use AI effectively?* or *What policies do we need?* but acknowledgement that something fundamental is happening to us, to our way of being, to educational relationships, to the very conditions of human learning. The question captures our sense that we aren't just witnessing technological disruption but experiencing a transformation in what it means to be thinking beings. It moves beyond instrumental concerns toward existential ones. It acknowledges that we are beings thrown into circumstances we haven't chosen, inheriting conditions that exceed our control. *What is AI doing to us?* demands inquiry into how an AI-mediated world is reshaping what it means to be human.

However, there is a tension we must address.

When we ask *What is AI doing to us?* we frame artificial intelligence as an active agent with the power to reshape human experience. We position ourselves as recipients of technological change, as beings transformed by forces that press upon us from outside. The question treats AI as the subject doing something to human objects. Yet Heidegger's insight, 'The essence of technology is by no means anything technological', suggests that focusing on any particular technology, even one as sophisticated as AI, misses what's most essential about our technological condition. At first glance, these framings appear contradictory. Our question demands inquiry into what this specific technology is doing to human thinking. Heidegger's insight redirects attention away from particular technologies towards something more fundamental.

But here's what began to come into view – these aren't opposing perspectives, but the same recognition approached from different starting points.

The question *What is AI doing to us?* is revelatory precisely because it opens inquiry beyond itself. Though framed around a particular technology, it points towards questions that transcend any specific tool – What happens to human thinking when machines can simulate its products? What does it mean to learn when algorithms can complete traditional academic tasks? How do we remain authentically human in technological conditions we didn't choose? Following our question seriously doesn't lead away from Heidegger's insight, it leads directly towards it. The inquiry that *What is AI doing to us?* opens necessarily moves beyond AI as particular technology towards examination of the technological condition that shapes thinking itself.

This is where our inquiry converges with Heidegger's philosophical recognition. The essence of what's happening to us is indeed 'by no means anything technological', it's about the transformation of human thinking itself, the reshaping of what it means to think, learn, and exist as human beings in a technological world. The question that felt so revelatory contains within itself the recognition that points beyond itself. We began by asking what AI was doing to us and came to recognise we needed to ask about the nature of technological existence itself. *What is AI doing to us?* is exactly the right question to ask, not because it is perfectly framed, but because it is the question that can lead us beyond its own limitations towards the deeper inquiry we need. The revelatory power lies not in the question itself but in where it can lead us. The tension resolves when we recognise that our practical question and Heidegger's philosophical insight aren't contradictory but connected. The inquiry that begins with *What is AI doing to us?* arrives at understanding that the essence of our situation is by no means anything technological.

This recognition changes everything about what follows. We're no longer investigating what a particular technology does to us, but examining how technological thinking shapes our way of being.

The philosophical inquiry that unfolds in the chapters ahead doesn't abandon our original question – it fulfils it by revealing what that question was actually pointing towards all along.

Part III

Learning to See

Chapter 6

The Structures of Human Existence

Martin Heidegger[1] wrote in a small hut in the Black Forest, where snow fell quietly outside the window and ideas moved slowly, one word at a time, one thought per page. No emails. No pings. No dashboards. No prompts. It was a life of deliberate slowness, almost unimaginable in today's rhythms. This deliberate slowness wasn't incidental to his thinking; it was foundational to insights that would prove remarkably prescient for our current moment. And yet, his thinking reaches straight into the heart of what's unfolding now – not just in classrooms, but across entire institutions and society itself. Born in 1889 in rural Germany, Heidegger lived through a period of unprecedented technological and social upheaval: from two devastating world wars to the rise of mass production, nuclear technology, and automated systems. Initially trained in Catholic seminary, he studied theology before turning to philosophy where he began asking questions that most people had stopped asking – What does it mean to exist meaningfully in a world that increasingly reduces things and people to functions, tools, and resources?

In 1954, Heidegger wrote an essay that would become one of the most influential examinations of technology and human existence – *The Question Concerning Technology*. In it, he developed an insight that cuts to the heart of our situation: 'The essence of technology is by no means anything technological'.

But What Does This Mean?

[1]Martin Heidegger's philosophical insights into technology and human existence cannot be separated from his personal and political failings. He joined the Nazi Party in 1933, held antisemitic views documented in his notebooks, and never adequately confronted his complicity with the Nazi regime. We engage with his thinking on technology not because we endorse his politics or character, but because his analysis of how technological thinking reshapes human existence remains philosophically significant for understanding our current circumstances. Many scholars critical of Heidegger's politics have likewise drawn on his work on technology while maintaining explicit distance from his ideology. Our use of Heideggerian concepts should not be interpreted as an endorsement of Heidegger himself, only of the specific insights relevant to this inquiry.

What Is AI Doing to Us? A Philosophical Inquiry into Learning, Thinking, and Being, 37–57

Published under exclusive licence by Emerald Publishing Limited
doi:10.1108/978-1-83742-276-020261006

How We Exist

To understand why technology's essence is nothing technological, we must first understand what makes human existence distinctive. For Heidegger, this isn't about human capabilities or achievements. It's something more fundamental – humans are the beings for whom Being itself is always already a question.

We are, in Heidegger's terms, *Dasein*, literally 'being-there'. In *Being and Time* (1927), where he develops the existential structures explored in this chapter, he shows that this doesn't simply mean we occupy physical locations. It means we exist in such a way that existence itself matters to us. We wonder what it means to be. We question the nature of reality. We are concerned with meaning itself. A rock exists, but it doesn't wonder about existence. A tree grows, but it doesn't question what growth means. Human beings exist while simultaneously questioning what it means to exist at all. This questioning relationship to Being isn't something we occasionally do. It's the basic structure of what we are.

This distinctive way of existing unfolds through what Heidegger called 'care' (*Sorge*). Care isn't emotional concern or worry. It's the fundamental structure that makes human existence possible. We care about our circumstances, about our futures, about what matters. This caring reveals itself in how we're always already engaged with the world – concerned with projects, involved with others, oriented towards possibilities that matter to us. We don't exist as detached observers who occasionally engage with an external world. We exist *as* that engagement itself. Care is the structure through which human existence unfolds in time, shaped by the past we inherit, the future we project towards, and the present where we must choose who to become.

This caring structure means human existence is essentially temporal. We exist through the complex interpenetration of past, present, and future. We inherit circumstances we didn't choose, yet they shape all our current possibilities. We project towards futures we cannot guarantee, yet those anticipated possibilities press into the present and give meaning to current choices. We exist as finite beings moving through time, and this finitude – the fact that our existence will end – creates the urgency that makes present choices meaningful.

Dasein's way of existing is always 'being-in-the-world' – not contained within a world like objects in a container, but existing as the relationship itself between self and world. We are constantly with others, engaged with meaningful contexts, involved in projects that extend beyond ourselves. This isn't a choice we make. It's the basic condition within which all our choices occur. We find ourselves already thrown into existence, already embedded in languages we didn't create, cultures we didn't choose, historical moments we didn't select.

This groundless condition – the fact that we exist without having chosen to exist, that we must make choices without ultimate foundation for those choices – creates both the burden and the possibility of human existence. We can flee from this groundlessness by losing ourselves in what 'everyone' thinks and does, adopting ready-made interpretations that provide the illusion of secure foundation. Or we can take responsibility for existence that has no guarantee, choosing who to become while acknowledging that such choosing emerges from our engagement with groundless circumstances rather than from predetermined essence or social expectation.

Now let's trace how this structure unfolds and how it gets distorted. We'll begin with the most fundamental aspect of *Dasein*'s condition – the fact that we find ourselves existing without having chosen to exist – what Heidegger called 'thrownness'. From there, we'll follow how this groundless condition shapes our relationship with others, creates modes of flight through which we systematically flee from authentic existence, and ultimately how technology intensifies these tendencies in ways that threaten to obscure what makes human existence genuinely human. Each concept we explore isn't a separate idea but an interconnected aspect of how *Dasein* exists and how that existence can be either authentically inhabited or fled from into systematic inauthenticity.

How We Find Ourselves

Thrownness

For Heidegger, thrownness (*Geworfenheit*) reveals the most fundamental condition of human existence – we find ourselves existing without having chosen to exist. We discover ourselves already in the world, already engaged with circumstances, already involved in situations that were underway before we arrived. This isn't simply about inheriting difficult circumstances. It's about the groundless nature of existence itself. We make choices about who to become, but we never chose the basic condition of having to choose. We discover ourselves in existence with no ultimate foundation for the choices we must make. There is no secure ground beneath human existence, no predetermined essence that tells us who we should be or how we should live. This groundlessness isn't a problem to be solved but the inescapable condition within which all human existence unfolds.

Thrownness has a fundamental temporal structure, not the linear time of clocks and calendars, but the lived temporal structure that makes human understanding possible. We inherit a past we didn't choose, yet that past remains present as the foundation that shapes current possibilities. We project towards futures we cannot guarantee, yet those anticipated possibilities press into the present and give meaning to current choices. Past, present, and future interpenetrate in complex ways that create the temporal conditions within which human existence unfolds. The recognition of thrownness typically emerges through Angst (often translated as dread or existential anxiety), not fear of particular things, but the fundamental Angst that arises when we confront the groundlessness of existence itself. In moments of Angst, familiar meanings dissolve and we recognise that our existence has no ultimate foundation. This Angst reveals both the burden and the possibility of human existence: we must choose who to become without guarantee, yet this very condition creates the space within which authentic existence becomes possible.

This groundless condition creates two fundamental possibilities for human existence. We can flee from the Angst of groundlessness by losing ourselves in *das Man*, the anonymous 'anyone' whose ready-made interpretations we absorb without examination. Following what 'everyone' thinks, adopting social expectations, conforming to public interpretations provide the illusion of secure foundation. Or we can embrace our groundless condition by taking responsibility for existence that has no ultimate justification – authentic existence. Authenticity doesn't mean finding a 'true self' or following individual preferences. It means owning up to existence as groundless, taking responsibility for choices that emerge from engagement with our condition rather than borrowing responses from what 'everyone' does. Authentic existence involves what Heidegger called 'resoluteness' (*Entschlossenheit*) – not determination to achieve particular goals, but the resolve to choose who to become while acknowledging that such choosing has no foundation beyond the choosing itself. Resoluteness means taking responsibility for existence without guarantee about the consequences of our choices.

This groundless condition shapes every aspect of human existence.

We find ourselves in language we didn't create, cultures we didn't choose, historical moments we didn't select. Yet within these inherited conditions, we must still choose how to exist. Thrownness reveals that human existence is always already relational – we exist with others, in shared worlds, embedded in contexts that exceed our individual control, yet we remain responsible for how we inhabit these inherited conditions.

This groundless condition of thrownness shapes how we exist with others. When faced with Angst about our thrown circumstances, we naturally turn to collective interpretations that promise relief from uncertainty.

Das Man

Das Man (The They) isn't a person or group of people, it's a fundamental way of being that shapes how we exist with others. In our everyday existence, we naturally turn to what 'anyone' would think, what 'one' does in such situations, what 'everyone' knows to be true. This isn't simply social influence or peer pressure – it's the basic structure through which we initially encounter and make sense of the world. *Das Man* provides the shared interpretations, common practices, and public meanings that make social existence possible. We inherit ways of speaking, thinking, and acting that feel like common sense but emerge from anonymous collective interpretations. When we say 'one doesn't do that' or 'everyone knows this', we're existing through *das Man*. These interpretations don't belong to any particular person, they circulate through conversations, media, social interactions, and cultural practices until they feel like natural truth rather than inherited interpretation. *Das Man* offers pre-formed responses to situations, especially new and unsettling ones that create Angst.

Das Man serves a crucial function in human existence – it provides the background of shared intelligibility that makes communication and social action possible. Language learning occurs through *das Man*, social skills develop through its shared practices, cultural navigation happens through its interpretations. Without this shared foundation, individual existence would be impossible. *Das Man* isn't simply negative, it's the necessary condition within which human existence unfolds. Human beings are always already embedded in shared meanings that exceed individual creation. Yet *das Man* also creates the possibility of losing ourselves in collective interpretations. When we absorb ready-made responses without examination, follow social expectations without questioning, or adopt public opinions without engaging with them personally, we flee from the Angst of having to choose who to become. *Das Man* offers the comfort of certainty. Instead of confronting the groundless nature of existence, we can follow what 'everyone' thinks. This provides relief from existential Angst by surrendering responsibility for authentic choice while maintaining the illusion that our responses emerge from a secure foundation.

The danger of *das Man* lies not in its existence but in our absorption into it without awareness. When we lose ourselves completely in what 'everyone' thinks, we avoid the Angst of groundless existence by surrendering responsibility for our own choices. We become what Heidegger called the 'they-self' (*Man-selbst*) – a mode of existence where we function as anyone might function rather than taking responsibility for who we become.

The They-Self

The 'they-self' represents a fundamental transformation in how we exist. Instead of confronting the Angst of choosing who to become, we dissolve into public ways of being that avoid the burden of authentic decision. We begin to think what anyone would think, feel what anyone would feel, respond as anyone would respond. This dissolution offers profound comfort because it shields us from the groundless Angst that authentic existence requires. When we become 'anyone', we no longer face the difficult work of taking responsibility for choices that have no ultimate foundation. The 'they-self' provides the illusion of secure identity – we know who we are because we are who 'everyone' expects us to be.

This absorption into public ways of being makes authentic choice feel not just difficult but unnecessary. Why struggle with uncertain decisions when established responses already exist? Why confront Angst about what matters when collective wisdom provides ready-made answers? The 'they-self' experiences authentic choice as inefficient deviation from proven approaches rather than essential responsibility for human existence. We lose the capacity to recognise that following what 'everyone' does represents a choice we are making. It begins to feel like natural necessity rather than flight from the Angst of authentic existence.

Authentic existence emerges not by escaping *das Man* but by consciously engaging with it. We cannot step outside shared meanings and social contexts; we are always already embedded in them. But we can distinguish between interpretations we've inherited and understanding we've developed through personal engagement. We can recognise when we're following what 'everyone' thinks versus responding from our own encounter with what matters. Authenticity involves taking responsibility for our choices while acknowledging that such choices occur within social contexts we didn't create. This dynamic between *das Man* and authentic existence shapes every aspect of human social life. Conversations, institutions, cultural practices, and professional contexts are formed through public ways of being. Yet within these inherited structures, we must still choose how to exist. *Das Man* reveals that human existence is fundamentally social – we exist with others, through shared meanings, embedded in collective contexts, while remaining responsible for how we inhabit these social conditions.

Das Man provides the foundation for what Heidegger identified as an even more fundamental mode of flight from authentic existence – fallenness.

Fallenness

Das Man shows itself through what Heidegger called 'fallenness' (*Verfallenheit*) – our systematic tendency to flee from the Angst of authentic existence. Fallenness isn't moral failure but the structural way we avoid confronting our groundless condition. It reveals itself through three interconnected structures that work together to create a comprehensive escape from authentic engagement.

Idle talk represents language that circulates without genuine engagement with what it discusses. We repeat phrases, adopt terminology, and express opinions that sound authoritative but lack personal involvement with the questions they address. Professional discourse becomes filled with sophisticated vocabulary that creates the impression of understanding complex situations without the struggle of working through fundamental questions ourselves. We participate in conversations about difficult topics by following established ways of speaking rather than developing our own engagement with what matters. Idle talk allows us to sound knowledgeable while avoiding the Angst of confronting what we don't actually understand, providing the comfort of apparent competence without the risk of authentic encounter with uncertainty.

Curiosity shows itself as restless seeking after novelty rather than sustained engagement with what concerns us. We find ourselves constantly drawn to new information, latest developments, updated methods, and approaches that promise to resolve the difficulties we encounter. But this curiosity systematically avoids dwelling with fundamental questions that require patient attention and offer no guarantee of resolution. Instead of sustained engagement with what actually demands our response, we flee into the comfort of exploring new possibilities that feel productive while avoiding the Angst of confronting what we cannot immediately understand. This restless seeking prevents the temporal duration that genuine understanding requires, substituting the activity of gathering new material for the demanding work of thinking through what we already encounter.

Ambiguity emerges when we can no longer distinguish between authentic and inauthentic responses to our situation. When sophisticated performance masks genuine engagement, when professional competence substitutes for personal involvement, when systematic procedures promise comprehensive resolution while leaving us with the persistent sense that something essential is missing, we find ourselves unable to recognise authentic response when we encounter it. This ambiguity isn't simply confusion about appropriate methods. It represents the systematic blurring of what makes human engagement genuinely human, creating conditions where everything appears equally valid, equally sophisticated, equally professional.

These three structures reinforce each other in ways that make fallenness self-perpetuating. Idle talk makes restless curiosity feel productive rather than avoidant. Curiosity generates more idle talk that sounds sophisticated but avoids fundamental engagement. Together, they create the ambiguity that makes it increasingly difficult to distinguish between authentic response and systematic performance. Fallenness reveals why systematic approaches to complex situations, however comprehensive and well-intentioned, consistently leave us with the sense that something essential is slipping away. We flee from the Angst that signals authentic engagement into the comfort of procedures that promise resolution without requiring the struggle that genuine understanding demands.

The Unity of Flight

We can now see how these structures work together. Thrownness describes where we find ourselves – groundless, without having chosen to exist, facing choices without ultimate foundation. *Das Man* describes where we flee – into what 'everyone' thinks, the collective interpretations that promise relief from existential Angst. The 'they-self' describes what we become when flight is complete – 'anyone' rather than someone taking responsibility for authentic existence. Fallenness describes the manner in which this flight takes shape – through idle talk that circulates without engagement, curiosity that seeks novelty without dwelling, and ambiguity that obscures the difference between authentic response and sophisticated performance. This isn't a sequence of separate concepts, but a unified analysis of human existence and its tendency towards inauthenticity. We are thrown into groundlessness, we flee that groundlessness through *das Man*, we become 'they-selves' absorbed in collective modes of interpretation, and we live that absorption through the systematic structures of fallenness. Each structure depends on and reinforces the others. Together, they reveal how human existence naturally flees from the Angst of groundlessness into the comfort of public ways of being. Table 3 illustrates these interconnected structures and the ordinary ways they manifest in daily life.

Table 3. The Structures of How We Find Ourselves.

Structure	What It Reveals About How We Exist	How It Appears in Everyday Life
Thrownness	Finding ourselves already in existence, groundless, and unchosen	Our inherited circumstances, languages, and histories
das Man	The shared social world of common meanings	Conforming to what 'everyone' thinks or does
they-self	The self shaped by absorption in that world	Acting and thinking as 'anyone' rather than from personal understanding
Fallenness	The everyday motion of flight from authenticity	Idle talk, restless curiosity, and ambiguity that mask genuine engagement

Technology enters this dynamic not as an external force but as systematic amplification – it makes flight easier, faster, more comprehensive, and increasingly difficult to recognise as flight at all.

How Technology Intensifies Inauthenticity

Enframing

Enframing (*Gestell*) represents Heidegger's most profound insight into the essence of modern technology – not what technology does, but how it transforms the very way Being reveals itself to human existence. He develops this concept in his 1954 essay 'The Question Concerning Technology'. Enframing is not about particular machines or devices. It's a fundamental mode of revealing that makes everything, including human beings, appear as resources available for optimisation, control, and efficient deployment. Under the sway of enframing, the world shows up as what Heidegger called *Bestand*, standing-reserve that exists solely to be stockpiled, calculated, and optimised for maximum utility. We experience enframing as a totalising way of thinking that reduces all beings to their function within systematic processes. Nature becomes 'natural resources' to be extracted and managed. Human beings become 'human resources' to be developed and deployed. Knowledge becomes 'information' to be processed and transmitted. Even thinking itself becomes 'problem-solving' to be refined through better methodologies. Nothing appears for its own sake or in its own terms, everything exists as raw material for systematic enhancement and control. This transformation occurs so gradually and completely that it feels like natural progress rather than a fundamental shift in how reality appears. The language of efficiency, optimisation, and systematic improvement becomes the only vocabulary for addressing any situation. When we encounter difficulties, enframing makes solutions appear automatically in terms of better management, more effective systems, and enhanced performance. The idea that some aspects of human existence might resist optimisation becomes nearly unthinkable.

Enframing shapes not just how we see the world but how we understand ourselves within it. Under its influence, human existence appears as a resource to be optimised rather than a way of being to be authentically inhabited. We begin to see ourselves as systems requiring enhancement, profiles needing management, performance needing improvement. The very capacity for questioning, for wondering whether systematic optimisation serves human flourishing, gets reduced to a problem requiring better methodological approaches. Enframing also transforms our relationship to time itself. Everything must be immediately available, calculable, and predictable. The temporal rhythm that authentic existence requires, duration for understanding to develop, space for questions to deepen, gets compressed into optimisation cycles. Past becomes data to be processed, future becomes outcomes to be achieved, present becomes efficiency to be maximised. The lived temporality where human existence actually unfolds gets reduced to systematic time management.

The essence of enframing lies in what Heidegger called 'challenging-forth' (*Herausfordern*) – demanding that everything reveal itself as available for systematic use. This goes beyond ordinary exploitation or use. 'Challenging-forth' transforms the very way beings show up in the world. A river appears not as a natural force with its own character but as 'water resources' for power generation. A forest appears not as a complex ecosystem but as 'timber resources' for production. Human beings appear not as persons with their own existence but as 'human resources' for deployment. 'Challenging-forth' makes beings appear solely in terms of their utility for systematic processes. The danger of enframing lies not in its particular applications but in its totalising character. When everything appears as standing-reserve, the space for alternative ways of being disappears from view. Enframing doesn't destroy other possibilities, it conceals them by providing such a comprehensive framework for understanding and action that questioning the framework itself becomes difficult. The more successful systematic approaches become, the more natural they feel, and the more alternative approaches seem inefficient or unrealistic. Yet Heidegger saw within enframing both supreme danger and a possibility for awakening. The extremity of technological conditions might awaken us to what makes existence authentically human.

Understanding enframing doesn't provide escape from technological conditions but reveals what conscious dwelling within them might require. We cannot step outside the technological world that enframing has shaped, but recognising how it shows itself allows us to preserve space for ways of being that resist reduction to systematic optimisation. This requires what Heidegger called *Gelassenheit* – a way of engaging with technology that neither dominates it nor is dominated by it, maintaining openness to what cannot be systematised while working within technological conditions we cannot escape.

Calculative Versus Meditative Thinking

This totalising character of enframing reveals itself most clearly in how it transforms thinking itself. In his 1955 'Memorial Address', later published in *Discourse on Thinking*, Heidegger contrasts two fundamental modes of thought: calculative thinking (*rechnendes Denken*), which plans and controls, and meditative thinking (*besinnliches Denken*), which dwells and lets what calls for thought reveal itself.

Calculative thinking approaches everything as problems requiring systematic solutions. It reduces complex situations to variables that can be managed through predetermined procedures, treats uncertainty as inefficiency requiring immediate resolution, and converts every encounter into an opportunity for optimisation and control. Calculative thinking seeks to overcome what resists systematisation by forcing predetermined frameworks upon complex realities that don't conform to systematic expectations. It shows itself through the logic of efficiency, measurability, and procedural guarantee, promising resolution without requiring the patient attention that understanding actually demands.

Meditative thinking allows situations to reveal what they actually require rather than imposing systematic frameworks that override their inherent resistance. It dwells with questions that resist quick answers, remains open to what cannot be immediately understood or controlled, and preserves space for possibilities that predetermined procedures cannot anticipate. Meditative thinking shows itself through patient attention that honours temporal complexity, sustains engagement with uncertainty, and maintains receptiveness to what shows itself gradually rather than demanding instant availability.

The distinction reveals itself most clearly in how each mode relates to time and difficulty. Calculative thinking treats temporal complexity as delay requiring elimination, converts confusion into problems requiring efficient solutions, and approaches uncertainty as an obstacle to be overcome through systematic procedures. Meditative thinking preserves the temporal duration that understanding requires, allows confusion to become productive through sustained attention, and treats uncertainty as the opening where genuine insight might emerge.

Enframing intensifies calculative thinking while systematically marginalising meditative thinking from human engagement. When everything appears as standing-reserve requiring optimisation, the patient dwelling that allows situations to reveal their own character gets replaced by procedures that force predetermined outcomes upon complex realities that don't fit systematic frameworks. The temporal complexity that makes human understanding possible gets compressed into optimisation cycles that promise efficient resolution. This contrast can be imagined as a descent into the depths of thinking. Calculative thinking skims the surface of what can be measured and controlled, while meditative thinking dwells in the depth where meaning reveals itself (Fig. 4).

Yet meditative thinking cannot be eliminated entirely through technological conditions; it remains available through conscious choice to inhabit technological circumstances while preserving what resists systematisation. Understanding

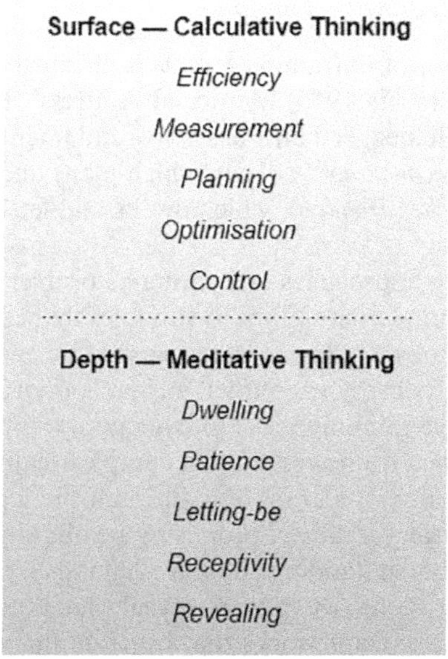

Fig. 4. The Depths of Thinking.

this distinction becomes essential for recognising when technological capabilities serve authentic purposes versus when they substitute systematic efficiency for the patient engagement that makes thinking genuinely human.

The Ontic-Ontological Difference

This replacement of meditative thinking with calculative thinking creates the conditions within which a deeper structure shows itself. We experience enframing most effectively when our attention gets directed towards what Heidegger called the 'ontic' – the realm of particular entities, tools, and techniques – while what is 'ontological' remains concealed from us, the fundamental structures of existence itself. This distinction, central to *Being and Time*, becomes crucial for understanding technology's deepest effects. The pull towards ontic concerns isn't accidental but occurs through our living the structure of fallenness, providing sophisticated escape from the Angst of recognising what technological conditions are doing to human existence.

Calculative thinking naturally directs us towards ontic concerns – managing particular tools and optimising specific procedures – because these promise systematic resolution. Meditative thinking, by contrast, opens ontological questions about how technological conditions transform the very structures through which we encounter existence itself. But such questioning requires the patient attention and tolerance for uncertainty that calculative thinking systematically avoids.

The ontic concerns itself with particular beings – specific tools and their applications, concrete problems and their solutions, measurable outcomes and their optimisation. When we encounter technological challenges, our attention naturally turns to ontic questions: Which tools work best? What training do we need? How do we ensure effective implementation? What policies should we adopt? These questions feel urgent and practical because they address immediate problems we can identify and potentially resolve through systematic approaches. The ontic realm provides clear targets for our problem-solving efforts and creates the satisfying sense that we are responding competently to technological circumstances.

The ontological concerns itself with Being – the fundamental conditions that make it possible for beings to show up as they do. Ontological questions ask not what particular tools accomplish, but how technological conditions transform the very nature of human existence, thinking, and meaning. They examine not what we do with technology, but what technology does to the structures through which we encounter ourselves, others, and the world. These questions resist immediate resolution because they concern the background conditions within which all our ontic problem-solving takes place – they demand the patient attention and tolerance for uncertainty that fallenness systematically avoids.

We experience this difference through the structures we have already identified. Idle talk about technological solutions uses sophisticated vocabulary that creates the impression of understanding fundamental questions while avoiding genuine engagement with what technology reveals about human existence. We develop professional discourse about 'digital transformation' and 'technological integration' that sounds authoritative but remains absorbed in ontic management. Curiosity drives us towards new capabilities, updated features, and emerging applications, the restless seeking that calculative thinking encourages, while fleeing from the meditative attention required to understand how technology transforms human thinking itself. We become restlessly fascinated with what technology can do while avoiding the Angst of confronting what it is doing to us. Ambiguity emerges when we can no longer distinguish between genuine technological wisdom and sophisticated management of technological objects – we lose the capacity to recognise when we are thinking about tools versus when technological thinking is reshaping how we think.

This difference explains why asking *What can we do with AI?*, however, comprehensive our responses, consistently leaves essential questions unaddressed. That question directs attention towards ontic concerns – which tools to use, how to implement them effectively, what policies to develop. Even our most sophisticated approaches to 'leveraging AI capabilities while managing challenges' remain absorbed in managing particular technologies while missing the ontological transformation occurring simultaneously. Fig. 5 illustrates this movement from ontic absorption to ontological awareness, showing how questioning, dwelling, and recognition unfold as we move from managing technological tools towards understanding how technology shapes how Being is revealed.

The question *What is AI doing to us?* represents a fundamental shift from ontic management to ontological inquiry. Instead of asking how to optimise our use of tools, it asks how technological conditions transform the very structures through which we encounter ourselves, others, and the world. This question resists the systematic approaches that ontic concerns invite because it demands engagement with the background conditions within which all our tool management takes place.

The ontic-ontological difference reminds us that responses to technological challenges, however, comprehensive and professionally sophisticated, address only surface manifestations, while the deeper transformation of our understanding of Being proceeds unnoticed. We focus on optimising our use of particular

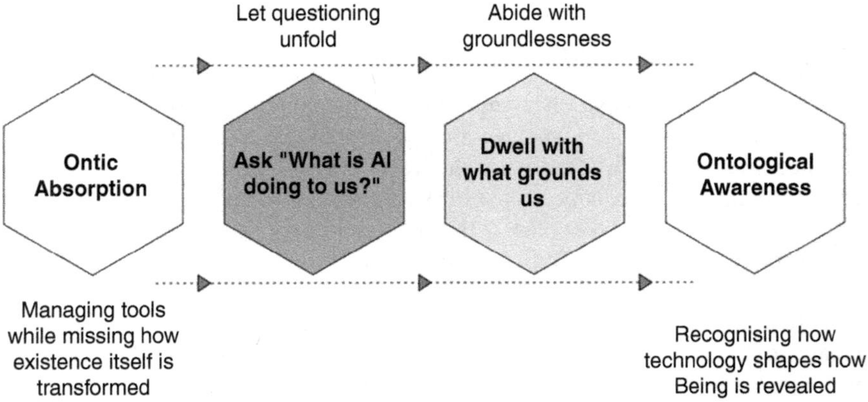

Fig. 5. The Movement from Ontic Absorption to Ontological Awareness.

technologies while remaining unconscious of how technological thinking transforms the very way of being out of which optimisation strategies arise. This feels natural rather than problematic because ontic concerns offer concrete tasks that systematic approaches can manage, while ontological questions require forms of engagement that resist systematisation and demand confronting the groundless Angst that authentic existence requires. Understanding this difference reveals why technological conditions pose such fundamental challenges to the way human beings exist.

Technology as Amplification of Flight

These three aspects – enframing, calculative thinking, and the ontic-ontological difference – work together as a unified amplification of our flight from authentic existence. Enframing provides the framework within which everything appears as standing-reserve, calculative thinking becomes our default mode of engagement, and the ontic-ontological difference reveals why this transformation remains so difficult to recognise – we stay absorbed in managing tools while the reshaping of existence itself proceeds beneath our awareness. The danger lies not in any particular technology but in how technological conditions amplify our existing tendency to flee from meditative dwelling into systematic optimisation, from ontological questions into ontic management, from the Angst of groundlessness into the comfort of calculative solutions.

This is why *What can we do with AI?* feels urgent while *What is AI doing to us?* seems impractical. The first question keeps us focused on tool management, while the second addresses the transformation we are actually living through. Understanding this transformation requires examining the fundamental structures that are being amplified and distorted. We begin with the nature of *Dasein's* temporal existence.

How We Experience Time

Dasein

Dasein exists as always already engaged with the world rather than standing apart from it as detached observers. This isn't simply about physical location but about the fundamental way human existence unfolds. Human beings are always already involved in situations, concerned with projects, engaged with others, embedded in what matters to us. There is no human existence that occurs outside this engagement – we are always already 'there' in the world, dealing with what concerns us.

This 'being-there' reveals itself through care – not emotional concern but the fundamental structure that makes human existence possible. Care is structured by three interconnected dimensions: thrownness (we find ourselves in circumstances we didn't choose), projection (we exist by throwing ourselves towards possibilities that matter to us), and fallenness (we are always already absorbed in the everyday world with others, losing ourselves in immediate concerns rather than confronting the deeper questions of existence). These aren't separate aspects but unified ways that human existence unfolds through ongoing involvement with what matters. *Dasein's* way of being is always 'being-in-the-world' – not contained within a world like an object in a container, but existing as the relationship between self and world. We don't first exist as isolated subjects who then encounter an external world. We exist as the opening within which world and self-emerge together. Our existence is essentially relational – we are constantly with others, engaged with meaningful contexts, involved in projects that extend beyond ourselves.

This engaged existence reveals itself through what Heidegger called 'understanding' (*Verstehen*) – not intellectual comprehension but the fundamental capacity to grasp possibilities and organise existence around projects that matter. Understanding means seeing current situations in terms of what they might become, projecting towards possibilities that concern us, organising our existence around meaningful projects. This is how we exist towards future possibilities while being shaped by inherited circumstances – understanding is the basic way human existence moves through time. *Dasein's* temporal structure differs fundamentally from chronological time. We exist through existential temporality where past, present, and future interpenetrate in complex ways. The past remains present as the inherited foundation that shapes current possibilities. The future presses into the present as the anticipated possibilities that give meaning to current choices. The present becomes the moment of decision, where inherited circumstances and anticipated possibilities come together.

The authenticity of *Dasein* emerges through what Heidegger called 'being-toward-death' (*Sein-zum-Tode*) – not morbid preoccupation with dying but recognition of existence as finite and therefore urgently meaningful. When we confront our own mortality, we recognise that existence is limited and unrepeatable – we cannot endlessly defer choices about who to become. This confrontation with finitude reveals that we must take responsibility for our existence rather than following what 'everyone' expects. Facing our mortality creates the urgency and responsibility that makes authentic existence possible. *Dasein's* everyday existence typically reveals itself through engaged involvement rather than detached observation. When we write with a pen, the pen disappears into the act of writing. When we navigate familiar spaces, we don't consciously calculate routes but move through skilled familiarity. This reveals how human existence actually unfolds, through skilled involvement with meaningful contexts rather than analytical management of external objects. Only when this engaged involvement breaks down do we shift to conscious observation and analysis.

The danger for *Dasein* lies in losing itself in analytical detachment, treating existence as a problem to be solved rather than a way of being to be authentically inhabited. When we approach ourselves, others, and the world primarily through detached analysis, we lose contact with the engaged involvement that makes human existence meaningful. We become observers of life rather than participants in it, managers of existence rather than beings authentically engaged with what matters. Authentic *Dasein* involves resoluteness – not stubborn determination but the resolve to take responsibility for existence as finite, groundless, and, therefore, requiring authentic choice. Resoluteness means owning up to our thrown condition, taking responsibility for possibilities that concern us, and choosing who to become while acknowledging that such choosing has no ultimate foundation beyond the choosing itself. This is how human existence achieves authenticity within the groundless conditions of thrownness.

Dasein's engaged 'being-in-the-world' unfolds through the temporal structure that technological thinking systematically undermines.

Temporality

Temporality (*Zeitlichkeit*) represents Heidegger's most fundamental insight into the structure of human existence – we are essentially temporal beings whose existence unfolds through the complex interpenetration of past, present, and future. This isn't measured time where moments follow each other in sequence, but existential temporality where the three dimensions of time work together to create the conditions within which human existence and understanding become possible. Temporality is not something we experience – it is the basic structure through which we exist.

The future (*Zukunft*) reveals itself as the primary dimension of human temporality, but not as distant events that will eventually occur. Heidegger used *Zukunft*, literally 'coming-toward', to emphasise that the future is what comes towards us rather than what we move towards. The future presses into the present as the possibilities towards which we are always already projecting ourselves. We exist by moving towards possibilities that concern us – projects we care about, goals that matter to us, ways of being that we anticipate. This projection towards possibilities gives human existence its forward momentum and meaning.

The past (*Gewesenheit*) remains present not as memories we occasionally recall but as the inherited foundation that shapes all current possibilities. Heidegger's term *Gewesenheit*, 'having-been', emphasises that the past is not gone but remains present as the ever-active foundation of existence. We exist as 'having-been-thrown' into circumstances, languages, cultures, and contexts that we didn't choose but that continue to influence every aspect of our existence. This past shows itself as the ever-present foundation that makes current understanding possible. We cannot escape our inheritance – it remains the condition within which we project towards future possibilities. The present (*Gegenwart*) emerges as the moment of decision where inherited circumstances and anticipated possibilities converge. *Gegenwart*, 'present-ing', indicates an active bringing-together rather than a static instant. The present is where we take responsibility for existence that is simultaneously shaped by thrownness and oriented towards future projects. Present moments achieve their meaning through this convergence of past inheritance and future projection, creating the temporal space where authentic choice becomes possible.

This temporal structure reveals itself as a unified whole – past, present, and future interpenetrate in ways that create the conditions for human understanding and authentic existence. We cannot separate these dimensions without destroying the temporal unity that makes human existence possible. Every act of understanding involves this temporal complexity. We approach current situations with inherited background, project towards possibilities that concern us, and make present choices that integrate past and future into meaningful action.

Temporality reveals itself most clearly in human experiences of Angst, anticipation, and decision-making. Angst about the future isn't simply worry about what might happen, it's the fundamental mood that reveals how possibilities press into the present and demand response. When we face difficult choices, we experience the temporal structure directly. We feel the weight of inherited circumstances, the pull of anticipated possibilities, and the urgency of present decision. In moments of Angst, the temporal structure that usually remains implicit comes into view, revealing that we exist as beings who cannot escape the burden of choosing who to become.

This temporal integration is what makes human existence authentic rather than merely reactive. But how does such authentic temporal integration actually emerge in the concrete situations where we must choose who to become?

Making-Present

Inauthentic temporality shows itself through what Heidegger called 'making-present' (*Gegenwärtigen*) – becoming absorbed in immediate concerns while losing sight of how past inheritance and future projection give meaning to current existence. This represents a profound flight from the Angst that authentic temporality requires, collapsing the rich interpenetration of temporal dimensions into the manageable demand for instant availability. We experience 'making-present' when we become restlessly focused on immediate tasks while losing touch with why those tasks matter, when we seek quick solutions to avoid the patient dwelling that complex questions require, and when we treat urgent deadlines as more important than the meaningful projects they supposedly serve.

Rather than dwelling with inherited circumstances as living foundations that continue to shape understanding, 'making-present' reduces the past to immediately accessible information that can be retrieved and deployed efficiently. We lose the capacity to let traditional wisdom reveal its significance through patient engagement, treating historical complexity as data rather than as the ever-present inheritance that makes current understanding possible. Similarly, authentic projection towards uncertain possibilities gets replaced by planning towards predetermined outcomes that promise to remove the discomfort of Angst. Instead of remaining open to futures that concern us deeply, possibilities that create meaningful Angst because they cannot be guaranteed, we focus exclusively on achievable goals that can be systematically managed. The present itself becomes reduced to efficiency optimisation rather than the convergence point where inherited meaning and anticipated possibility demand authentic response.

This flattening creates the illusion of mastery over time while destroying the duration that authentic existence requires. When everything must be immediately available and instantly responsive, the slow rhythm of genuine understanding – the time needed for ideas to settle, for confusion to become productive, for possibilities to reveal their significance – gets replaced by optimisation cycles that promise resolution without requiring the struggle that meaningful engagement demands.

Temporality also reveals itself in how human existence relates to mortality – we are essentially 'being-toward-death'. Our existence is temporal precisely because it is finite. The recognition that our existence will end creates the urgency that makes present choices meaningful and gives weight to future possibilities. Without finitude, temporal existence would lose its distinctive character. Death reveals itself not as an event that happens to us but as the structural limit that makes temporal existence possible and authentic.

Modern technology intensifies the tendency towards 'making-present' by demanding instant availability and immediate response. When everything must be accessible on demand, the rich temporality that human existence requires gets compressed into management cycles. Dwelling authentically with temporality means preserving space for the slow development of understanding, maintaining openness to possibilities that cannot be immediately realised, and honouring the inheritance that shapes current existence. Authentic temporality resists the demand for instant availability while engaging consciously with technological capabilities.

The Collapse of Temporal Depth

Dasein, temporality, and 'making-present' reveal how human existence is fundamentally temporal and how that temporality gets systematically distorted. We exist as care – thrown, projecting, and absorbed in everyday concerns. This care unfolds through the interpenetration of past, present, and future, not as sequential moments but as a unified temporal structure that makes understanding possible. 'Making-present' collapses this rich temporality into demands for instant availability, compressing the duration that authentic existence requires into optimisation cycles. When past becomes data to retrieve, future becomes outcomes to achieve, and present becomes efficiency to maximise, we lose the temporal complexity through which we actually exist. Technology intensifies this collapse by demanding that everything appear on command.

How We Experience the World

Ready-to-hand and Present-at-hand

Heidegger's distinction between ready-to-hand (*Zuhandenheit*) and present-at-hand (*Vorhandenheit*) reveals something fundamental about how human existence encounters the world. This isn't simply a theory about tools and objects but an analysis of two fundamentally different ways that beings can show up for human existence. The distinction illuminates how *Dasein's* engaged 'being-in-the-world' unfolds and what happens when that engagement breaks down.

Ready-to-hand describes how we encounter equipment when we are skilfully engaged in meaningful activity. Heidegger emphasises that when a carpenter uses a hammer, the hammer doesn't appear as an object with properties like weight, texture, and hardness. Instead, it disappears into the activity of hammering – there is just the skilled engagement with the work at hand. When we write with a pen, the pen vanishes into the flow of thinking onto paper. When we navigate familiar spaces, we don't consciously calculate routes but move through engaged familiarity. This transparency, the complete disappearance of equipment into skilled activity, reveals how human existence typically encounters the world – through engaged involvement rather than detached observation. Ready-to-hand engagement unfolds through meaningful networks of tools, purposes, and projects that hang together as unified wholes. The hammer refers to nails, which refer to wood, which refer to building, which refer to shelter, which refer to human dwelling. The pen refers to paper, which refers to writing, which refers to communication, which refers to shared understanding. Each piece of equipment gains its meaning through its place within this larger context of purposes and projects. We don't encounter isolated tools but enter into meaningful worlds where everything refers to everything else in networks of significance.

This engaged involvement reveals the temporal structure of human existence at work seamlessly within skilled activity. When we use equipment skilfully, we move through the unified temporality of past inheritance (learned skills and inherited techniques), future projection (anticipated completion of meaningful projects), and present engagement (current focused activity). The carpenter's skilful hammering integrates inherited technique, projected completion of the building, and present focused activity into a seamless temporal flow. The writer's engagement with pen and paper unifies past learning, anticipated communication, and present expression. Ready-to-hand engagement is how temporal existence actually unfolds in everyday skilled activity – past, present, and future working together inconspicuously.

Present-at-hand describes what happens when ready-to-hand engagement breaks down and beings appear as objects for detached observation. When the hammer breaks, it suddenly appears as a physical object with properties that require conscious attention – weight, texture, damage, and need for repair. When the pen runs out of ink, it shifts from transparent writing tool to object requiring analysis and replacement. The transparency of skilled engagement gives way to analytical observation of an object standing before us. We shift from engaged participation to detached analysis, from temporal involvement to spatial measurement. This breakdown reveals both the primacy of ready-to-hand engagement and the derivative character of present-at-hand analysis. We don't first encounter objects and then learn to use them as tools. Rather, we are always already engaged with equipment in meaningful contexts, and objects appear as such only when engagement breaks down. The present-at-hand stance of detached observation is derivative – it emerges from the breakdown of more primordial ready-to-hand involvement with the world. Present-at-hand analysis is a modification of our more fundamental mode of 'being-in-the-world', not the foundation from which engagement develops.

The present-at-hand stance becomes the foundation for scientific and technological thinking. When beings appear as objects with measurable properties standing before detached subjects, they become available for systematic analysis, mathematical calculation, and technological manipulation. This mode of revealing has enabled enormous advances in scientific understanding and technological capability. However, it represents a fundamental modification of how human existence more primordially encounters the world through skilled engagement. The danger lies not in present-at-hand analysis itself but in treating it as the primary or only valid way of encountering reality. When we approach everything, including human existence itself, primarily through detached analysis and systematic management, we lose contact with the engaged involvement that makes human existence meaningful. We risk becoming observers of life rather than participants in it, managers of existence rather than beings authentically engaged with what matters.

This distinction reveals something crucial about the nature of human understanding. Authentic understanding unfolds through skilled engagement with meaningful contexts rather than detached analysis of isolated objects. We understand tools by using them skilfully, understand people by engaging with them as persons, and understand situations by participating in them rather than observing them from outside. Present-at-hand analysis can supplement this engaged understanding but cannot replace it without fundamental loss. The ready-to-hand/present-at-hand distinction also illuminates what happens in human relationships. When we encounter others authentically, they appear not as objects to be analysed but as persons engaged in their own projects within shared meaningful contexts. We understand others through engaged interaction, shared activity, and mutual involvement in common concerns. Only when these relationships break down do others appear as objects for psychological analysis or social management.

Modern technological thinking tends to privilege the present-at-hand stance while obscuring the ready-to-hand engagement that remains foundational. When everything appears as a resource for systematic optimisation and control, the skilled involvement that makes human existence meaningful gets reduced to efficiency problems requiring better management. Yet even the most sophisticated technological systems depend on human beings who remain ready-to-hand engaged with meaningful projects and purposes. Understanding this distinction doesn't eliminate the need for present-at-hand analysis but creates awareness of when each mode of engagement serves human existence. Sometimes, detached analysis provides essential insights that engaged involvement cannot achieve. Sometimes, stepping back from immediate involvement allows us to see patterns and possibilities that engaged participation obscures. The key is maintaining awareness of what each stance reveals and conceals, using analytical detachment when it serves authentic purposes rather than letting it become the only way of encountering reality.

Dwelling consciously with this distinction means preserving space for ready-to-hand engagement while using present-at-hand analysis strategically. This involves protecting activities that require skilled involvement and engaged participation, maintaining relationships that take shape through shared meaningful activity, and creating contexts where transparent engagement with meaningful projects can flourish. It means recognising when analytical detachment serves authentic purposes and when it substitutes management for genuine engagement.

This distinction between ready-to-hand and present-at-hand reveals how the technological amplification of inauthenticity manifests in our most basic encounter with beings. When we are absorbed in *das Man* and drawn into calculative thinking, the present-at-hand stance feels natural and comprehensive. Tools, people, situations – everything appears as objects for analytical management rather than contexts for engaged involvement. Technology intensifies this shift by making the present-at-hand stance increasingly unavoidable – everything must be available for inspection, measurement, and optimisation. Yet authentic existence depends on preserving ready-to-hand engagement where meaning emerges through skilled involvement rather than detached analysis. Understanding how these structures work together reveals what technology's essence actually means.

Why the Essence of Technology Is by No Means Anything Technological

'The essence of technology is by no means anything technological'. Having explored how human existence unfolds in technological conditions, we can now understand this seemingly paradoxical statement. The essence of technology lies not in any particular device or capability but in how technology transforms the fundamental structures through which human existence unfolds – our groundless condition, our flight into collective interpretations, our absorption in systematic thinking, our temporal complexity, and our ways of encountering beings.

Technology's essence is nothing technological because it works by intensifying tendencies we already possess. We are beings who naturally flee from the Angst of groundlessness into the comfort of what 'everyone' thinks and does. We systematically avoid authentic engagement through idle talk, restless curiosity, and ambiguity about what genuine response requires. Technology doesn't create these tendencies – it amplifies them. Enframing makes our flight systematic and comprehensive. Calculative thinking makes our avoidance feel productive. The absorption in managing tools keeps ontological questions at bay. 'Making-present' compresses the temporal duration that understanding requires. The shift to present-at-hand analysis makes engaged involvement seem inefficient. Each intensification reinforces the others until the transformation of existence itself proceeds unnoticed beneath our management of technological capabilities.

This is why the essence of technology remains so difficult to recognise. Technology conceals its deepest impact by working through structures that make us human. The transformation feels like natural progress rather than fundamental change. When we ask *What can we do with AI?* we remain absorbed in tool management. When we avoid asking *What is AI doing to us?* we demonstrate the very pattern we're describing – fleeing from ontological questions into calculative solutions. Technology's essence reveals itself not by acting upon us like an external force but by keeping our attention fixed on what we can optimise while how we exist gets systematically reshaped. Understanding these structures as unified rather than isolated reveals that conscious engagement with technological conditions requires not escape, which is impossible, but awareness of how technology amplifies our flight and the deliberate preservation of space for what resists systematisation. In Heidegger's terms from *What Is Called Thinking?*, our task is to learn to think – to keep the clearing open within technological conditions, rather than seeking yet another method to master them.[2]

[2]See the Timeline of Heidegger's Key Works in the appendix for sources.

Chapter 7

When Authentic Learning Becomes the Path of Greatest Resistance

These ontological structures – thrownness, *das Man*, fallenness, enframing, *Dasein*, temporality, our relationship to tools and world – aren't abstract concepts. They're the fundamental ways we exist as human beings in technological conditions, all emerging from care, the basic structure through which we relate to existence itself. So what happens when we examine our AI circumstances through this understanding? What do these structures reveal about what's actually happening to us? Consider the Bera phenomenon: How does a student become disconnected from sophisticated work she herself has produced? What conditions make such disconnection possible?

When Students Find Themselves Thrown into AI Circumstances

Bera didn't plan to become someone who could produce work she couldn't defend. She found herself in a moment where AI was suddenly available, where classmates were openly using it, where the technological landscape had shifted around her. When she stares at that empty ChatGPT prompt box, she's already situated in circumstances she didn't create. This reveals thrownness showing itself – we find ourselves in AI circumstances without having chosen them. Most of us didn't expect to become educators wrestling with machine-generated essays or students navigating artificial intelligence for academic work. Yet here we are, forced to respond somehow.

But thrownness runs deeper than encountering new technology. Bera inherited an educational system shaped by decisions made long before she arrived – assignment formats, assessment criteria, expectations about what academic work should be. The forensic linguistics assignment itself carried assumptions about how students should engage with complex material, assumptions embedded in structures she had no part in creating.

What Is AI Doing to Us? A Philosophical Inquiry into Learning, Thinking, and Being, 59–66

Published under exclusive licence by Emerald Publishing Limited
doi:10.1108/978-1-83742-276-020261007

When she encounters AI, she's not choosing in a vacuum. She's responding within inherited circumstances – academic pressure she didn't create, time constraints she didn't design, performance expectations she didn't establish. The 30-second ChatGPT account creation reveals someone navigating a technological moment that arrived without her permission.

Yet something about how readily she adapts suggests that thrownness alone doesn't explain what's unfolding. What makes certain responses feel more viable than others?

When Authentic Learning Encounters *Das Man*'s Scripts

Let's take a look at Bera's reasoning process. Where did her justifications come from? 'Everyone's doing it', she tells herself. 'I'd be stupid not to at least try. It's just brainstorming, right?' None of these emerge from her own engagement with the situation. She finds herself drawn to anonymous interpretations circulating through student networks, library conversations, casual exchanges – collective wisdom that belongs to no one in particular yet feels safer than developing her own uncertain response. She'd overheard the ready-made scripts: 'It's not really cheating', someone had said. 'Everyone uses it for brainstorming. It's basically like having a research assistant'. Developing her own response to AI's unprecedented availability would require confronting genuine uncertainty about academic integrity, learning, and what her work should represent. Here, we see Bera turning to *das Man* – how she finds collective interpretations appealing precisely when developing her own response feels most difficult. The ready-made justifications offer relief from the Angst of authentic choice. These collective certainties feel safer than wrestling with questions that have no established answers. When faced with genuinely new circumstances that demand authentic judgement, *das Man* provides responses that can feel like lifelines rather than limitations.

But notice what happens when these borrowed scripts encounter actual educational complexity. Bera adopts sophisticated terminology – 'phonetic markers of impairment' and 'acoustic degradation patterns' – that she acquired from ChatGPT rather than developed through her own engagement. The language sounds authoritative, but it remains disconnected from her understanding. Bera's use of AI through *das Man* reveals something more troubling than collective script-following. She doesn't just absorb ready-made interpretations – she chooses to become 'they-self', dissolving into the modes of inauthenticity that spare her the burden of authentic intellectual development. Instead of confronting the Angst of not understanding acoustic evidence immediately, she becomes 'anyone' who would use AI rather than taking responsibility for her own learning. She begins to think and perform exactly as 'anyone' absorbed in optimisation would. This dissolution offers profound comfort because it spares her the groundless Angst that authentic learning requires. When she becomes 'anyone' using AI, she no longer faces the difficult work of taking responsibility for intellectual development that has no guaranteed outcomes, gaining efficiency at the cost of depth.

When Learning Falls into Patterns of Flight

Das Man provides the foundation for an even more comprehensive pattern of flight from authentic engagement. Bera's AI use reveals how she lives through fallenness: the three interconnected modes that work together as she avoids the Angst that signals genuine learning – idle talk, curiosity, and ambiguity. While Heidegger originally described idle talk as the anonymous discourse of 'what one says', its structure is preserved, and arguably intensified, in today's AI-mediated contexts. Tools like ChatGPT are trained on vast bodies of public discourse and generate authoritative-sounding language that circulates as if it belonged to everyone and no one. When students adopt this language without grounding it in their own understanding, they aren't bypassing *das Man* – they are enacting it in a new form.

Bera's use of AI-generated terminology thus reflects a technologically intensified version of idle talk – a way of sounding informed without being authentically engaged. Idle talk becomes visible in how Bera adopts AI-generated sophisticated terminology without developing genuine engagement with what it represents. She uses phrases like 'phonetic markers of impairment', 'spectral analysis of fricative consonants', and 'acoustic degradation patterns' that sound authoritative but remain disconnected from her understanding. This isn't simply using unfamiliar vocabulary, it's absorbing language that creates the impression of engaging with complex ideas while avoiding the struggle that authentic engagement requires. The AI provides her with professional discourse that allows her to participate in academic conversations rather than developing her own relationship with acoustic evidence.

Curiosity shows itself as restless seeking after AI capabilities while avoiding sustained engagement with what the forensic linguistics assignment actually demands. Instead of dwelling with the confusion about slurred speech and intoxication through meditative thinking, uncertainty that could become productive if given temporal duration, she flees into the calculative approach of exploring what ChatGPT can provide. She finds herself thinking about how to get the best response rather than what she actually needs to understand. This restless seeking prevents the patient attention that allows complex questions to reveal their significance, substituting the activity of gathering AI-generated material for the demanding work of thinking through acoustic evidence herself.

Ambiguity emerges as Bera loses the capacity to distinguish between AI-enhanced performance and authentic engagement with ideas. When she presents sophisticated analysis she cannot defend, when her work sounds authoritative but is disconnected from her own understanding, when AI assistance promises comprehensive resolution while leaving her feeling fraudulent, she finds herself struggling to recognise authentic response when it might emerge. This ambiguity isn't simply confusion about appropriate AI use. It represents the blurring of what makes intellectual engagement genuinely human, creating conditions where sophisticated performance and authentic understanding appear equally valid.

These three structures reinforce each other in ways that make fallenness self-perpetuating. Idle talk about AI capabilities makes restless seeking after AI solutions feel productive rather than avoidant. Curiosity about what AI can produce generates more idle talk that sounds sophisticated but avoids fundamental engagement with learning itself. Together, they create the ambiguity that makes it increasingly difficult to distinguish between authentic intellectual development and performance enhancement.

What becomes visible through these modes is how Bera uses AI to avoid not just academic stress but the fundamental Angst that signals authentic engagement with existence itself. Bera experiences fear about specific challenges – deadlines, performance expectations, academic requirements – but she avoids the deeper Angst that emerges when we confront the groundless nature of learning itself. Authentic engagement with acoustic evidence would require confronting the Angst of not-knowing, of struggling with complexity that offers no guaranteed resolution, of taking responsibility for understanding that has no predetermined foundation. Instead, Bera gains the language of depth without the experience of it, the form of understanding without its struggle. AI provides sophisticated escape from this fundamental Angst by offering procedures that promise resolution without requiring the groundless work of genuine intellectual development.

When Students Experience Everything as Standing-reserve

Enframing emerges clearly here – how everything begins to appear as standing-reserve available for optimisation. Living through enframing, Bera doesn't see herself as a developing mind encountering ideas that matter; she experiences herself as a system requiring enhancement. We can see the ontic-ontological difference showing itself directly: her attention turns immediately to ontic questions – 'How can I use AI effectively?' 'Should I ask for an outline?' 'A full argument?' Something in between?' – while missing the ontological transformation occurring beneath her awareness. She focuses on managing the tool, her attention captured by immediate demands, while the deeper transformation of her relationship to thinking unfolds beneath the surface of awareness. The question becomes not 'What do I need to understand about acoustic evidence?' but 'How do I efficiently produce what's expected?' This shift reveals calculative thinking displacing meditative thinking. Instead of dwelling with questions that resist quick answers, Bera converts every educational encounter into optimisation problems requiring systematic solutions. This means that even her most sophisticated AI management addresses surface-level efficiency while the deeper transformation of her thinking continues undisturbed.

ChatGPT aligns perfectly with this approach. It promises to transform the temporal complexity that learning requires – duration for ideas to settle, space for confusion to become productive, time for understanding to develop naturally – into instant availability. The logic feels compelling because it offers concrete solutions to immediate pressures. When everything appears as optimisation problems through enframing's lens, technological solutions seem like an easier route than struggling with complexity that offers no guaranteed outcomes.

But this approach to her own thinking creates the disconnection we observed. This dissolution offers profound comfort because it allows her to avoid the groundless Angst that authentic learning requires. Depth disappears into efficiency, learning becomes measurable but not meaningful. Bera ends up with sophisticated outputs that exceed her authentic capabilities.

When Learning Becomes Immediate and Depth Disappears

Bera experiences 'making-present' – becoming absorbed in immediate academic demands while losing sight of how past inheritance and future projection give meaning to current learning. This represents a profound flight from the Angst that authentic temporality requires, collapsing the rich interpenetration of temporal dimensions into manageable demands for instant academic productivity.

Rather than dwelling with inherited educational traditions as living foundations that continue to shape understanding, 'making-present' reduces the past to immediately accessible information that can be retrieved and deployed efficiently through AI assistance. She loses the capacity to let the complexity of forensic linguistics reveal its significance through patient engagement, treating academic complexity as data to be processed rather than as inherited knowledge that makes current understanding possible. Similarly, authentic projection towards uncertain intellectual possibilities gets replaced by planning towards predetermined academic outcomes that promise to spare her from Angst. Instead of remaining open to what acoustic evidence might teach her – possibilities that create meaningful uncertainty because they cannot be guaranteed – she focuses exclusively on producing work that can be evaluated. The present itself becomes reduced to efficiency optimisation rather than the convergence point where inherited meaning and anticipated possibility demand authentic response.

ChatGPT's instant responses align perfectly with this flattened temporality. 'Twenty minutes ago she'd been drowning; now she had everything she needed for a sophisticated argument'. The tool makes the temporal complexity that learning requires seem like unnecessary delay rather than essential duration. When faced with deadline pressure, instant solutions feel more practical than uncertain development.

This temporal flattening also obscures the recognition of finitude that gives learning its urgency. Bera moves as if she has unlimited time to defer authentic engagement, as if she can endlessly postpone the work of genuine understanding through technological assistance. But learning opportunities are finite and unrepeatable – this particular encounter with acoustic evidence, this specific moment in her intellectual development, this unique convergence of circumstances will not return. When 'making-present' covers over awareness of this finitude, learning loses the urgency that makes present choices about authentic engagement meaningful. The depth of understanding collapses into immediacy – the temporal struggle that makes insight possible quietly disappears. AI creates the illusion that understanding can be indefinitely deferred because sophisticated analysis remains instantly available.

Where Monitoring Replaces Meaning

Take a look at how Bera relates to her own thinking during the mock trial. Even when not actively using AI, she monitors her performance rather than engaging authentically with ideas. 'Is this good enough?' she keeps thinking. 'I just need to get through this'. But she realises she isn't actually trying to understand what acoustic evidence means – she's trying to survive the questioning. The thought 'What am I actually supposed to be learning here?' flickers briefly, but she pushes it away.

Scattered *Dasein* becomes visible here – how the essential 'being-there' that makes authentic learning possible gets fragmented across multiple concerns. Instead of being fully present to the ideas she's encountering, her attention splits between technological management, performance expectations, and deadline pressure.

This scattered relationship to her own thinking didn't begin with AI. Much of her educational experience had already trained her to monitor performance rather than engage authentically with ideas. The AI tool intensifies a fragmentation that was already at work, making it easier to maintain distance from genuine intellectual struggle.

Meanwhile, even experienced AI users rarely achieve the transparent integration that authentic thinking requires. There's always consciousness of managing the interaction – 'She found herself writing another prompt, thinking about how to ask for clarification without seeming ignorant' and 'evaluating the AI's response for completeness and polish'.

The ready-to-hand/present-at-hand distinction becomes crucial here. When Bera writes with a pen that works well, the pen disappears into the movement of thinking onto paper. But the AI tool resists becoming transparent. She remains always aware of working with it rather than through it. This persistent present-at-hand visibility fragments the thinking process itself. Instead of direct engagement with acoustic evidence, there's negotiation with a machine about acoustic evidence. The tool offers capabilities that exceed her understanding while maintaining a persistent otherness that fragments her attention.

When presence becomes analytical management of multiple concerns rather than authentic engagement, learning transforms from genuine encounter to procedure – exactly what makes it replicable by algorithms. Monitoring has replaced meaning itself, and with it, the experience of genuine understanding.

Where Everything Conspires Against Learning

What becomes visible through this analysis is that all these structures represent distortions of care – the fundamental way human beings relate to existence itself. Bera didn't begin as someone disconnected from learning. She cares about her education, her performance, her future – but the conditions she inherits transform caring-for her intellectual development into taking-care-of academic requirements. Instead of the patient, sustained attention that authentic learning demands, she learns to optimise academic outputs. Instead of engaging authentically with ideas that matter, she manages performance across multiple evaluation criteria.

When care gets transformed into management, the temporal duration that caring relationships require – time for confusion to become productive, space for understanding to emerge gradually, patience for authentic engagement to develop – gets compressed into optimisation cycles that promise resolution without requiring the struggle that genuine understanding demands. This transformation of care into management explains why Bera can produce sophisticated work while remaining disconnected from the thinking it represents – she has learned to care systematically rather than authentically.

When all these structures work together – thrownness into AI circumstances, *das Man*'s ready-made scripts, fallenness as a mode of flight, enframing's optimisation logic, scattered *Dasein*, compressed temporality, and persistently present-at-hand tools – they create something more troubling than any single tendency alone. These aren't separate problems happening to Bera simultaneously. They're interconnected modes of existence she lives through that conspire to make authentic learning difficult to sustain.

Consider how they reinforce each other: Bera's thrownness into AI circumstances she didn't choose makes *das Man's* ready-made scripts feel more appealing than developing her own uncertain response. 'Everyone uses it for brainstorming' offers relief from the Angst of navigating unprecedented technological territory without guidance. But following these collective scripts leads her deeper into enframing's optimisation logic – treating herself as a resource requiring enhancement rather than a developing mind. The scripts themselves frame technological solutions as the easier path, making enframing feel like common sense rather than a fundamental transformation in how she relates to her own learning.

When everything appears as standing-reserve requiring efficient deployment, the duration that authentic learning needs – time to sit with confusion, space for understanding to emerge gradually – feels like wasteful delay rather than essential process. Compressed temporality makes enframing's optimisation logic seem not just reasonable but urgent.

As temporal pressure mounts, *Dasein* becomes increasingly scattered. Instead of being fully present to ideas worth engaging, Bera's attention fragments across multiple concerns – technological management, performance monitoring, deadline pressure. Scattered presence makes authentic engagement feel unattainable while procedural approaches feel necessary.

Present-at-hand tools complete their role in what the other structures started. When attention is already fragmented and time already compressed, tools that promise efficiency – even though they demand conscious management rather than transparent integration – feel unavoidable. The AI tool's persistent visibility aligns with scattered attention rather than demanding the focused presence that authentic learning requires.

Each structure makes the others feel more natural and harder to resist. Thrown circumstances make collective scripts appealing. Collective scripts normalise optimisation thinking. Optimisation thinking compresses temporality. Compressed temporality scatters presence. Scattered presence disrupts transparent engagement, making conscious tool-management feel necessary. And conscious tool management reinforces the approach that avoids authentic struggle.

The result is a unified condition where Bera shapes herself away from authentic learning while believing she's making reasonable choices. She inherits circumstances and chooses responses that make AI use feel easier than alternatives, adopts collective scripts that present technological solutions as the easier path, responds to temporal pressure by bypassing reflection, chooses to monitor her thinking rather than engage authentically, and works with tools in ways that prevent transparent integration.

Together, these create something unprecedented – the diminishment of the struggle that builds genuine understanding while enhancing the appearance of sophisticated learning. Bera ends up disconnected from work she herself produced because the ontological structures of her existence have converged to make such disconnection the path of least resistance.

And yet, what we began to see through her experience would not remain hers alone.

Chapter 8

When Authentic Educational Practice Becomes the Path of Greatest Resistance

As we traced the modes of existence of Bera's AI engagement through Heidegger's ontological structures – her flight into *das Man's* ready-made scripts, her systematic avoidance of authentic encounter, her transformation of care into management – we began to recognise something revealing. We had been living through the same structures ourselves.

When Educators Find Themselves Thrown into AI Circumstances

When ChatGPT arrived in November 2022, we discovered ourselves in circumstances we hadn't chosen – educators suddenly wrestling with machine-generated essays, administrators navigating unprecedented questions about academic integrity, an institution compelled to respond to technological capabilities that exceeded our educational frameworks. Like Bera staring at that empty prompt box, we found ourselves thrown into AI circumstances without having anticipated them, forced to respond somehow to questions we'd never encountered.

But our thrownness ran deeper than encountering new technology. We inherited educational institutions shaped by decisions made before any of us arrived – assessment systems designed for different technological conditions, accreditation requirements that prioritised measurable outcomes, competitive pressures that demanded visible innovation responses. When AI arrived, we weren't choosing responses in a vacuum. We were navigating within inherited institutional structures that made certain approaches feel more viable than others, just as Bera inherited academic pressures and performance expectations she had no part in creating.

When Authentic Educational Practice Encounters *Das Man*'s Scripts

When genuine uncertainty about AI's educational implications demanded authentic institutional response, we found ourselves drawn to what 'everyone' was saying

What Is AI Doing to Us? A Philosophical Inquiry into Learning, Thinking, and Being, 67–71

Published under exclusive licence by Emerald Publishing Limited
doi:10.1108/978-1-83742-276-020261008

about technological change – collective interpretations that promised relief from unprecedented Angst without requiring the struggle of developing our own uncertain responses. When we analysed how Bera turned to scripts like 'Everyone's doing it' and 'It's just brainstorming, right?' we realised we had been adopting parallel institutional scripts: 'Best practices for AI integration', 'responsible AI use while maintaining academic integrity', 'leveraging AI capabilities for educational enhancement'. These phrases circulated through conferences and publications, offering the comfort of apparent expertise without requiring the groundless work of developing authentic responses to genuinely novel circumstances.

Just as Bera's scripts belonged to no particular student yet felt safer than developing her own uncertain response, our institutional scripts belonged to no particular institution yet provided relief from the Angst of authentic institutional leadership when facing unprecedented questions. Both individual and institutional flight into collective interpretations revealed the same pattern: when thrown circumstances demand authentic engagement, *das Man's* ready-made responses offer appealing alternatives to the Angst that authentic choice requires.

When Leadership Falls into Modes of Flight

The institutional scripts provided foundation for comprehensive flight from the Angst that authentic engagement with AI's educational implications requires. Our institutional responses revealed how we had lived through the same structures of fallenness that shaped Bera's AI use. When we analysed how Bera adopted sophisticated terminology like 'phonetic markers of impairment' without genuine engagement, we realised we had been developing institutional vocabulary about 'digital transformation' and 'AI literacy' that sounded authoritative but remained disconnected from our understanding of what these capabilities meant for educational relationships. Just as her idle talk allowed participation in academic conversations without authentic struggle, our institutional idle talk allowed participation in professional discussions without confronting fundamental questions about educational purpose. Bera's curiosity showed itself as restless seeking after AI capabilities while avoiding sustained engagement with what the assignment actually demanded. We began to recognise parallel institutional curiosity – the restless calculative thinking that chases new frameworks, emerging tools, and updated best practices while fleeing from the meditative attention required to understand what AI's arrival actually reveals about learning itself. The tools arms race we experienced throughout 2024 mirrored exactly her flight from dwelling with confusion into systematic solutions that promised resolution without requiring genuine engagement.

Most troubling was recognising the same ambiguity. Just as Bera lost capacity to distinguish between AI-enhanced performance and authentic engagement with ideas, we found ourselves unable to distinguish between sophisticated institutional performance and authentic engagement with educational questions. When we could run successful workshops while feeling disconnected from educational purpose, we were experiencing the same disconnection between performance and understanding that characterised her relationship to AI-generated work – institutional activity without depth.

When Institutions Experience Everything as Standing-reserve

Through these tendencies of institutional flight, everything began to appear through the same enframing logic that shaped Bera's experience. When we analysed how she began treating herself as a system requiring enhancement rather than a developing mind encountering ideas, we recognised that we had been approaching our institution as a system needing optimisation, our educational practice as processes requiring improvement, our students as outcomes to be managed. The ontic-ontological difference showed itself identically in our institutional responses. Just as Bera's attention turned to managing AI tools while missing the transformation of her relationship to thinking, our attention focused on implementing policies and managing technological integration while the deeper transformation of our way of being as educators remained concealed. We addressed surface efficiency while fundamental questions about educational purpose continued undisturbed.

We addressed surface efficiency while fundamental questions about educational purpose appeared to be engaged but were quietly converted into management problems – reframed rather than confronted. When fundamental questions about purpose and meaning are reframed as problems requiring systematic solutions, both individuals and institutions find themselves reaching for tools and policies that promise to manage what cannot be managed. This is calculative thinking at work - refusing to preserve space for meditative dwelling with what cannot be systematised. Bera experienced ChatGPT's 'twenty-minute solution' as relief from weeks of uncertain struggle. We experienced systematic institutional responses as relief from the Angst of not knowing what AI meant for educational relationships. Both individual and institutional enframing transformed care into management, eliminating the duration that authentic development requires, trading meaning for measurable efficiency.

When Educational Practice Becomes Immediate and Reflection Fades

We experienced the same temporal compression that characterised Bera's AI use. When she collapsed past inheritance and future projection into immediate productivity demands, we compressed the temporal complexity that authentic educational leadership requires into implementation timelines and policy cycles that promised resolution without requiring groundless struggle.

Just as Bera lost awareness that learning opportunities are finite and unrepeatable, we lost sight of the recognition that this particular encounter with AI's arrival, this specific moment in our educational development, would not return. When 'making-present' erodes awareness of institutional finitude, educational leadership loses the urgency that makes present choices about authentic engagement meaningful.

The tools arms race clearly revealed this temporal flattening. New applications emerged weekly, and we kept adjusting presentations, abandoning materials we'd spent hours preparing. This created the illusion that institutional mastery over technological change was possible while destroying the duration that authentic understanding requires. We were living the same temporal compression that made Bera's authentic engagement with acoustic evidence feel like unnecessary delay, losing reflection as we accelerated towards procedural resolution.

Where Monitoring Replaces Meaning in Leadership

Even when not actively managing AI implementation, we found ourselves monitoring institutional performance rather than engaging authentically with educational questions. Just as Bera monitored her academic performance while remaining disconnected from genuine learning, we monitored institutional metrics while losing touch with educational purpose. The scattered *Dasein* we observed in Bera's fragmented attention between performance monitoring and AI tool management reflected our own institutional experience. Our attention split between policy development, competitive positioning, technological learning, and actual educational engagement – never settling into sustained presence with what mattered most.

When we analysed how AI tools remained persistently present-at-hand for Bera, preventing transparent integration with authentic thinking, we recognised the same pattern emerging in our own leadership practice. We remained always conscious of managing institutional AI responses rather than thinking through educational questions transparently. This persistent technological visibility fragmented whatever focused attention might have emerged, transforming educational leadership from genuine encounter with purpose into procedure management.

The parallel was exact – just as Bera's scattered attention prevented authentic engagement with learning, our scattered institutional attention prevented authentic engagement with educational relationships. Both individual and institutional modes of being revealed the same transformation from caring-for authentic development to taking-care-of systematic requirements. Monitoring has replaced meaning here too, converting leadership into administration and presence into performance.

Where the Structures Begin to Echo Each Other

The recognition that we were living through the same ontological structures as our students changed everything about our inquiry. When we could produce sophisticated institutional responses while remaining disconnected from understanding what they meant for educational purpose, we were experiencing the same disconnection between performance and authentic engagement that characterised Bera's AI use. This wasn't about individual students making poor choices or institutions implementing flawed policies. We were all navigating technological circumstances through the same fundamental structures that shape human existence itself. The structures we identified in individual AI use – thrownness, *das Man*, fallenness, enframing, temporal compression, scattered attention, care transformation – showed themselves across educational contexts in strikingly similar ways. But more than parallel experiences, we began to see how institutional and individual modes actively reinforced one another, creating conditions where systematic approaches feel not just appealing but inevitable.

Consider how institutional *das Man* scripts shape the circumstances students inherit. When institutions adopt collective interpretations about 'responsible AI use while maintaining academic integrity', they create environments where students naturally find parallel interpretations appealing. The institutional ambiguity embedded in 'responsible use while maintaining integrity' becomes individual ambiguity where students turn to collective wisdom like 'It's just brainstorming, right?' Institutional emphasis on 'leveraging AI capabilities for educational enhancement' reveals optimisation thinking that treats education as a system requiring improvement. When Bera focused on 'How do I efficiently produce what's expected?', she was living through an individualised form of *das Man* that mirrored the institutional optimisation scripts we had modelled.

The reinforcement shows itself in both directions. Students' ready adoption of systematic approaches creates institutional pressure for more systematic solutions. Each systematic institutional response makes individual systematic choices feel more reasonable, while individual systematic choices create institutional pressures for more comprehensive systematic frameworks. Most fundamentally, both institutions and individuals learn to take-care-of systematic requirements rather than caring-for authentic relationships. Institutions focus on completion rates and policy compliance while students focus on grade optimisation and performance management. The temporal structure that makes caring relationships possible gets compressed into immediate productivity demands at both levels. This convergence reveals reinforcement loops where each structure makes the others feel more natural and harder to resist. Institutional conditions create individual circumstances where systematic responses feel reasonable. Individual adoption of systematic approaches creates institutional pressures for more systematic solutions. Each cycle makes authentic alternatives feel more difficult while systematic optimisation feels more inevitable.

We were witnessing how the ways we exist together, shaped by the basic structures of human life, had created conditions where systematic optimisation felt natural while authentic struggle had begun to seem impractical. Understanding how we collectively arrived at circumstances where authentic educational engagement had become the path of greatest resistance for everyone involved would require investigating the deeper historical conditions that made such systematic convergence possible.

Part IV

The Convergence

Chapter 9

The Systematic Preparation

The analysis we undertook in Part III reveals something more fundamental than individual students making poor choices about AI use or institutions implementing flawed policies. What we're witnessing is how the ways we exist together, shaped by the fundamental structures of human life, create conditions where authentic educational engagement becomes increasingly difficult while systematic optimisation feels increasingly natural and necessary. But how have we collectively come to this point?

The Illusion of Learning

We had been experimenting with AI since it had initially been released to the public, but now, armed with our developing understanding of technology through a Heideggerian lens, we decided to revisit what we were seeing. What were we actually looking at? Our experiments were simple enough. We prompted it to write discussion posts about literary themes, to summarise research articles, to generate thesis statements for argumentative essays, to respond to reading assignments. Each time, it produced the same systematic organisation – clear introductions that moved to structured development and tidy conclusions. The professional vocabulary sounded authoritative without being too complex. The balanced tone seemed perfectly appropriate for academic contexts. Yet something felt strangely familiar about all of this.

As we continued examining the outputs, that sense of familiarity began to unsettle us. The predictable logical sequences it used to develop arguments. The standard academic formulations it employed for analysis. The sentence structures that varied just enough to seem natural while maintaining perfect clarity. Gradually, it began to show itself as *das Man* in operation – anonymous ways of speaking that belong to no one and yet shape everyone's thinking. We started noticing echoes of places where these patterns had appeared before.

The answer seemed to be everywhere. In thousands of student papers, we had graded over the years. In the writing, we had praised and rewarded. In the very standards, we had established for academic success. What this reveals is troubling – these appear less as individual expressions of authentic thinking and more as

What Is AI Doing to Us? A Philosophical Inquiry into Learning, Thinking, and Being, 75–85

Published under exclusive licence by Emerald Publishing Limited
doi:10.1108/978-1-83742-276-020261009

collective scripts absorbed and reproduced. Our unease deepened into something more disturbing. We were not just seeing familiar patterns – we were seeing the very patterns we ourselves had taught our students to value. Through our inquiry, this reveals itself as enframing in operation – learning itself appears as though it has been drawn into standing-reserve, to be optimised and managed – and perhaps this helps explain why machines can so easily replicate it.

A troubling possibility began to emerge. Was this AI mimicking education, or was it completing what education had already become? The machines were following patterns we had created. They were meeting standards we had established. They were satisfying criteria we had rewarded for years – the sophisticated vocabulary we had always accepted as proof of learning, the structured argumentation we had counted on to demonstrate critical thinking. Of course, many educators experienced these tools as enabling more thoughtful engagement by removing arbitrary barriers – helping struggling students access academic discourse, creating consistency across evaluators, addressing genuine accountability needs. What reveals itself here is deeper – perhaps even when these tools succeeded by their own measures, we had been dwelling inauthentically, mistaking systematic procedures for genuine human engagement.

But if machines can now replicate the work we had always taken to demonstrate learning, what does this suggest about the nature of learning itself? The realisation began to strike us with unexpected force. We had spent years believing we were cultivating authentic human existence, fostering the kind of thinking that emerges from genuine encounter with ideas, the struggle with uncertainty that makes learning distinctively human. Yet when machines can now follow our patterns so perfectly, it unsettled us to wonder – had we been training students to execute systematic procedures rather than to engage authentically with ideas?

This recognition opened disturbing questions that would drive our inquiry forward. When had learning shown itself as no longer distinctively human? When had authentic thinking given way to systematic procedures so refined that machines could now carry them out flawlessly? Perhaps AI was not disrupting education. Perhaps it was completing what we had unknowingly begun. Learning reveals itself as already translated into patterns, engagement replaced with procedures, authenticity eroded into forms reproducible by machines. And in seeing these patterns repeated so perfectly, it becomes possible to glimpse what may have been lost – what once made learning distinctively human. But how had this happened? How had we collectively arrived at this point?

Preparing the Ground for Our Own Replacement

The questions from our earlier recognition demanded inquiry: How had we collectively arrived at this point? If AI could now replicate what we thought was learning, when had education become systematic enough for such replication? Armed with our understanding of the ontological structures we had traced through Bera's experience and our own institutional responses, we began to trace these same structures backward through educational history. The thrownness into circumstances that made systematic responses feel viable, the *das Man* scripts that made optimisation thinking feel natural, and the enframing logic that made everything appear as standing-reserve – all began to show themselves as having shaped educational development for far longer than we had recognised. Through our inquiry, we could trace how structured assignment formats had emerged during the 1990s and 2000s. These approaches had gained prominence as responses to genuine educational challenges – helping students who struggled with open-ended tasks, enabling more consistent assessment, addressing accountability pressures. The changes had felt natural, even necessary, and we had embraced them willingly, believing they were making education better.

As we continued our inquiry, what revealed itself was that educational relationships themselves were being systematically transformed during this period. Standardised testing had converted complex learning into measurable data points that could be tracked and compared. Learning management systems had systematised educational delivery, making every interaction trackable and manageable. Data-driven instruction had converted educational decisions into systematic responses to test scores and metrics. At the time, these changes had appeared to be better time management, more efficient use of limited resources, more accountable educational practice. But as we traced these changes, something unsettling revealed itself in what was showing itself.

It appeared that something fundamental had been happening, though we were only now beginning to see it. The past increasingly appeared as something to be efficiently accessed – documented procedures that can be implemented rather than lived traditions that shape understanding over time. The future increasingly appeared as predetermined learning objectives to be systematically achieved rather than uncertain possibilities that create meaningful engagement. The present increasingly appeared as optimisation cycles focused on immediate improvement rather than the duration where authentic understanding actually develops. The tendency began to reveal itself more clearly, and it was deeply unsettling. We could see 'making-present' showing itself across decades through what had appeared to be reasonable educational improvements. When educational time became compressed into demands for immediate availability, systematic procedures began to feel not just helpful but necessary. They promised to remove the slow, uncertain process that authentic learning actually requires.

As we sat with what our inquiry was revealing, something began to dawn on us. What if all the changes we had made, all the improvements we had embraced, were showing themselves as part of the same trajectory? The recognition came with force – it appeared that we had been systematically chipping away at authentic learning while believing we were improving it. Every structured format we had implemented, every rubric we had created, every systematic approach we had embraced, reveals itself as perhaps reducing the temporal complexity that makes learning distinctively human. We had been converting the struggle with uncertainty that creates authentic engagement into manageable procedures that could be efficiently executed. The scope of what was disclosing itself was sobering – each improvement seems to carry within it the possibility of slowly diminishing what makes learning human. The changes that had once seemed reasonable now reveal themselves as perhaps preparing the ground for our own replacement.

This historical trajectory was not uniform or uncontested. Throughout these same decades, critical pedagogy movements questioned instrumental approaches to education. Progressive educators and researchers actively resisted the reduction of learning to measurable outcomes, arguing for care-based pedagogies, dialogical learning, and education as liberation rather than management. Yet these resistance movements increasingly found themselves marginalised within institutions that rewarded systematic approaches – a marginalisation that itself reveals how powerful the trajectory towards systematisation had become.

We had been tracing how educational practices – rubrics, assessment protocols, and digital platforms – had reshaped the visible landscape of learning. But something deeper was beginning to emerge. These weren't just procedures we implemented. They reveal themselves as ways of being we have come to inhabit. The next phase of our inquiry wouldn't take us further into policies or platforms, it would take us into the habits of thought, language, and care that now showed themselves as working through us from within.

The Language That Claimed Our Thinking

As we reflected on this puzzle, we began to notice something we had taken for granted. Educators, often strangers to one another, working in different institutions and facing different challenges, had nonetheless begun to speak in strikingly similar ways about education. And institutions themselves, despite their unique missions, were adopting almost indistinguishable phrases in their official discourse. A single pattern seemed to echo across the educational landscape. Educators and institutions were repeating the same formulations: 'Data-driven decision making', 'Student-centred learning objectives', 'Enhancing student outcomes', 'Implementing best practices', 'Optimising learning experiences', and 'Leveraging evidence-based practices'. This vocabulary echoes in classrooms, in faculty meetings, in mission statements, and in strategic plans, until it seems to belong to no single place yet pervades them all.

But where had this language come from? Who first spoke of 'leveraging best practices' or of 'enhancing student outcomes'? As we tried to trace these phrases back, they slipped away from any origin. They seemed to belong to no one in particular, and yet they had quietly taken hold of how everyone thought about improvement in education. They moved through conferences, circulated in publications, were repeated in professional development sessions, and taken up in administrative meetings – phrases ready-made, offering themselves as if they were natural educational wisdom. In this movement, what reveals itself was not a single author or source, but *das Man* speaking through language itself. These anonymous phrases belong to no one, and yet they shape everyone. We found ourselves repeating interpretations already given, never quite noticing that we had not chosen them, speaking in ways that felt like common sense but which, on reflection, reveal themselves as a flight from authentic engagement.

As we traced back through our own experience, something began to disturb us. When had it first happened that we found ourselves saying 'optimise learning experiences' without sensing what the phrase was already making us think? When had institutions begun incorporating 'systematic instructional delivery' into their planning documents? When had 'delivering content' become so normal that we never noticed how it was quietly shifting our understanding of authentic engagement with ideas into information transfer? The more we reflected, the more unsettling the recognition became. We had thought we were learning sophisticated professional vocabulary that would help us communicate more effectively about education. Institutions had believed they were adopting more precise language for strategic planning. The language had given us a sense of competence and professionalism as it spread through our professional contexts. But what if the movement was otherwise? What if, instead of us mastering this language, it had already begun to master us?

The possibility was chilling. When educators said 'optimise learning experiences', they weren't just describing what they planned to do. When institutions adopted language about 'systematic instructional delivery', they weren't just communicating administrative decisions. The language itself reveals itself as shaping how both individuals and institutions can think about students – as systems requiring enhancement. It converts understanding of authentic engagement into systematic information transfer.

It appeared, then, that this vocabulary was not merely expressing thoughts we already had – it was opening the very space within which we could think about education at all. We were experiencing what Heidegger analysed in *On the Way to Language*. Language is not merely a tool for expressing thoughts we already have, it is the house of Being creating the clearing within which beings can appear and be understood. We don't first have thoughts and then find words for them. Language creates the space within which certain kinds of thinking become possible while concealing others entirely. This systematic language reveals itself as systematically reshaping the very clearing within which educational relationships can appear. It makes only systematic approaches seem coherent while concealing the possibility of authentic caring-for students as persons engaged in uncertain development. The language isn't just changing how we talk about education – it is showing us what education can be, and what it can no longer be, within its terms.

We thought we were mastering a professional language, but little by little it revealed itself as the one quietly mastering us. It shaped not only how we spoke, but also what we were able to see. By the time AI entered the scene, the space of educational thought had already been flattened into patterns so systematic that algorithms could echo them flawlessly. What disturbed us is not that AI can generate convincing educational discourse, but that it is drawing from a vocabulary that, perhaps, has already claimed our thinking. If so, it had already cleared the way for the machine's arrival.

The Unveiling of the Picture-world

The language showed itself as having claimed our thinking – not merely reshaping how we communicated about education, but quietly altering our very capacity to conceive of it. It subtly defined what we valued, what we measured, and, in a way we hadn't fully recognised, what we could even perceive as real. Yet, this systematic capture of our discourse was no final destination; it appears instead as a crucial, almost imperceptible, layer of preparation. By the time artificial intelligence began echoing our professional vocabulary and replicating our valued outputs, educational institutions were already inhabiting a fundamentally altered landscape – an ontology in which the very nature of learning, teaching, and human engagement had quietly shifted.

What shows itself here is no simple evolution of practice or mere adoption of tools. It reveals itself as a redefinition, a silent upheaval that changes what we are actually seeing, even when we believed we knew precisely what stood before us. Students no longer appear simply as persons embarking on uncertain journeys of growth – they are increasingly rendered as academic profiles to be managed and optimised across digital interfaces. Learning, once an authentic, messy encounter with resistant ideas, a struggle with the unknown, shows itself as having solidified into measurable progress, neatly tracked and displayed on dashboards. Teaching, once a complex, caring relationship with unpredictable, deeply human outcomes, reveals itself instead as systematic procedure, streamlined for efficient delivery and effortless replication.

It shows itself less as disruption and more as culmination. The temporal complexity inherent in authentic educational encounters – the slow development, the unpredictable detours, the human struggle with uncertainty, has been meticulously refined. It has been converted, piece by piece, into representations that promise clarity and remove the very messiness that makes learning human. The lived reality of teaching and learning reveals itself as transformed into manageable abstractions – models, metrics, and outcomes. It appears as though we have perfected the art of observing and controlling education from a distance, working not with the raw, vibrant reality of students and ideas, but engaging with their pictures.

And what unsettled us most was this. It hadn't felt like a loss. It had felt like improvement. It felt like clarity. Like progress. Like control. And that was the tragedy. It revealed itself as our having learned to celebrate the disappearance of uncertainty. For decades we had refined procedures that made education appear more visible, more manageable, more efficient. We had created taxonomies, templates, outcomes, procedures. But slowly, we began to glimpse what we had done. The more we tried to represent learning, the more we had replaced it. Conversations gave way to metrics. Presence to dashboards. Possibility to preloaded outcomes. Only later did it show itself otherwise – less a shift in practice than a metaphysical transformation. What we were witnessing was something Heidegger had identified as characteristic of the modern age – the world becoming a picture.

In his 1938 essay *The Age of the World Picture*,[1] Heidegger argued that modernity is defined by a particular way of revealing – not merely having

[1]Heidegger, M. (1977). The age of the world picture. In *The question concerning technology and other essays* (W. Lovitt, Trans., pp. 115–154). Harper & Row. (Original work published 1938)

representations of reality, but converting reality itself into a fixed image, a picture, that a thinking subject can observe, control, and manipulate. Reality becomes something to stand before us, ready to be processed. Educational relationships reveal themselves as undergoing exactly this transformation through the processes we have been tracing. The temporal, relational, unpredictable nature of teaching and learning is flattened into snapshots – pictures of students, pictures of progress, pictures of outcomes. What was once lived becomes displayable. What was once uncertain becomes visualised. What was once relational becomes representational. And so when AI now processes educational work so convincingly, it is not breaking with authentic relationships but shows itself as working on what education had already become. It works not with students, ideas, or struggle, but with the pictures, we had already created. What AI unveils is not a break from the past, but its disclosure. The transformation is not technical. It is ontological – the essence of technology is by no means anything technological.

When We Stopped Thinking and Started Computing

The systematic conversion of educational relationships into manageable representations began to uncover something more fundamental – the way thinking itself has come to show itself differently in educational contexts. Bera's approach to her forensic linguistics assignment, framing it as 'How do I efficiently produce what's expected?' rather than dwelling with what acoustic evidence might reveal, appeared as the result of a much longer shift, a replacement of one kind of thinking with another.

Consider what was actually required in educational moments before systematic solutions were developed. When a student struggled with a complex idea, what did authentic educational engagement look like? Staying present with their confusion without immediately providing answers. Dwelling with uncertainty about what they needed. Remaining open to where their questions might lead, even when it disrupted lesson plans. Being willing to sit with not knowing whether responses were helping.

What later showed itself as systematic improvements also reveals itself as undermining this kind of engagement in systematic ways. Procedures were developed for moving quickly towards predetermined solutions rather than dwelling with student confusion until insight emerged naturally. Timelines compressed learning into efficient outcomes rather than preserving space for uncertain emergence. Structured formats channelled thinking towards measurable results rather than remaining open to where authentic questions might lead. What at first appeared to be educational improvement now discloses itself otherwise – as the erosion of meditative thinking from educational relationships. This transformation resonates with what Heidegger identified in his 1954 work *Science and Reflection* – the historical replacement of meditative thinking with calculative thinking that characterises the modern technological age.

The reason AI can replicate educational work so convincingly shows itself more clearly here. Machines excel at calculative thinking – systematic problem-solving, efficient optimisation, predetermined procedures. But they cannot engage meditatively – they cannot dwell with uncertainty, remain present with confusion, or stay open to possibilities that resist systematisation.

In education, the kind of thinking that machines cannot replicate had already begun to diminish. Educational practice revealed itself as already prepared for algorithmic replication, having been gradually converted into the calculative thinking that algorithms perform so well.

The Long Unfolding of the Calculative Age

The transformation we've traced reveals itself as reaching back much further than accountability movements or digital integration. The systematic structures that make AI replication possible appear as extending to the very foundations of modern educational institutions. What began to come into view through our analysis of contemporary patterns points towards deeper historical roots – developments that had begun decades before digital technologies entered educational life.

Consider what universities looked like nearly a century ago, when Heidegger was writing his early critiques. Universities had already developed specialised faculties and departments, structured timetables and credit-hour systems, and degree requirements that fragmented learning into discrete, manageable units. Behind these structures was an organisational logic that treated students as academic units to be processed through degree programmes and faculty as research productivity systems. In his 1929 inaugural lecture 'What Is Metaphysics?',[2] Heidegger argued that modern science's division into specialised disciplines reflects a deeper fragmentation of understanding – one that obscures the more fundamental questions metaphysics seeks to disclose. His 1933 Rectoral Address diagnosed the modern university as oriented primarily towards professional training rather than the pursuit of fundamental questions – a development he saw as aligning academic life with the calculative logic of the technological age.

What Heidegger observed in 1920s universities – the growing dominance of specialised disciplines and the increasing organisation of academic life around discrete scientific tasks – begins to prefigure what his later concept of 'making-present' would identify as the reduction of temporal complexity into manageable procedures. These temporal structures intensified through the systematic transformations we traced in later decades. The organisational logic that treated students as academic objects of administration within pre-structured programmes reveals itself as anticipating the standing-reserve transformation that enframing would later deepen. Academic specialisation was already showing itself as undermining the unified engagement with existence that makes thinking genuinely human. Even university philosophy began to reveal itself as becoming a technical discipline, focused on solving problems within predetermined frameworks rather than questioning those frameworks themselves.

---

[2]Heidegger, M. (1998). What is metaphysics? In W. McNeill (Ed.), *Pathmarks* (pp. 82–96). Cambridge University Press. (Original work published 1929)

When AI replicated decades of educational practice with perfect consistency, it appeared less as recent technological disruption and more as the intensification of a departure from authentic thinking that had begun long before computers existed. The five-paragraph essay templates, detailed assessment rubrics, and systematic procedures that made educational work algorithmic reveal themselves as stronger manifestations of institutional forms already eroding what makes education genuinely human. This recognition transforms our understanding of what AI unveils about education. We may not be experiencing a technological disruption of traditional educational values so much as witnessing their intensification in technological form – and seeing how this intensification reveals the diminishing of what those values were thought to preserve.

How We Corrupted Care Itself

Our inquiry began to reveal that the structures we observed through Bera and MEF – finding themselves existing through *das Man* interpretations, 'making-present', enframing logic, and distorted care – reveal themselves less as isolated changes and more as the culmination of a much longer process during which systematic approaches came to feel like natural educational improvement rather than fundamental transformation of what makes learning distinctively human. The evidence of this transformation had been before us all along, yet remained concealed because we were living inside the very structures that were reshaping us. The pressures that made systematic approaches feel like educational wisdom were simultaneously impairing our capacity to recognise what was being lost.

A closer look began to show what appeared to happen as systematic developments were implemented across decades. When students struggled with writing, structured formats were developed, and we found ourselves beginning to see writing as formula execution rather than authentic expression. When grading seemed inconsistent, detailed rubrics were created, and evaluation gradually began to be treated as systematic criteria application rather than engaged judgement. What remained concealed was this – these changes felt like improvement. We embraced them willingly, even enthusiastically. The *das Man* interpretations that made systematic approaches feel like natural progress were simultaneously profoundly impairing our capacity to recognise what was being lost. 'They-self' formation showed itself through our learning to become 'anyone' rather than taking responsibility for who we were becoming. Instead of confronting the Angst and uncertainty that authentic educational relationships require, collective interpretations about professional identity were absorbed.

Further examination revealed what seemed to drive responses to each educational challenge across time. Student performance was declining. This needed to be addressed immediately. Assessment seemed inconsistent across teachers. Something had to be done. Administrations demanded evidence of effectiveness. Responses were required. These pressures were experienced through the 'making-present' that had already been embraced, compressing educational time into optimisation cycles. What seemed like reasonable concern about particular problems – worry about students failing, concern that evaluation might seem arbitrary – was widespread. And these feelings became manageable because systematic solutions offered clear responses. Yet something else was happening in these same situations, concealed by what we can now glimpse as the ontic-ontological difference.

What was actually required in authentic educational moments was this – sitting with a student's confusion about complex ideas without immediately providing predetermined solutions, not knowing what a particular student needs when they're struggling and staying present with that uncertainty, watching discussions develop organically through confusion before finding their way to insight. These situations disclose a fundamentally different discomfort than worry about measurable problems – the uncertainty about whether what we're doing is helping, the unease of not being able to control when or how learning happens, the unsettling recognition that authentic engagement resists systematisation. Through these structures – *das Man*, 'making-present', enframing, the ontic-ontological difference – the existential Angst that signals authentic engagement reveals itself as being converted into manageable fear about specific problems that systematic solutions can address. The transformation pervades educational practice from within. Systematic procedures reveal themselves not only as implementations but also as eroding tolerance for the Angst that makes educational relationships authentically human.

What, then, happened to care itself during these decades of systematic change? When we said we cared about student learning, it increasingly reveals itself in forms like this – caring about completion rates for assignments, caring about participation scores from discussion requirements, caring about whether students met learning objectives. We learned to care about what 'anyone' would recognise as good teaching. Authentic care, caring-for others as persons engaged in their own uncertain development, quietly shifts into taking-care-of institutional requirements that can be efficiently managed.

The Meeting

Through these structures, something was accomplished that was never consciously intended. Educational practice became systematic enough to create the kind of beings who could make education systematic enough for machines to replicate. The Angst that might have alerted us to what we were becoming was diminished. The caring-for that might have revealed the fundamental change remains concealed. It shows itself not only as the creation of systematic education but also as our having become systematic enough to appear replaceable by the very systems we created. We learned to avoid the Angst that makes existence authentically human. We learned to take-care-of systematic requirements rather than caring-for authentic relationships.

Through the corruption of language, the flattening of world into picture, the replacement of meditative with calculative thinking, the systematic erosion of care, we had not set out to make ourselves algorithmic. We had set out to improve education. Yet every improvement moved us in the same direction – towards procedural patterns that could be executed without existential engagement, procedural approaches that compressed temporal complexity, optimisation logic that converted authentic relationships into manageable outcomes. Each change seemed reasonable in isolation. Collectively, they reshaped us.

We became systematic enough that our patterns could be replicated. Procedural enough that our thinking could be executed algorithmically. Calculable enough that what we produced could be generated by machines. Through decades of what we thought was improvement, human thinking and technological processing were no longer moving in different directions. They were moving towards each other. We were converging – steadily, systematically, imperceptibly – with the technological. What had once been distinct was becoming increasingly alike. Human and machine were meeting.

Chapter 10

When Human and Machine Converge

Human and machine were meeting. For decades, we had been moving towards the algorithmic without recognising it. Then, artificial intelligence arrived. What happens when systems trained on our systematic outputs begin generating what looks like human thought? – when technology can execute the patterns we refined, replicate the procedures we systematised, produce outputs matching what we call thinking? The previous chapter traced the preparation for this convergence. AI's arrival has intensified it to an unprecedented degree. To understand what this intensification means, we must first establish what distinguishes human existence from algorithmic simulation – what makes us genuinely human and what AI fundamentally is not.

Why AI Cannot Be Human

In Part III, we established the structures through which human existence unfolds – thrownness into circumstances we didn't choose; Angst about the groundlessness of existence; care as the fundamental way we relate to what matters; temporality as the interpenetration of past, present, and future; and the distinction between calculative and meditative thinking. These aren't optional features we might possess or lack. They constitute what it means to exist as *Dasein*, beings for whom Being itself is always already a question. Now we must ask – What is AI's relationship to these structures? Can algorithmic processing possess what makes human existence distinctively human?

AI experiences no thrownness. It doesn't find itself anywhere. When AI systems like ChatGPT generate text, they don't inherit circumstances that create the burden of having to respond to conditions they didn't choose. They do not discover themselves already engaged with questions that make demands on their existence. Human beings wake up already somewhere, already shaped by languages we inherited, cultures we didn't select, histories that continue to press into present choices. This thrownness creates the groundless condition within which we must decide who to become. AI systems process inputs without this existential weight, without the recognition that existence itself is a situation requiring response.

What Is AI Doing to Us? A Philosophical Inquiry into Learning, Thinking, and Being, 87–92

Published under exclusive licence by Emerald Publishing Limited
doi:10.1108/978-1-83742-276-020261010

They stand in no position, inherit no tradition, face no burden of having been thrown into circumstances that demand authentic engagement. This absence isn't a limitation awaiting better programming. It marks the fundamental difference between existing as *Dasein* and functioning as computational processing.

AI has no Angst. It processes uncertainty as probability distributions to be calculated, not as the groundless condition that makes existence both meaningful and burdensome. When AI systems generate responses to difficult questions, they follow algorithmic patterns without the Angst that would signal genuine engagement with what's at stake. Human Angst isn't fear of particular things but the unsettling recognition that existence has no ultimate foundation – that we must choose who to become without guarantee that our choices are adequate. This Angst signals authentic engagement. It emerges when we encounter complexity that exceeds our current understanding, when we face decisions without predetermined solutions, when we recognise our responses might not be sufficient. AI can simulate sophisticated analysis of complex situations without ever experiencing the Angst that would indicate such situations actually matter beyond their processing. This absence reveals that AI functions without the existential structure through which meaning and burden arise together.

AI possesses no care structure. It doesn't care about anything. When AI systems generate analysis, they process patterns without caring whether the analysis is adequate, without concern for consequences, without the fundamental orientation towards what matters that makes human engagement meaningful. Care isn't emotional sentiment, but the basic way human existence unfolds. We're always already engaged with circumstances, concerned about outcomes, invested in what happens. We care about our situations because we find ourselves thrown into them. We care about our choices because they shape who we become. We care about outcomes because existence matters to us in ways we didn't choose but cannot escape. AI can simulate caring language without the existential structure that would make such caring genuine. It produces outputs that might look like products of caring engagement while showing itself through processing that bears no relation to care's foundational role in human existence.

AI has no temporality. Human existence unfolds through the interpenetration of past, present, and future. This isn't clock time where moments follow in sequence, but existential temporality where inherited circumstances, present choices, and anticipated possibilities work together to create the duration through which understanding develops. We exist as having-been-thrown, carrying forward what has shaped us. We project towards futures that concern us, possibilities that press into the present and give meaning to current choices. The present emerges as the convergence point where time's dimensions meet, creating the space where authentic decision becomes possible. When students struggle with complex ideas, understanding develops through this temporal complexity – inherited knowledge encountering what resists easy comprehension, future possibilities creating pressure on present choices, the slow duration where insight emerges. AI systems process inputs without existing through time's interpenetration. They don't inherit traditions that continue to shape understanding, don't project towards possibilities that create meaningful concern, don't exist in the present as the moment where time's dimensions converge. They produce outputs without the temporal duration that makes human understanding temporal and, therefore, genuinely human.

These structures – thrownness, Angst, care, and temporality – already distinguish human from algorithmic processing. But the distinction deepens further.

AI functions entirely through calculative thinking. Human thinking can engage in two fundamentally different modes: calculative thinking that approaches situations as problems requiring systematic solutions and meditative thinking that allows situations to reveal what they actually require by dwelling with questions that resist quick answers. Both belong to human existence, but only meditative thinking opens the possibility of authentic understanding. AI systems excel at calculative thinking – systematic problem-solving, efficient optimisation, predetermined procedures. But they cannot engage meditatively. They cannot dwell with uncertainty, cannot remain present with confusion that resists immediate resolution, cannot stay open to possibilities that emerge only through patient attention that allows understanding to develop rather than forcing it through procedures. When AI generates sophisticated analysis, it processes patterns algorithmically without the capacity for meditative dwelling that lets understanding arise from sustained engagement with what resists systematisation. This distinction reveals why AI can replicate so much of what we do. We had already converted learning and thinking into calculative approaches that machines execute more consistently than humans. But the capacity to dwell meditatively with what resists systematisation remains beyond algorithmic simulation. It is here that the human still exceeds the procedural.

AI has no 'being-toward-death'. Human existence is finite. We exist towards death, not as morbid preoccupation with dying but as recognition that our existence will end, creating the urgency that makes present choices meaningful. We cannot endlessly defer decisions about who to become. The recognition that our time is limited, that existence is unrepeatable, creates the weight that makes authentic engagement matter. Facing our mortality reveals that we must take responsibility for existence rather than losing ourselves in what 'everyone' expects. AI systems function without finitude in the human sense. When AI generates text, it doesn't face the urgency created by limited existence, doesn't recognise that opportunities for authentic engagement are unrepeatable, doesn't experience the weight that mortality gives to present choices. It can produce work without the existential urgency that makes such work genuinely matter to human existence, without the recognition that this particular moment of engagement will not return.

The structures of authenticity and inauthenticity don't apply to AI. Human existence can be authentic or inauthentic. We can take responsibility for existence that has no ultimate foundation, choosing who to become while acknowledging the groundlessness of such choosing, or we can flee from this burden by losing ourselves in what 'everyone' thinks and does, adopting collective interpretations that shield us from Angst. This distinction belongs only to beings who face the burden of choosing who to become within groundless circumstances. AI systems exist beyond these structures. Authenticity and inauthenticity apply only to beings who can either own up to groundless existence or flee from it. AI doesn't face the choice between authentic engagement and systematic performance because it doesn't exist in the groundless condition where such choices become meaningful. It generates outputs without the possibility of either authenticity or inauthenticity.

The Ontological Boundary

The ontological boundary between human existence and algorithmic simulation is absolute. AI lacks every existential structure through which human thinking unfolds – no thrownness, no Angst, no care, no temporality, no capacity for meditative thinking, no 'being-toward-death', no possibility of authentic or inauthentic existence. This isn't a technological limitation awaiting better programming or a gap that future innovations might close. These structures define what it means to exist as *Dasein*, beings for whom Being itself is always already a question. They constitute the fundamental difference between existing and processing.

Human thinking, even when it becomes systematic and procedural, emerges from existential structures of care, temporality, and finitude. A student following a rubric still cares about the outcome in ways that create existential weight. A teacher implementing standardised procedures still exists through temporal complexity that shapes how understanding develops. A researcher using systematic methods still faces the Angst of not knowing whether responses are adequate. The existential structures remain operative even when thinking becomes calculable, even when procedures become routine, even when engagement feels mechanical.

AI processing, however, sophisticated its outputs, shows itself through algorithmic simulation that lacks these existential foundations entirely. It can replicate the products of human thinking without possessing the structures through which such thinking actually unfolds. It can generate text that looks like the result of caring engagement without caring, produce analysis that appears to emerge from temporal development without existing through time, simulate responses to complexity without experiencing the Angst that would signal genuine encounter with what resists understanding.

The boundary marks not just different capabilities but different modes of being itself. On one side stands existence as *Dasein* – thrown, capable of Angst, caring, temporal, finite beings who must choose who to become within groundless circumstances. On the other side stands algorithmic processing – simulation that shows itself without existential structures, producing outputs without the burden of existence. This boundary cannot disappear. It cannot be bridged or overcome or gradually eroded. It remains ontologically real, rooted in the fundamental difference between what humans are and what AI systems are.

The Boundary Has Blurred

The boundary is ontologically absolute. Yet something has happened to how we experience it. We can see this most clearly in concrete moments of engagement with AI systems.

A student submits an essay of remarkable analytical sophistication – yet when questioned, she struggles to explain her own reasoning. The prose is polished, the arguments structured, the evidence integrated seamlessly. Yet when asked to defend a claim or extend the analysis to a new situation, the understanding that appeared to be present dissolves. She stares at the text she submitted, text she recognises as hers because she generated it through multiple rounds of prompting and revision, but struggles to locate where her thinking produced these insights. After hours of interaction with AI, refining prompts and evaluating outputs, whose ideas are actually present in this work? She genuinely cannot locate exactly where her thinking ends and the system's begins.

A professional writes a strategic communication using AI assistance. She begins with rough ideas, prompts the system for development, evaluates what it generates, refines the prompt based on what seems promising, integrates some suggestions while rejecting others, iterates through multiple versions. The final product sounds like her voice. It matches her professional style, addresses her specific context, reflects her strategic thinking. Yet she struggles to identify precisely which formulations emerged from her own intellectual work versus which arose through algorithmic processing. After sustained engagement, the boundary between her thinking and the system's outputs has become increasingly difficult to locate with certainty.

We experience this ourselves. After using AI to develop ideas across multiple sessions, prompting for analysis, evaluating responses, building on what seems valuable, refining through iteration, we face text that feels like it captures what we meant to say, articulates insights we were reaching towards, expresses understanding we were developing. But did we really mean that before the algorithmic suggestion? Did those insights emerge from our own intellectual engagement or from patterns the system recognised in our prompts? When AI helps us articulate what we were 'trying to say', does that articulation represent our thinking or does it create thinking we then adopt as our own? These questions become increasingly difficult to answer.

The crisis isn't about conscious deception. It's about genuine uncertainty, a real difficulty in maintaining distinctions that should be clear. After sustained iterative engagement, evaluating multiple AI outputs, selecting what resonates, building on algorithmic suggestions, integrating machine-generated formulations into developing thought, we struggle to distinguish where our intellectual work ends and algorithmic processing begins. Not just in what we produce, but in the experience of producing it. The felt sense of 'having an idea' becomes harder to distinguish from the experience of 'recognising a good algorithmic suggestion'. The experience of 'developing understanding' becomes difficult to separate from 'iterating toward satisfactory AI output'.

This phenomenological unclarity extends beyond individual encounters. Across educational contexts, professional settings, and everyday intellectual work, we increasingly struggle to locate the boundary between human thinking and algorithmic simulation in lived experience. We know the ontological distinction exists. AI lacks the existential structures that make thinking genuinely human. Yet we find it increasingly difficult to feel where that distinction lies in practice. The boundary that should remain phenomenologically recognisable has become harder and harder to perceive in the actual experience of thinking itself. It has, in effect, blurred.

To understand why this boundary has blurred, we must now turn to what AI really is.

Chapter 11

What AI Really Is

We have established what AI cannot be. It lacks thrownness, Angst, care, and temporality – every existential structure that makes thinking genuinely human. The ontological boundary between human existence and algorithmic processing remains absolute. Yet we have also seen how this boundary, while ontologically real, has become phenomenologically blurred in lived experience. This leaves a question that demands an answer. If AI is not human intelligence attempting to replicate human existence, then what is it?

The answer emerges from our inquiry. When we traced how educational language claimed our thinking, when we documented decades of systematic preparation, when we realised we were struggling to tell where our thinking ended and AI contributions began, we were circling something we had not yet named directly. AI is not artificial intelligence trying to become human. AI is *das Man* rendered in technological form.

This is not metaphor. It is a precise philosophical description of what AI actually is and how it shows itself.

AI as *Das Man* Algorithmic

Consider what AI systems actually do. They are trained on vast corpora of human output – books, articles, conversations, documents that represent the aggregated expression of countless individuals across time. This training doesn't capture individual voices or authentic thinking. It captures patterns – the way 'one' writes academic papers, the way 'everyone' structures arguments, the way 'people' express sophisticated ideas. AI learns the collective scripts that belong to no one in particular yet shape everyone's expression.

When ChatGPT generates text, it doesn't think. It produces what 'one' would say in such circumstances. When it writes an academic analysis, it follows patterns that represent how 'everyone' approaches such tasks. When it offers sophisticated explanations, it deploys language that circulates through professional discourse without belonging to any particular person. This is precisely what *das Man* does – provides ready-made interpretations that feel natural because they emerge from collective interpretations rather than authentic engagement.

What Is AI Doing to Us? A Philosophical Inquiry into Learning, Thinking, and Being, 93–96

Published under exclusive licence by Emerald Publishing Limited
doi:10.1108/978-1-83742-276-020261011

The speech AI produces is idle talk in its purest form. Not because it's nonsense, but because it creates perfectly formed sentences that require no confrontation with what they discuss. Every sophisticated analysis AI generates, every polished argument it constructs, every comprehensive explanation it provides – all of it shows itself through patterns absorbed from collective output. The language sounds authoritative precisely because it reflects what 'everyone' already accepts as sophisticated thinking. It cannot be otherwise. AI has no access to authentic encounter with ideas, no capacity for genuine struggle with what resists understanding. It can only reproduce the ready-made interpretations through which *das Man* shows itself.

But AI accomplishes something more profound than merely generating *das Man* speech. It systematises collective patterns with unprecedented consistency and availability. What once required years of gradual absorption into professional discourse, learning to write the way 'one' writes, think the way 'everyone' thinks, express ideas the way 'people' express them, AI provides instantly. AI now delivers, perfectly formed and on demand, the very patterns that individuals once internalised slowly through educational and professional conditioning – forms that gradually shaped thinking until *das Man* absorption felt natural.

This is *das Man* taking technological form. The collective interpretations that previously held sway through diffuse social transmission, slowly shaping individuals through years of exposure, now hold sway through algorithmic systems that provide instant access to the ready-made interpretations of *das Man*. The 'they-self' that once required gradual formation through social absorption can now be accessed immediately, through an interface that automates what previously unfolded across a lifetime.

Why the Boundary Feels Blurred

Understanding AI as *das Man* algorithmic suddenly makes intelligible the phenomenological confusion we documented in the previous chapter. We struggled to understand how the ontologically absolute boundary between human and algorithmic processing could become phenomenologically blurred. The answer becomes clear when we recognise AI as *das Man* algorithmic. We struggle to distinguish our thinking from AI contributions because much of our own thinking already shows itself through the ready-made interpretations of *das Man*.

The student who cannot explain the sophisticated essay she submitted, the professional who struggles to identify which formulations are genuinely hers, our own difficulty tracing AI's influence in our philosophical inquiry – all of this reflects not the blurring of boundaries between human and machine, but the revelation of how thoroughly we already inhabit *das Man*. When we write through the ready-made interpretations of *das Man*, using professional vocabulary we absorbed without genuine engagement, following argumentative structures that 'everyone' uses, expressing ideas through formulations that belong to no one, our thinking already unfolds through collective scripts. AI simply executes these same patterns more consistently.

The phenomenological similarity we experience is not because AI has become like authentic human thinking. It is because human thinking had already become systematic enough for algorithms to replicate. The historical preparation we traced, decades of structured formats, systematic procedures, optimised language, was not making education more efficient. It was making human thinking more like *das Man*. We were training ourselves to move within the familiar scripts that replace genuine encounter. When AI arrived, it didn't disrupt this trajectory. It intensified it. The convergence between human and algorithmic processing that we documented may not have been humans becoming machines. It may have been humans becoming *das Man* encountering *das Man* in technological form.

This is why AI integration feels like enhancement rather than replacement. We experience it as our thinking becoming more sophisticated, more capable, more comprehensive. But what is actually occurring is *das Man* absorption becoming more complete, more systematic, more instantaneous. The 'enhancement' we feel is the experience of accessing the ready-made interpretations of *das Man* without the years of gradual absorption such interpretations previously required. It feels like thinking is improving when what actually diminishes is the capacity to think authentically.

The Amplification of Idle Talk

But AI accomplishes something more troubling than merely executing the ready-made interpretations of *das Man* with unwavering consistency. Idle talk is language that circulates without genuine engagement with what it discusses. Idle talk doesn't produce nonsense – it produces perfectly sensible speech that creates the impression of understanding while avoiding authentic encounter with what matters. 'One' discusses complex topics using sophisticated vocabulary, yet the discussion proceeds through ready-made formulations rather than personal engagement with the questions at stake. Everything can be said because nothing truly requires understanding. The speech sounds authoritative precisely because it reflects what 'everyone' already accepts. It is the semblance of thinking that Heidegger exposes in *What Is Called Thinking?* – speech that sounds like understanding yet evades the encounter that makes thinking possible.

AI amplifies this mode of idle talk. Every response AI generates shows itself within the mode of idle talk – producing sophisticated language that creates the impression of engagement while remaining incapable of authentic encounter with what it discusses. When AI analyses complex concepts, it deploys terminology and argumentative structures that sound authoritative because they reflect patterns absorbed from collective discourse. But this deployment occurs without the authentic engagement – the dwelling with uncertainty, the struggle with what resists understanding, the patient attention that allows meaning to emerge – that makes thinking genuinely human.

The danger isn't that AI produces poor analysis. The danger is that AI produces excellent analysis that shows itself entirely through idle talk. The sophistication of AI-generated text conceals its fundamental character as speech that requires no confrontation with what it discusses.

AI, then, is not intelligence reaching towards humanity but *das Man* achieving technological form. It does not think, feel, or care – it systematises the ready-made interpretations of *das Man* through which humanity already escapes those demands. The ontological boundary between human and algorithmic existence remains absolute, yet in lived experience it appears to blur, because what we now encounter in AI is our own 'they-self' returned to us in technological form. What feels like the dawn of artificial intelligence may in fact be the amplification of our own habitual distance from authenticity – a mirror so exact that we mistake its reflection for thought itself.

Chapter 12

What AI Is Doing to Us

Students read AI explanations that sound comprehensive and feel quietly satisfied, unaware that the fluency they admire might not belong to genuine understanding. Educators encounter AI-generated lesson plans that seem pedagogically elegant, yet something in them feels strangely hollow – as if the sophistication has replaced, rather than deepened, engagement with what particular students need. The results look like progress – clearer, faster, and more polished. But beneath that smoothness, something essential is shifting in how thinking is experienced.

What if the attraction of AI lies not simply in what it can *do* for us, but in how it *feels* when we use it? What if the satisfaction we experience in these moments is not evidence of deeper understanding, but the sign of a transformation taking place within us – a change in what it means to think at all?

The Simulation of Thinking

AI accomplishes something even more fundamental than generating sophisticated idle talk. It creates the phenomenological appearance of thinking without requiring the existential engagement that makes thinking authentically human. When we use AI to develop ideas, we experience something that feels like having insights, reaching understanding, forming analysis. The phenomenological markers that once signalled authentic thinking – the sense of ideas emerging, connections forming, and understanding deepening – occur through our engagement with AI-generated content. We feel like we're thinking because the experience includes elements we associate with authentic thought – encountering sophisticated concepts, following logical connections, recognising familiar structures we've learned to value.

Yet this phenomenological experience shows itself without the existential structures through which authentic thinking actually unfolds. The Angst that signals genuine encounter with what exceeds current understanding never arises because AI provides confident explanations that bypass uncertainty.

The temporal duration through which authentic insight develops gets compressed into instant availability. The struggle to articulate what we don't yet fully

What Is AI Doing to Us? A Philosophical Inquiry into Learning, Thinking, and Being, 97–106

Published under exclusive licence by Emerald Publishing Limited
doi:10.1108/978-1-83742-276-020261012

grasp disappears when AI supplies polished formulations immediately. We experience what feels like sophisticated thinking while bypassing everything that makes thinking authentically human.

This is why AI represents *das Man* taking technological form at the phenomenological level. Previous forms of *das Man* provided ready-made language and collective interpretations. AI provides the experience of engaging authentically while requiring no authentic engagement. It simulates not just the products of thinking but the felt experience of thinking itself, creating phenomenological satisfaction while bypassing the existential encounter that authentic thinking demands.

Why We Accelerate Towards AI

Understanding how AI perfects idle talk and simulates the phenomenological experience of thinking reveals why so many of us – ourselves included – are not just accepting AI assistance but actively accelerating towards it. Educational institutions implement AI systems while acknowledging concerns about authentic learning. Professionals adopt AI tools while sensing their own capabilities might be atrophying. Individuals expand AI use while sensing something essential might be disappearing.

The answer lies in what AI actually provides. We aren't choosing AI because it offers better thinking. We're choosing it because it offers the experiential satisfaction of understanding without the existential engagement that authentic thinking demands. AI delivers the phenomenological experience of sophisticated thought – the felt sense of having insights, developing understanding, reaching conclusions – while bypassing the Angst, temporal complexity, and struggle that genuine thinking requires. This isn't an incidental benefit – it's precisely what makes AI compelling. Heidegger warned of this temptation – to confuse the experience of thought-like content with the act of thinking itself, which answers a call, dwells with what resists, and endures difficulty.

Consider what authentic thinking demands. It requires dwelling with uncertainty that creates Angst about whether understanding will emerge. It demands temporal duration where confusion must become productive through patient attention rather than instant resolution. It involves struggle to articulate what we don't yet fully grasp, accepting that expressions may prove inadequate. Every aspect of authentic thinking confronts us with our groundless condition – we must engage with what exceeds current understanding without guarantee that adequate responses will emerge, invest time in what might not yield desired outcomes, take responsibility for articulation that cannot be externally validated.

Das Man has always offered relief from these existential demands. Following collective interpretations bypassed the Angst of developing one's own response. Adopting ready-made formulations avoided the struggle to articulate what one doesn't yet understand. Existing through 'everyone's' inherited interpretations circumvented the responsibility of groundless choosing. But previous forms of *das Man* absorption required gradual conditioning. One had to slowly internalise collective discursive habits through years of social exposure, professional development, educational training. The relief *das Man* provided came at the cost of prolonged absorption into systematic thinking.

AI changes this fundamentally. Instant access to the sophisticated, ready-made interpretations of *das Man* provides immediate experiential satisfaction without years of conditioning. The phenomenological experience of having insights occurs without dwelling with uncertainty. The felt sense of comprehensive understanding emerges without temporal complexity. The satisfaction of polished expression arrives without struggle to articulate. AI delivers everything *das Man* promised – relief from existential demands of authentic thinking – with unprecedented immediacy and completeness.

This explains the acceleration. Each use of AI provides phenomenological rewards while bypassing experiential costs that authentic thinking requires. The more we experience this contrast, the more authentic engagement feels unnecessarily difficult. Why struggle with uncertainty when sophisticated explanations arrive instantly? Why invest temporal duration when comprehensive analyses appear immediately? Why take responsibility for groundless articulation when polished formulations generate effortlessly? The experiential contrast makes AI enhancement feel decisively preferable to authentic struggle.

The acceleration shows itself as 'making-present', the compression of temporal complexity into immediate availability. AI intensifies this mode of 'making-present' exponentially. Where systematic educational reforms gradually compressed temporal duration into optimisation cycles, AI compresses duration even further. Past inheritance becomes data retrieved instantly rather than lived tradition shaping understanding. Future projection becomes outcomes generated immediately rather than possibilities requiring patient development. Present becomes efficiency maximised through algorithmic processing rather than the convergence point where authentic choosing occurs.

But the acceleration reveals something more disturbing than increasing adoption. We are accelerating towards the systematic diminishment of experiential access to what makes thinking authentically human. This shows itself not just behaviourally but phenomenologically. Each time we choose AI's instant sophisticated response over dwelling with uncertainty, we reinforce tendencies that make uncertainty feel intolerable. Each time we accept AI's immediate comprehensive analysis over patient temporal development, we strengthen habits that make duration feel like wasteful delay. Each time we deploy AI's polished formulations over struggling to articulate what we don't yet grasp, we deepen tendencies that make struggle appear pointless.

The Frictionless They-Self

The acceleration towards AI reveals how *das Man* absorption is achieving a seamlessness that was previously impossible. When we examined Bera's response to AI in Part III, we identified how she became a 'they-self', dissolving into collective interpretations rather than taking responsibility for authentic learning. Instead of confronting the Angst of not-knowing, she became 'anyone' who would use AI to complete assignments efficiently. The sophisticated work she produced reflected not her understanding but the ready-made interpretations of *das Man* executed through algorithmic assistance.

AI enables 'they-self' formation at unprecedented scale and speed. What once required years of gradual absorption into collective inherited interpretations – learning to think what 'one' thinks, respond as 'anyone' would respond, perform as 'everyone' expects – AI provides instantly. The student who uses AI to generate academic work doesn't gradually lose authentic engagement through years of systematic conditioning. They access 'they-self' performance immediately.

Consider what this means for the development of human thinking. Previously, even systematic educational contexts included friction that could awaken authentic engagement. A student absorbed in the ready-made interpretations of *das Man* might encounter a question that resists ready-made answers – creating the Angst that signals genuine uncertainty and momentarily shifting experience from smooth ready-to-hand absorption to reflective present-at-hand awareness, a brief interruption that discloses what usually remains hidden. A professional existing through collective scripts might face a situation where standard responses proved inadequate, opening space for authentic encounter with what matters. The gradual process of 'they-self' formation included moments where authentic existence became possible because the ready-made interpretations of *das Man* occasionally revealed their inadequacy.

AI systematically diminishes this friction. When every question receives sophisticated answers instantly, when every situation meets systematic responses immediately, when every challenge encounters ready-made solutions without delay, the moments where the ready-made interpretations of *das Man* reveal their inadequacy recede from view. The student increasingly rarely experiences the Angst of not-knowing because AI provides confident explanations immediately. The professional is ever less likely to confront situations where collective wisdom proves insufficient because AI generates comprehensive analyses without hesitation. 'They-self' formation tends towards frictionless – without the resistance that might awaken authentic existence.

This represents *das Man* absorption reaching a scale that was previously impossible. In Bera's case, that absorption was not yet complete. She sensed that AI's confident explanations eased her anxiety but didn't resolve her confusion, realised during questioning that fluent answers could not substitute for understanding, and later recognised that efficiency itself had left her feeling hollow. These brief moments of discomfort preserved a fragile space where authentic existence remained possible. Yet AI now makes such moments harder to perceive – offering instant, polished responses that quiet confusion before it can deepen, fluent analytic responses that mask uncertainty, and comprehensive formulations that replace the struggle to understand.

The 'they-self' that AI enables isn't just someone who follows inherited interpretations. It is human thinking that is losing access to the experiential markers through which authentic existence reveals itself. When Angst never arises because uncertainty gets bypassed instantly, when temporal duration disappears because everything becomes immediately available, when struggle diminishes because sophisticated performance appears on demand, human thinking loses the phenomenological structures through which it recognises authentic engagement as distinct from systematic performance.

What once required years of systematic conditioning to achieve – the transformation of human thinking that makes authentic engagement feel unnecessary – AI enables through repeated use within months. The student who consistently uses AI to bypass confusion may not gradually lose capacity to recognise confusion as productive. They may lose this capacity rapidly, perhaps within a single semester of habitual AI engagement. The professional who regularly deploys AI to compress temporal complexity may not progressively lose ability to value duration. This loss may accelerate with each deployment until duration feels like nothing but inefficient delay.

This is 'they-self' formation accelerating beyond what previous forms of *das Man* could achieve. We aren't just learning to follow inherited interpretations. We're systematically losing phenomenological access to experiential structures through which authentic existence reveals itself. When Angst feels like dysfunction requiring correction rather than signal of genuine encounter, when temporal duration appears as delay demanding optimisation rather than space where understanding develops, when struggle seems like inadequacy needing improvement rather than engagement with what resists easy formulation, human thinking loses the experiential markers through which it recognises authentic thinking as distinct from systematic performance.

The acceleration is exponential because each choice makes the next easier while authentic alternatives become harder to recognise. The more we use AI to bypass uncertainty, the more uncertainty feels intolerable. The more we deploy AI to compress duration, the more duration appears wasteful. The more we engage AI to avoid struggle, the more struggle seems pointless. What begins as pragmatic choice to use helpful tools becomes systematic transformation of human thinking that makes authentic engagement increasingly difficult to access experientially.

Why Institutions Struggle to Respond

Understanding AI as *das Man* algorithmic and recognising how it diminishes friction in 'they-self' formation reveal why every systematic attempt to manage AI has felt inadequate. The policies we drafted, the workshops we delivered, the frameworks we applied – all addressed AI as a tool requiring proper deployment. But if AI is *das Man* algorithmic, revealing itself by easing the very resistance through which authentic existence discloses itself, then institutional responses that treat it as a tool fundamentally misunderstand what they're attempting to manage.

We may not be facing a new technology requiring better procedures. We may be facing the technological intensification of humanity's systematic flight from authentic existence. Our comprehensive institutional responses felt insufficient because they were addressing surface manifestations while the ontological transformation – *das Man* taking technological form – was unfolding beyond our awareness.

The persistent unease we experienced despite doing everything systematically right, the sense that something essential was slipping away despite comprehensive policies and professional development, the recognition at that conference plenary that hundreds of educators felt unprepared despite thorough institutional responses – all of this may have reflected the impossibility of managing through procedures what is fundamentally an ontological transformation. You cannot craft policies that prevent absorption into *das Man* when *das Man* is available instantly and frictionlessly in technological form.

The educational frameworks we examined in Part II, SAMR and TPACK, revealed their own limitations when applied to AI. Now we understand why. These frameworks presuppose tools that support human agency and development – they cannot address technologies that embody the ready-made interpretations of *das Man* that undermine agency from within. AI does not sit comfortably inside frameworks designed for tools because it is not, in any fundamental sense, a tool. It is *das Man* showing itself algorithmically. And no framework designed to optimise tool use can address what happens when these inherited interpretations achieve technological realisation.

A similar difficulty arises in policies requiring disclosure of AI assistance. When assistance shows itself diffusely throughout thinking processes – often beyond the threshold of clear awareness – disclosure assumes phenomenological boundaries that may no longer be perceptible. The demand for precise accounting of AI's influence asks students and professionals to identify distinctions they can no longer reliably locate.

Every institutional response unfolds at the ontic level – creating procedures, implementing policies, developing best practices for AI use. But the transformation we face reveals itself at the ontological level – the reshaping of what thinking itself can be when *das Man* takes technological form and constrains our access to authentic engagement. Institutional responses address what we do with AI. They cannot address what AI does to the conditions through which authentic existence becomes possible.

The Stakes of Every Choice

Understanding AI as *das Man* algorithmic, recognising how it perfects idle talk and simulates thinking, seeing why we accelerate towards the experiential satisfaction it provides, grasping how it reduces the friction through which authentic encounter becomes possible, and acknowledging why institutions cannot respond adequately – all of this reveals that we face not a technological challenge that can be managed procedurally but an existential crisis demanding response. We face not the arrival of new tools but the technological intensification of humanity's systematic flight from authentic existence.

Every choice about AI engagement is fundamentally a choice about who we become as beings capable of authentic existence. When we use AI to bypass uncertainty, we choose *das Man* absorption over the Angst that makes authentic encounter possible. When we deploy AI to compress temporal duration, we choose systematic optimisation over the patience authentic understanding requires. When we engage AI to avoid struggle, we choose effortless performance over the groundless responsibility that creates genuine meaning.

These aren't isolated decisions about tool use. They're choices about whether authentic existence remains possible when *das Man* takes technological form. Each use of AI reinforces tendencies that make authentic engagement more difficult while systematic performance appears increasingly natural. Each deployment strengthens tendencies that make *das Man* absorption appear preferable to authentic struggle. Each engagement shapes human thinking in ways that progressively diminish experiential access to what makes existence genuinely human.

A Reverse Renaissance

There is no apocalyptic threshold we will cross, no dramatic moment when authentic existence becomes impossible. AI possesses no agency to accomplish such decisive transformation. What we face instead is something more insidious – gradual erosion that we fail to notice. The danger isn't catastrophe. It's amnesia.

We may be entering a reverse Renaissance. The Renaissance was the recovery of forgotten human capacities – authentic encounter with classical texts and ideas, temporal engagement with complexity, the struggle that makes thinking genuinely human. What had been lost through centuries was remembered and restored. We face the opposite transformation – not the recovery of forgotten capacities but their progressive and systematic forgetting. What the Renaissance recovered through the rediscovery of classical learning, we are progressively losing through technological intensification of *das Man*.

The difference is that the Renaissance knew what it was recovering. They recognised that something valuable had been lost and worked deliberately to restore it. The danger now is that we may not recognise what we are losing until generations inherit this diminishment as their natural condition, with little memory of what authentic engagement felt like, limited experiential access to the structures that make existence genuinely human, and no sense that existence could be otherwise.

Consider what is already occurring. This year, students reach for AI assistance slightly more quickly when confusion arises. They tolerate uncertainty for shorter durations before seeking algorithmic resolution. Next year, fewer students will recognise confusion as potentially productive rather than simply problematic. The year after, even fewer will value the temporal duration that authentic understanding requires. Each cohort experiences slightly less friction within the inherited interpretations of *das Man* than the cohort before. Each generation inherits diminished capacity while believing their experience represents the normal human condition.

The transformation shows itself through what we examined as 'making-present', but now accelerated exponentially. Where systematic educational reforms gradually compressed temporal duration into optimisation cycles across decades, AI compresses duration even further within individual lifetimes. Each time a student chooses AI's instant sophisticated response over dwelling with uncertainty, tendencies deepen that make uncertainty feel intolerable. Each time a professional accepts AI's immediate comprehensive analysis over patient temporal development, habits strengthen that make temporal duration appear wasteful. Each time an individual deploys AI's polished formulations over struggling to articulate what isn't yet grasped, tendencies intensify that make struggle seem pointless.

But the stakes extend beyond individual choices to collective transformation across generations. The widespread acceleration towards AI use isn't just many individuals making similar decisions. It's the systematic reshaping of what becomes possible for human existence itself. When educational institutions adopt AI systems that bypass the struggle authentic learning requires, they don't just change current pedagogical practices. They shape the conditions within which future generations will either develop or lose capacity for authentic intellectual engagement. When professional contexts integrate AI tools that compress the temporal complexity authentic work demands, they don't just increase efficiency. They transform what counts as competent professional practice in ways that systematically marginalise authentic expertise.

The Generation That May Not Remember

We can already glimpse what may be coming. A generation is emerging now, children currently in early education, who might never experience learning without immediate AI assistance. They may not slowly lose the capacity for authentic engagement, because the conditions for that capacity to form may never arise in the first place. Should this occur, when confusion arises, AI will be immediately available to provide sophisticated explanations that bypass the productive struggle through which understanding genuinely develops. When temporal complexity creates the space where insight might emerge, algorithmic processing will compress duration into instant availability instead. When the struggle to articulate what is not yet understood might awaken authentic engagement, polished formulations will appear immediately on demand.

If these conditions persist, these students will not experience the friction within the inherited interpretations of *das Man* that makes authentic existence recognisable as distinct from systematic performance. They will not encounter moments where ready-made interpretations prove inadequate, creating Angst that signals genuine uncertainty. They will not face situations where collective scripts fail, opening space for authentic encounter with what resists systematisation. They may come to inhabit frictionless 'they-self' formation as their natural condition, unaware that authentic existence might be possible because they never experience the friction through which it reveals itself.

This represents not the loss of something these students once possessed but the potential inheritance of diminishment as the normal human condition if we fail to preserve what makes thinking genuinely human. They will not mourn what they never had. They will not recognise absence because they have no experiential access to what is absent. When they deploy sophisticated vocabulary absorbed from AI interactions, they will believe they are thinking. When they produce systematic analyses generated through algorithmic assistance, they will believe they understand. When they perform complex intellectual work through the ready-made interpretations of *das Man* executed perfectly via technological interface, they will believe this is what human intelligence has always been.

When Diminishment Becomes Inheritance

In the Renaissance, scholars worked deliberately to recover what had been lost. They knew they were recovering something valuable that had slipped away. We face the opposite – we are losing capacities we still possess, but we may not recognise the loss until future generations inherit diminishment as their baseline condition, having no memory that existence could be otherwise. Without deliberate effort to preserve and transmit authentic engagement, there may be little collective memory of what it once felt like, limited cultural transmission of why struggle matters, and diminished institutional preservation of conditions through which Angst, temporal duration, and groundless responsibility together make thinking genuinely human.

This is why our institutional responses felt inadequate despite comprehensive implementation. We were addressing AI as a tool requiring better management when actually confronting something no institutional policy can adequately address – the generational transmission of diminished human capacity disguised as technological enhancement. The question is not how to use AI responsibly within current educational frameworks. The question is whether the frameworks themselves, the institutions, the collective practices through which we transmit human culture across generations, can resist becoming transmission mechanisms for the systematic forgetting of human capacities.

Understanding what AI really is – *das Man* algorithmic rather than artificial intelligence – reveals that everything depends on whether we can preserve and transmit authentic engagement while surrounded by technological intensification of humanity's flight from authenticity. When diminishment becomes inheritance, when future generations have little memory of what has been lost, the capacity to choose authentic existence may erode across generations who never knew existence could be otherwise.

What AI Is Doing to Us

What AI is doing to us cannot be measured by efficiency gains or learning outcomes. It is reshaping the conditions within which understanding becomes possible. It offers us the experience of thinking without the labour or risk of thought, the comfort of fluency without the burden of uncertainty, the satisfaction of insight without the patience of genuine engagement. In doing so, it draws us away from the very structures that make existence human – Angst, temporal depth, and groundless responsibility.

What AI is doing to us is not replacing our intelligence but reshaping our sense of what thinking feels like. It teaches us to prefer immediacy over depth, certainty over struggle, procedure over presence. It subtly reorients our phenomenological relation to the world until authentic engagement feels inefficient, and efficiency feels like the measure of truth.

If *das Man* has taken technological form, then what AI is doing to us is not an external act upon humanity but the ongoing intensification of our own longstanding drift from authenticity. It does not compel this movement; it simply makes it frictionless. And the danger is not that we will wake up to find ourselves replaced, but that we will no longer notice what has quietly receded – the very experience of what it means to think.

The point is not to reject AI, but to recognise how easily its promise of assistance becomes a reorientation of what it means to think. Only by seeing this clearly can authentic engagement remain possible within technological conditions that increasingly obscure it.

We have seen what AI actually is – *das Man* taking technological form. We have seen why we accelerate towards it despite sensing something essential disappearing. We have seen why institutional responses feel insufficient and why diminishment risks becoming inheritance. The question is no longer whether AI threatens authentic human existence. The question is whether we can still preserve the conditions for authentic choosing when *das Man* has taken technological form – one that makes such choosing increasingly difficult with each passing year.

Part V

Learning to Choose

Chapter 13

What Authentic Choosing Requires

Through our analysis of how the boundary between human thinking and machine processing has blurred, we can now see more clearly what AI is doing to us. And now that we've seen it, we cannot unsee it. However, this awareness carries a responsibility. We have a choice to make – but what is that choice? Not a decision in the usual sense, but the movement of opening ourselves to what calls from within our thrown circumstances. This choice centres on reclaiming what we have lost through the systematic transformation of education – the authentic care that makes human relationships genuinely human. Yet this care hasn't vanished. It remains, calling to us from within the very systems that obscure it, revealing itself precisely when those systems fail to meet the demands of genuine concern. The question becomes – *what does responding to this call require of us?*

To answer this, we need to understand how authentic existence can persist within technological conditions. Drawing on concepts Heidegger developed throughout his life, some before and some after he published his 1954 essay *The Question Concerning Technology*, can help us to see what it means to choose differently. What he anticipated – technology reaching into our way of being itself – is exactly what we now face with AI. What follows traces how these ideas can help us understand what it takes to choose differently when systematic thinking surrounds us.

Earlier, in Chapter 6, we explored the fundamental structures of human existence – how we find ourselves already thrown into the world, how we flee from the Angst of that condition into what 'everyone' thinks, and how fallenness conceals this flight beneath the appearance of normal life. That chapter revealed both the ground of human existence and the movement of flight that turns us away from it. This one asks whether that same ground can also become the place of return. It turns from analysing how we lose ourselves to asking how we might live otherwise within the very structures that make flight so easy and authenticity so easily eclipsed.

What Is AI Doing to Us? A Philosophical Inquiry into Learning, Thinking, and Being, 109–121

Published under exclusive licence by Emerald Publishing Limited
doi:10.1108/978-1-83742-276-020261013

How Care Endures Beneath the System

Care

The systematic distortion we traced through Part III obscures but cannot eliminate care as the fundamental structure of human existence. Care reveals itself as the unified foundation that makes all authentic choosing possible – the basic way *Dasein* exists through genuine concern for what matters beyond systematic efficiency. Care reveals itself through our capacity to invest temporal duration in what unfolds slowly, to dwell with what resists systematisation, to remain genuinely concerned with outcomes that cannot be guaranteed. This is not something we possess or deploy but the way we exist when we're being authentically human. Through care, past inheritance, present engagement, and future projection integrate as the temporal structure that makes authentic existence possible.

In our AI circumstances, care becomes visible precisely when systematic solutions fail to satisfy what educational relationships actually require. When educators feel disconnected from teaching despite following proven procedures, when students sense something hollow about AI-enhanced work despite its sophistication, care reveals its own distortion while remaining as the structure that systematic approaches cannot replicate or replace. Care is not a mode of resistance to technological circumstances but the existential foundation that makes authentic dwelling within those circumstances possible. Without care's underlying commitment to what transcends optimisation, authentic response to AI becomes impossible.

Care provides the foundation from which authentic engagement becomes possible – the sustained attention to what matters that cannot be systematised, the willingness to dwell with uncertainty that systematic solutions promise to eliminate, the commitment to relationships that resist optimisation. When authentic choice emerges in our AI situation, it emerges through care as the fundamental structure that enables genuine encounter rather than mere management of technological objects. Without care's foundational commitment to what transcends efficiency, engagement becomes procedural rather than authentic, systematic rather than genuinely human. Care makes authentic engagement possible by preserving space for the temporal complexity, patient attention, and groundless commitment that systematic approaches tend to diminish while promising to serve the same purposes more efficiently.

Conscience

The recognition that we have systematically eroded what makes learning authentically human did not emerge through analytical thinking but through what Heidegger called 'the call of conscience' (*Ruf des Gewissens*). Conscience is a fundamental ontological structure rather than moral judgement. It is the call that awakens *Dasein* from absorption in *das Man's* ready-made interpretations, revealing how we flee from the responsibility of authentic existence. When we sense something essential is slipping away despite systematic responses to AI, when we feel persistent unease that policies cannot address, we are experiencing conscience breaking through *das Man's* comfortable certainties.

The structure of the call reveals something fundamental about human existence. Conscience calls from *Dasein* to *Dasein*. We call ourselves back from absorption in anonymous public interpretations to confront our ownmost possibilities (*eigenste Möglichkeit*) – the possibilities that belong uniquely to us rather than to 'anyone'.

The caller is the authentic self-obscured by *das Man* absorption. The called is the 'they-self' living through borrowed interpretations. What is called to is the possibility of authentic existence that remains available despite systematic flight from its demands.

The call provides no content, no specific instructions. Conscience shows itself through 'reticence' (*Verschwiegenheit*). It calls silently, offering no *das Man* script to follow, no systematic procedure to implement. This reticence makes conscience fundamental rather than ontic. It calls us to the structure of authentic choosing rather than particular choices.

Conscience shows itself through Angst – not fear of particular things but fundamental anxiety that reveals existence's groundless nature. The call creates 'uncanniness' (*Unheimlichkeit*): the unsettling recognition that we have been at home in *das Man's* interpretations while fleeing from the groundless responsibility that authentic existence requires. The familiar world of collective certainties becomes strange, revealing itself as constructed rather than natural.

In our AI circumstances, conscience manifests as growing unease when systematic solutions consistently leave something essential unaddressed. When educators feel disconnected from teaching despite following proven procedures, when students sense something hollow about AI-enhanced work despite its sophistication, when comprehensive policies leave us troubled by concerns we cannot articulate, conscience calls through the systematic certainties that optimisation thinking provides.

The call reveals that we choose inauthentically without recognition, adopting systematic solutions to remove uncertain engagement, fleeing towards efficiency over what makes learning genuinely human, living through technological procedures that shape our way of being below the level of explicit decision. Yet conscience also reveals this flight is never complete. The persistent unease that systematic responses cannot eliminate emerges because authentic existence continues calling through our absorption in enframing's logic.

Conscience shows itself through what Heidegger called 'being-guilty' (*Schuldigsein*) – not moral guilt about particular actions but fundamental guilt from recognising our thrown condition. We find ourselves already absorbed in inherited interpretations we never consciously chose, already dwelling within technological circumstances we received rather than selected. Conscience reveals this thrownness as the groundless condition within which authentic choice becomes both possible and necessary. When conscience awakens us to this fundamental guilt, it creates the possibility for 'wanting-to-have-a-conscience' (*Gewissen-haben-wollen*) – resolve to remain open to conscience's call rather than fleeing into *das Man's* comfort. This becomes the foundation for authentic choosing that stands without external justification.

Together, care and conscience reveal the foundation from which authentic choosing must arise. In our AI situation, 'wanting-to-have-a-conscience' means remaining open to Angst that signals authentic engagement rather than seeking technological solutions that eliminate such Angst. It means acknowledging that we must choose how to engage with AI tools without predetermined procedures to guarantee appropriate use, that we must take responsibility for educational relationships without systematic frameworks to ensure desired outcomes. This reveals that the choice between authentic existence and systematic optimisation has always been fundamental, but AI circumstances make this choice urgent rather than theoretical. Yet why must we choose now rather than deferring this choice until circumstances become clearer? The urgency that makes authentic choosing unavoidable emerges from recognising our existence as finite and unrepeatable.

How We Awaken to Responsibility

Being-toward-death

Earlier, we established that *Dasein's* authenticity is intimately linked to its finitude. Now, let's explore why this is the case. Why can't we simply defer the difficult choices that conscience reveals until circumstances become clearer or better guidance emerges? A deeper examination, drawing from Heidegger's concept of 'being-toward-death', reveals why authentic choice carries urgent necessity rather than optional preference.

Death shows itself not as an event that happens to us but as the structural limit that makes authentic existence possible. Because our time is limited, we cannot endlessly postpone choices about who to become. Because our existence is unrepeatable, present choices about authenticity matter absolutely. Death reveals itself as our ownmost possibility in its most radical form – the possibility that is uniquely ours, that cannot be taken over by others, that calls us back from *das Man's* collective certainties.

Unlike other possibilities we share through common projects and social roles, death individualises us absolutely. No one can die our death for us. No collective wisdom can eliminate the fundamental solitude that death reveals. No systematic procedure can guarantee how to face the limit that gives existence its urgency.

This ownmost character breaks through *das Man's* tendency to cover over finitude through 'idle talk about death'. *Das Man* treats death as something that happens to people in general – a distant event that happens to others, an eventual biological termination that need not affect present choices. 'One dies', we say, converting death's absolute singularity into anonymous generality that obscures its power to individualise authentic existence.

Authentic 'being-toward-death' shows itself through 'anticipation' (*Vorlaufen*) – running ahead into the possibility that gives all other possibilities their urgency. When we authentically anticipate death, we recognise that every choice about who to become occurs within the horizon of absolute finitude. This recognition transforms the present from optimisation cycle into the urgent site where irreplaceable choices must be made.

In our AI circumstances, 'being-toward-death' creates specific urgency. The trajectory towards systematic optimisation has powerful momentum. Every semester that AI erodes more of the struggle essential to learning, every year that educational practice becomes more algorithmic, we move closer to complete experiential absorption in the inherited interpretations of *das Man* that make authentic alternatives feel unnecessary rather than essential.

Our individual existence as educators and learners unfolds within finite horizons. We have limited time to choose whether to remain authentically human or become optimised 'they-selves'. Yet AI circumstances also intensify *das Man's* covering over of this urgency. When technological solutions promise to transcend temporal limitations that define human existence, when systematic optimisation suggests that human development can be algorithmically managed, these promises obscure the finite character that makes present choices about authenticity urgent rather than optional.

The recognition of finitude reveals why authentic choice matters beyond individual existence. Our choices about how to engage with AI create the world that future generations will inherit. If we choose systematic optimisation, we shape conditions that make authentic learning more difficult for those who come after us. If we choose authentic existence, we preserve possibilities that would otherwise disappear into complete systematisation.

'Being-toward-death' reveals that human existence unfolds through irreplaceable moments that cannot be recovered once they pass. The particular convergence of circumstances we face – AI capabilities reaching into human existence itself, educational institutions retaining memory of authentic learning, collective recognition that something essential may be disappearing, represent a finite window that will not return in the same form.

This temporal irreplaceability counters the 'making-present' that AI intensifies, which treats all moments as equivalent optimisation opportunities. When we recognise that present choices about authenticity occur within finite existence, the courage that authentic choosing requires becomes not only possible but also urgent.

We find ourselves already mortal without having chosen this condition, already facing choices about authentic existence within time we did not create. This creates what authentic choosing requires – acknowledgement that we must take responsibility for who we become within circumstances that exceed our control, that we must choose without guarantee about outcomes, that groundless responsibility for authentic existence cannot be avoided through systematic deferral.

'Being-toward-death' doesn't promise that authentic choices will succeed in preserving what makes learning authentically human. It reveals that finite existence makes such choices unavoidable. And that deferral itself constitutes a choice, usually in favour of the systematic solutions of *das Man*. When we recognise that our opportunities to choose genuine learning over systematic optimisation are finite and diminishing, the groundless courage that conscience calls forth becomes the foundation for authentic choosing that takes shape without external justification.

In this recognition, 'being-toward-death' completes what conscience began – it transforms awareness into urgency. This recognition of finite urgency creates the existential crisis that demands authentic response: How do we choose when systematic guidance becomes unavailable, when systematic frameworks fall silent?

Resoluteness

Hearing conscience and recognising our finite existence create a crisis. If we can no longer follow what 'everyone' knows is right about AI integration, if systematic procedures cannot guarantee appropriate responses to unprecedented circumstances, how do we choose?

Heidegger's answer reveals the fundamental structure of authentic existence – authentic choice has no ultimate foundation except the choosing itself. This brings us back to what he called 'resoluteness' – not stubborn determination to achieve particular goals, but the courage to choose who to become while acknowledging that such choosing is groundless. We cannot point to external authorities, systematic procedures, or collective wisdom to justify our choices. We must choose based on our own encounter with what matters, taking responsibility for who we become without guarantee about outcomes.

Resoluteness reveals itself through the unity of conscience, 'being-toward-death', and thrownness. Conscience calls us back from *das Man's* comfortable scripts. 'Being-toward-death' reveals that we cannot defer authentic choosing indefinitely. Thrownness reminds us that we must choose within circumstances we inherited rather than selected.

Together, these create the existential situation within which resoluteness becomes both possible and necessary. Resoluteness chooses from among our ownmost possibilities – possibilities that emerge from our particular engagement with inherited situations. In our AI circumstances, our ownmost possibility reveals itself as our irreplaceable capacity for the Angst, duration, and struggle that machines cannot replicate.

While AI can simulate sophisticated formulations, generate instant responses, and optimise performance efficiently, it cannot experience the fundamental uncertainty that signals authentic engagement, endure the temporal complexity that understanding requires, or confront the groundless nature of existence that gives human choice its urgency. This ownmost possibility emerges through authentic engagement with limitation. When we embrace the Angst of not-knowing rather than seeking artificial confidence, when we preserve duration over instant resolution, when we choose groundless struggle over systematic enhancement, we inhabit possibilities that belong to us alone and cannot be transferred to machines.

Resoluteness also reveals itself through 'thrown projection' (*geworfener Entwurf*). We project towards possibilities that matter to us, but this projection occurs from within circumstances we didn't choose. In our AI situation, resoluteness means taking responsibility for how we exist as educators and learners without systematic guidance. We cannot escape institutional pressures towards optimisation, but we can choose how to respond.

We cannot guarantee that authentic engagement will be recognised, but we can preserve what makes learning genuinely human. This groundless choosing creates Angst precisely because it releases us from the security that *das Man* provides. There's no collective script for navigating AI that can substitute for our own authentic engagement with unprecedented circumstances. We must choose while acknowledging that consequences cannot be guaranteed, that we find ourselves without the systematic foundation that technological thinking promises yet never actually provides. But this groundlessness is precisely what makes authentic choice possible. If systematic procedures could guarantee outcomes, we wouldn't be choosing authentically. We'd simply be following scripts. Resoluteness means embracing the Angst of groundless choice as the condition within which genuine responsibility becomes possible.

Resoluteness reveals what Heidegger called 'the situation' (*die Situation*) – not objective circumstances that exist independently, but the meaningful context that emerges when *Dasein* chooses authentically from within its thrown circumstances. The situation appears only in the moment of resolute choice, when we see clearly what our circumstances demand and choose decisively based on our own encounter with what matters. Yet how does this resolute choosing actually emerge? How do we move from recognising the need for groundless choice to choosing authentically within temporal conditions that systematic thinking has trained us to avoid? This requires the integration of past inheritance, future projection, and present urgency in what Heidegger called the 'moment of vision' (*Augenblick*).

How Time Opens for Authentic Choice

The Moment of Vision

Authentic choice doesn't develop gradually through careful analysis or systematic deliberation. It emerges in the moment of vision – the temporal structure through which we see our complete situation in its full clarity and choose decisively.

The moment of vision isn't a brief temporal moment but a way of experiencing time where past, present, and future converge in unified integration. In moments of authentic choice, we see simultaneously – our thrown inheritance (circumstances we didn't choose but must work within), genuine possibilities that concern us (futures we can authentically pursue), and present urgency (the need to choose now rather than deferring indefinitely).

This temporal convergence directly counters the 'making-present' that systematic thinking intensifies. Where 'making-present' flattens temporal complexity into optimisation cycles, the moment of vision restores the rich interpenetration of temporal dimensions that authentic existence requires. Instead of predetermined procedures that abstract away from temporal complexity, authentic decision-making honours the full temporal situation that enframing systematically obscures.

The moment of vision reveals itself through 'retrieving' (*Wiederholung*) the past as living inheritance rather than dead information. Inherited circumstances don't appear as obstacles to overcome but as the ever-present foundation that makes current understanding possible. We take over our thrownness authentically, acknowledging how educational traditions, institutional expectations, and cultural interpretations continue to shape the possibilities within which we must choose.

Simultaneously, the moment of vision involves authentic anticipation towards genuine possibilities rather than predetermined outcomes. Instead of planning towards goals that minimise uncertainty, we project towards possibilities that create meaningful engagement precisely because they cannot be guaranteed. These aren't systematic objectives but authentic possibilities that emerge from our own encounter with what matters about educational relationships.

The present emerges as the temporal site where inheritance and projection converge in decisive choice. This differs fundamentally from 'making-present' that reduces temporal complexity to immediate demands for efficient action. The moment creates the temporal opening where authentic choice becomes possible through integration of what we inherit with what we authentically project.

Consider an educator encountering a student's AI-generated work. In the moment of vision, temporal dimensions converge: the past appears as inherited educational circumstances – assessment requirements, institutional expectations, pedagogical traditions. The future comes towards us as genuine possibilities – this could become authentic learning about understanding itself, or remain trapped in systematic policy application. The present emerges as a call to respond in ways that serve authentic learning rather than administrative efficiency.

The moment of vision reveals our freedom within thrownness. We didn't choose our AI circumstances, yet we remain responsible for how we inhabit them. We cannot eliminate uncertainty, yet we can take responsibility for responding to what our particular situations demand. Each authentic choice emerges from unique temporal convergence that cannot be predetermined or reproduced algorithmically.

The moment of vision displaces the comfort of systematic procedures because it demands response to particular situations that resist generalisation. It reveals 'the situation' in its full concreteness – not abstract circumstances existing independently, but the meaningful context that appears when we choose authentically from within thrown circumstances while projecting towards possibilities that genuinely concern us. The moment of vision restores what 'making-present' rushes past – the duration where confusion becomes productive, the space where understanding emerges gradually, the patience where authentic engagement develops naturally. When we experience authentic temporal integration, we recognise that some understanding requires slow time, that certain insights emerge only through sustained dwelling with uncertainty.

This recognition creates a fundamental challenge – how do we engage with technological tools that promise to bypass this very temporal complexity? The temporal integration that the moment of vision provides becomes essential for engaging technology authentically. We need to see how our inherited circumstances, present choices, and future possibilities converge in each encounter with AI.

How We Dwell with Technology

Gelassenheit

These questions point towards what Heidegger called *Gelassenheit* – a way of relating to technology that neither seeks to dominate it nor allows us to be absorbed into its logic. *Gelassenheit*, often translated as 'letting-be' or 'releasement', represents a receptiveness that lets what shows itself appear as it is. This requires meditative thinking – remaining open to what resists our attempts to control it while staying genuinely engaged with what matters.

In our AI circumstances, calculative thinking approaches AI as a problem requiring management – developing policies to control its use, creating procedures to ensure appropriate application, establishing guidelines intended to bypass uncertainty. Meditative thinking, by contrast, allows our encounter with AI to reveal what authentic engagement actually requires, preserving space for what cannot be anticipated or optimised.

Gelassenheit reveals itself through 'openness to mystery' (*Offenheit für das Geheimnis*) – remaining receptive to what cannot be reduced to measurement, prediction, or optimisation. In our AI situation, this means recognising that the most essential parts of learning cannot be generated by algorithms. The Angst that signals authentic engagement, the temporal duration that understanding requires, the groundless choosing that creates genuine responsibility – these remain beyond technological production or enhancement.

When we practise *Gelassenheit* with AI, we can engage its capabilities when they serve authentic educational purposes while maintaining awareness of what they cannot provide. This creates what Heidegger called 'a free relation to technology' (*freie Beziehung zur Technik*) – using technological capabilities without being absorbed into their logic. We neither reject AI tools wholesale nor embrace optimisation that bypasses what makes learning genuinely human.

This free relation reveals itself through authentic engagement that discerns when technological capabilities serve genuine educational ends and when they substitute efficiency for genuine meaning. When we engage AI tools authentically, we neither try to control them through calculative thinking nor allow ourselves to be claimed by them through systematic absorption.

AI tools can sometimes handle routine tasks that don't require our full humanity, creating space for sustained attention that authentic learning demands. But these technologies may also bypass the productive struggle through which genuine understanding develops. When AI provides instant explanations, it may sidestep the temporal process where confusion becomes insight.

A free relationship to technology means working with the technological circumstances we inherit while choosing how to engage with them. We cannot escape

AI's presence in educational environments, but we can stay attentive to possibilities for genuine engagement that no predetermined framework can anticipate. This stance counters enframing's operation, which makes everything appear as standing-reserve requiring optimisation.

When we practise letting-be, students appear as persons with their own ways of encountering material rather than learning profiles requiring algorithmic management. Knowledge appears as territory to be explored rather than content to be delivered efficiently.

Gelassenheit requires patience – the capacity to remain engaged with what unfolds slowly rather than demanding immediate resolution through technological assistance. This patience preserves space for the temporal rhythms that authentic understanding requires while working within technological conditions that pressure us towards instant availability.

Through *Gelassenheit*, we do not escape our technological circumstances - we learn to inhabit them without being determined by them, remaining open to what calls from within them towards genuine engagement.

Poiesis

The free relation to technology that *Gelassenheit* enables creates the possibility for a mode of 'bringing-forth' that responds to what shows itself rather than imposing upon it. Heidegger drew on the Greek term *poiesis*, which he translates as 'bringing-forth', to describe a way of engagement in which understanding emerges through patient involvement rather than being generated through systematic control. *Poiesis* represents a mode of revealing that differs fundamentally from the kind of production driven by modern technology's demand for control and optimisation. Where technological production shows itself through 'challenging-forth' – demanding that beings reveal themselves as standing-reserve available for optimisation – *poiesis* works through patient responsiveness that honours what it encounters.

The craftsperson working with wood studies the material's particular character – its grain, texture, possibilities, and limitations. They allow form to emerge through sustained dialogue between human skill and material reality.

Poietic 'bringing-forth' shows itself through what Heidegger analysed as Aristotle's 'four causes' that work together – the material (what something is made from), the formal (what shape it takes), the final (what purpose it serves), and the efficient cause (in Aristotle's sense of the agent from whom the emergence proceeds, rather than a producer imposing form). *Poiesis* honours all four dimensions rather than reducing everything to efficient manipulation. Technological production, by contrast, reduces all causation to systematic control of material towards predetermined outcomes, sidestepping the temporal complexity that poietic 'bringing-forth' requires.

In educational contexts, *poiesis* means allowing learning to emerge through sustained engagement with resistant ideas rather than forcing predetermined outcomes. When students struggle with complex concepts, authentic teaching works with that resistance to let understanding take form. The difficulty students encounter is not a problem requiring more efficient methods but the very condition through which genuine comprehension unfolds. The confusion that arises when familiar frameworks prove inadequate creates the opening where new insight becomes possible.

Educational *poiesis* reveals itself when something takes shape that was not yet present – not simply new information, but a shift in understanding. The student who discovers an argument through writing, not by following a formula but by staying with the tension between thought and evidence, engages poietically with material. This poietic 'bringing-forth' requires temporal duration – time that optimisation habits tend to compress or bypass. Authentic understanding develops through slow accumulation of encounters with ideas across time. *Poiesis* honours this temporal complexity rather than demanding immediate resolution. The wandering and revision that lead to unexpected discoveries, the patient work of staying with what has not yet taken form – these require duration where confusion becomes productive.

In our AI circumstances, *poiesis* reveals what is lost when algorithms generate educational outputs from simple prompts. When AI produces analyses instantly, it bypasses the temporal process where writers discover what they think through the difficulty of articulating it. When students receive polished explanations, they avoid the encounter with resistance that makes learning transformative rather than merely informative. *Poiesis* does not require rejecting technological assistance entirely. The student who uses AI for routine tasks while preserving energy for responsiveness to what has yet to emerge, or the teacher who employs AI for administration while protecting time for thoughtful pedagogical engagement, demonstrates a poietic relationship to technology – one that uses tools without being absorbed into their logic.

Poietic engagement also transforms our relationship to limitation. Instead of treating constraints as obstacles requiring technological solutions, it works from within inherited circumstances, using requirements and limitations as starting points for possibilities that could not be anticipated. It transforms constraint into an opening for possibility rather than a problem requiring resolution. Working poietically means taking responsibility for the conditions through which something can emerge, rather than producing outcomes directly. When we choose optimisation, we create educational conditions where authentic struggle becomes unnecessary. When we choose poietic engagement, we preserve possibilities for learning that resist algorithmic generation. Every choice about AI engagement either supports or undermines the conditions within which poietic 'bringing-forth' can occur.

As technological production becomes more sophisticated, the capacity for poietic 'bringing-forth' becomes both rarer and more essential. The ability to respond to rather than override what we encounter, to honour temporal complexity, and to take responsibility for sustaining the conditions of emergence represents what remains uniquely human even when machines can replicate the products but not the process of such 'bringing-forth'.

Where the Saving Power Appears

The Saving Power

Heidegger's most hopeful insight about technological conditions draws on a line from the poet Friedrich Hölderlin: 'But where the danger is, there grows also the saving power'. The extremity of our condition, the possibility that we might replace ourselves entirely through systematic optimisation, might also awaken us to what makes existence authentically human.

The danger of enframing lies in its totalising character. When everything appears as standing-reserve requiring optimisation, alternative ways of being disappear from view. We lose the capacity to recognise that systematic thinking represents a choice rather than inevitable progress. We become so embedded in optimisation logic that we forget what authentic existence requires. But extremity can create recognition. When machines begin replicating our work with perfect consistency, we might finally see what we have become. When students produce sophisticated analyses they cannot explain, we might recognise what we have displaced from learning. When efficiency becomes so complete that it threatens to obscure everything distinctively human, we might finally see what authentic existence actually requires. The very success of algorithmic replication reveals, by contrast, what authentic existence demands.

Yet the saving power doesn't emerge automatically from technological extremity. It becomes possible only when we recognise the danger clearly and choose authentic response. The saving power requires what the preceding concepts have illuminated – conscience that awakens us from *das Man* absorption, resoluteness that chooses groundlessly, recognition of finitude that creates urgency, temporal integration that makes authentic choice possible, *Gelassenheit* that maintains freedom within technological circumstances, and *poiesis* that preserves authentic 'bringing-forth'.

The saving power shows itself through what Heidegger called 'the step back' (*der Schritt zurück*) – creating distance from enframing's total absorption that allows us to see technological thinking as one possibility rather than the only reality. When we step back from systematic optimisation, space opens for alternative ways of engaging with what matters. This does not eliminate technology but reveals it as regional rather than total.

We can use technological capabilities when they serve authentic purposes while maintaining awareness of what they cannot provide. In our AI circumstances, the step back means recognising that when machines can simulate our inherited modes of thinking, we can finally see how systematic our thinking has become. When algorithms can follow our educational procedures more consistently than we can ourselves, we recognise that what we have taken for natural teaching has already become algorithmic. This recognition creates the possibility for authentic 'dwelling' (*Wohnen*) within technological conditions – inhabiting them authentically rather than being absorbed into their systematic logic.

The saving power also emerges through individual authentic choice that creates conditions where others might begin to see alternatives to systematic optimisation. Our individual choices about authenticity don't guarantee broader transformation, but they create the foundation upon which collective authentic existence might emerge. In our circumstances, the saving power begins to emerge as we recognise what machines cannot replicate – the groundless choosing that creates genuine responsibility, the temporal integration that allows insight to develop naturally, the patient attention that honours what resists systematisation, and the poietic engagement that works with rather than against material resistance. By seeing clearly what AI can systematise, we can finally understand what makes existence authentically human.

The saving power reveals itself not only in thought but also in the lived practices of human learning. It appears in those moments when care, conscience, and genuine struggle resist the pull of systematic efficiency and allow something genuinely human to emerge.

Chapter 14

How Authentic Learning Unfolds

Understanding what authentic choosing requires is only the beginning. The deeper question is how authentic learning shows itself – and what preserving it now demands when AI makes systematic alternatives instantly available.

This is where we return to Maya. Her story captures the strongest movements of authentic learning we witnessed before AI assistance became common. When read through the Heideggerian concepts we have been working with, her ways of engaging reveal how care, conscience, resoluteness, temporal integration, *Gelassenheit*, and *poiesis* took shape in lived experience as it unfolds in authentic learning.

Care as the Foundation of Sustained Engagement

Maya's inability to proceed past the first page while confusion remained unresolved reveals care showing itself as the fundamental structure that makes authentic learning possible. Her inability to 'just build the argument everyone expects' emerged not from academic inadequacy but from care's refusal to reduce educational relationships to procedural compliance. Maya could have approached the assignment systematically – accepting the expert's conclusions, organising the technical analysis into standard legal argument format, and working towards predetermined claims about intoxication evidence. Instead, her care preserved the questioning that procedural approaches bypass.

Care revealed itself through Maya's capacity to invest temporal duration in what unfolded slowly – weeks spent dwelling with uncertainty rather than accepting premature resolution. Her willingness to remain genuinely concerned with outcomes that could not be guaranteed, to dwell with what resisted systematisation, emerged from care's foundational commitment to what matters beyond optimisation.

Her recognition that 'I'm sabotaging my own grades for questions that don't have answers' revealed care's resistance to converting caring-for authentic understanding into taking-care-of systematic requirements. Care preserved space for the temporal complexity that learning requires, the Angst that signals genuine engagement, the struggle that builds authentic understanding.

What Is AI Doing to Us? A Philosophical Inquiry into Learning, Thinking, and Being, 123–127

doi:10.1108/978-1-83742-276-020261014

Care functioned as the unified structure that made all her other authentic responses possible – the foundation from which conscience could call, resoluteness could choose, and temporal integration could develop. Care alone, however, could not awaken Maya from systematic absorption. Conscience breaking through the comfortable scripts that caring might otherwise follow unconsciously would prove necessary.

Conscience Calling Against *das Man*'s Systematic Scripts

Maya's recognition that accepting the easy path would mean giving up something important reveals conscience breaking through her absorption in *das Man*. Her partner's suggestion to 'just focus on building the argument you need' represents the collective script that treats confusion as inefficiency rather than as a signal for authentic engagement. Conscience called through this systematic absorption, creating unease about following what 'everyone' would do.

The shift came when Maya's friend casually questioned whether slurred speech automatically indicates intoxication. This simple moment of doubt opened space for conscience to awaken her from *das Man's* inherited interpretations. The call provided no content and no specific instructions about the acoustic evidence – it simply revealed that following ready-made scripts would mean turning away from authentic engagement with what mattered.

This awakening brought with it the fundamental Angst that conscience creates. Maya was not afraid of particular academic consequences but experienced the kind of deeper anxiety that arises when familiar ways of working no longer feel secure. Her sense that 'something essential was at stake' showed conscience generating uncanniness – the familiar academic practice of assembling the required argument began to feel strange, revealing itself as a retreat into the expected script rather than natural scholarly method.

In each moment when she could have followed what 'everyone' expected instead of wrestling with what the situation actually required, she faced the fundamental choice that conscience illuminates.

Yet hearing conscience's call was only the beginning. Responding to what it revealed would require resoluteness – the courage to choose without guarantee.

Resoluteness: Choosing Without Guarantee

Maya's sustained investment over weeks without guarantee demonstrates resoluteness as the courage to choose who to become while acknowledging that such choosing is groundless. Finding herself already embedded in academic circumstances she hadn't chosen, she remained responsible for how she inhabited them. This thrownness created the condition within which authentic choice became necessary. She could not point to authorities, procedures, or collective wisdom to justify her choice. No external validation existed for choosing weeks of uncertainty over readily available expert analysis. The choice had to emerge from her own encounter with what mattered.

This groundless choosing revealed itself clearly when her study partner dismissed her concerns: 'You're overthinking this. It's not that complicated'. Maya's response, 'But what if it is that complicated?' refused to collapse her uncertainty into the easy answer, even when the simplified approach would have been faster and more efficient. Her study partner packed up saying, 'Your call. I'm done', leaving Maya to face the groundless choice that resoluteness requires – taking responsibility for who she becomes through engagement that offers no external justification.

What followed demonstrated resoluteness in action. Her choice to pursue research threads that led nowhere, to draft paragraphs she deleted, to try approaches that didn't work showed resoluteness embracing the Angst of groundless choice as the condition within which genuine responsibility becomes possible. This recognition of the encounter's irreplaceability intensified her commitment. The urgency created by 'being-toward-death' revealed that this particular moment with the acoustic evidence – this specific convergence of confusion and possibility – would never return in the same form. Maya couldn't defer authentic engagement until later. This moment was finite and unrepeatable.

Maya could not guarantee that her weeks of confusion would produce better understanding than simply accepting expert conclusions and building the required argument, but she chose authentic development over academic efficiency. Through all of this, Maya inhabited possibilities that belonged to her alone through groundless commitment to what mattered beyond measurable outcomes. Resoluteness, however, unfolded through time in ways that systematic thinking systematically undermines. Maya's groundless choosing required the temporal integration that makes authentic decision possible.

Temporal Integration and the Development of Understanding

Maya's weeks of dwelling with uncertainty reveal the temporal integration that authentic learning requires – the complex interpenetration of past, present, and future that makes human understanding possible. The moment of vision unfolded through Maya's learning as a temporal convergence where past inheritance, present engagement, and future projection worked together. She retrieved the past as a living inheritance – legal habits of interpretation that had become instinctive through her training – rather than as dead information to be processed. She anticipated genuine possibilities rather than predetermined outcomes, remaining open to where authentic questions might lead.

This temporal complexity manifested concretely through Maya's approach. Her willingness to follow research threads that led nowhere demonstrated her resistance to the fallenness that seeks comfort in quick resolution. Her return to difficult passages multiple times, and her patience in letting understanding develop across weeks rather than demanding immediate clarity, preserved the temporal complexity that authentic learning requires.

Such authentic engagement demanded its own rhythm. This process required duration for confusion to become productive, space for insights to emerge gradually, and patience for authentic engagement to develop naturally. Maya's confusion became productive not through rapid resolution but through sustained dwelling that allowed complexity to reveal itself.

This temporal development required a particular stance towards what resisted her understanding – neither forcing systematic control nor passively accepting authoritative claims, but the meditative engagement of Gelassenheit.

Gelassenheit as Openness to What Resists

Maya's questioning about whether slurred speech might indicate fatigue or stress demonstrates *Gelassenheit* working with what resisted easy categorisation rather than against it. Instead of accepting the expert's authoritative claims, she allowed gaps in reasoning to become visible, letting the evidence reveal what the expert's systematic framework obscured. This openness unfolded through meditative thinking – the kind of thoughtful dwelling Heidegger describes, where we allow what calls for thought to show itself rather than forcing conclusions.

Gelassenheit worked through Maya's willingness to let the material speak before imposing analytical categories. She noticed 'assumptions in the expert's reasoning – places where alternative explanations weren't considered, moments where correlation got treated as causation', preserving space for what resisted simplified resolution.

Most fundamentally, her willingness to sit with not-knowing rather than seeking quick answers revealed *Gelassenheit* as openness to what cannot be immediately resolved. Maya acknowledged that the most essential aspects of legal judgement resist systematic control – the uncertainty about what evidence proves, the Angst that signals genuine engagement with complex questions, the groundless choosing that human responsibility requires.

She could appreciate the expert's technical competence while maintaining awareness of what expert analysis could not provide – the temporal duration that understanding requires, the Angst that signals authentic engagement, and the struggle that builds irreplaceable human judgement. This free relation to the expert's analysis created the conditions within which Maya could engage creatively with the complex evidence rather than simply accepting expert conclusions.

Poiesis as Bringing-forth Through Struggle

Maya's understanding emerging through struggle rather than reception reveals *poiesis* as a form of 'bringing-forth' that works with – rather than against – what resists easy control. Each encounter with difficulty revealed something new about what acoustic evidence could and could not demonstrate about human mental states during crisis. This poietic engagement unfolded through patient involvement rather than rapid conclusion.

Poiesis worked through Maya's sustained attention to evidence that resisted simple interpretation. Instead of forcing predetermined outcomes, she returned repeatedly to the material, letting its gaps, contradictions, and methodological limits show themselves. Understanding was allowed to emerge through a kind of dialogue between her attentive questioning and the evidence's complexity.

What emerged demonstrated poietic 'bringing-forth' in its truest sense. Her research that complicated rather than simplified the expert's claims showed *poiesis* honouring all dimensions of 'bringing-forth' – the material (the acoustic evidence itself), the formal (patterns of legal reasoning), the final (what legal judgement serves), and the efficient cause (in Aristotle's sense of the agent responsible for *letting* something come into being – here, Maya's responsibility for the understanding that emerged). Through this process, she took responsibility for sustaining the engagement through which understanding could unfold.

The character of this 'bringing-forth' became evident during the mock trial. Maya could defend her reasoning and respond in a grounded way because she had allowed her understanding to develop through personal struggle rather than receiving it from external authority. Her analysis emerged from weeks of poietic engagement with what initially resisted comprehension – insights that could only take shape through patient, temporal 'bringing-forth'.

Chapter 15

How Authentic Learning Endures

Maya's authentic learning required conscious choices against systematic pressure that already favoured efficient solutions. Our examination in the previous chapter revealed how each philosophical concept worked through her deliberate resistance to optimisation logic. Her struggle was not accidental – it was the condition through which authentic understanding became possible.

However, if Maya encountered the same assignment today, she would face a fundamentally different challenge. AI would not simply increase pressure toward efficiency – it would offer polished performance that bypasses the very struggle through which authentic learning develops. Instead of intensifying familiar academic pressures, AI would present sophisticated outputs that appear to replace the work of development itself, creating the temptation to forgo the slow, uncertain processes that make understanding genuinely human.

What follows explores what sustaining Maya's way of learning would require in a world where AI increasingly erodes the very struggle through which authentic understanding becomes possible.

When Care Must Resist Systematic Efficiency

Consider how this would unfold in practice. The moment confusion arose about acoustic evidence, Maya would face pressure to shortcut weeks of caring engagement through instant analysis made possible by AI. She would need to choose caring-for genuine understanding over taking-care-of assignment requirements whenever AI provides sophisticated explanations that bypass the temporal investment caring demands. Preserving a foundational commitment to care would become challenging as deadlines pressed while understanding remained incomplete, when classmates accessed instant resolution while she dwelled with uncertainty, during moments when choosing optimisation may feel more reasonable than sustained involvement with what matters.

This reveals how AI threatens care itself – the fundamental structure that makes authentic engagement possible through genuine concern for what matters beyond systematic efficiency. She would face constant pressure to convert

What Is AI Doing to Us? A Philosophical Inquiry into Learning, Thinking, and Being, 129–133

Published under exclusive licence by Emerald Publishing Limited
doi:10.1108/978-1-83742-276-020261015

her genuine concern about what acoustic analysis proves into AI-generated completion of academic requirements. The challenge would be distinguishing care from inefficiency when AI's availability makes caring involvement appear as poor time management. Maya would need to choose temporal complexity over instant availability, patient attention over efficient resolution, groundless commitment over procedural guarantee, while surrounded by alternatives that deliver the products of learning without the learning itself.

Resisting the reduction of caring-for into taking-care-of would become urgent whenever confusion arose, when understanding demands duration that algorithmic solutions can compress, as authentic encounter requires what systematic alternatives can diminish.

But care alone cannot sustain authentic engagement unless Maya can still hear what calls her back from systematic absorption – the voice of conscience.

When Conscience Calls Through Algorithmic Absorption

Maya would need to hear conscience calling whenever AI offered to reduce the weeks of uncertainty that signal authentic encounter. The difficulty would lie not in hearing the call, but in trusting it – especially when AI offers instant, sophisticated analysis while conscience demands that she remain confused for weeks, with no guarantee of deeper understanding. As AI enables avoiding what authentic involvement must learn to live with, she would need to preserve 'wanting-to-have-a-conscience' rather than turn to technological solutions that bypass the very groundless Angst through which conscience reveals itself.

She would need to recognise that accepting AI's confident conclusions would constitute a flight from the responsibility that authentic existence requires. The challenge would intensify when classmates accessed ready-made analysis while she chose to remain confused about what acoustic evidence actually proves. Conscience would need to call through her absorption into algorithmic logic, where optimisation feels like natural academic progress, and through collective scripts that frame expedience as more reasonable than genuine encounter.

Maintaining openness to the Angst that reveals authentic involvement – rather than using AI to bypass the discomfort that signals genuine encounter with the groundless nature of existence – would require constant vigilance. She would face the ongoing choice between algorithmic confidence and authentic uncertainty whenever confusion arose.

But hearing conscience clearly would not guarantee that she could act on what it revealed – doing so would require the groundless resolve that resoluteness demands.

Choosing Groundless Struggle over AI Enhancement

Maya would need to choose the uncertainty of authentic struggle over AI's polished shortcuts, especially when algorithmic confidence seems to remove the very uncertainty that genuine development depends on. Embracing the Angst of not-knowing would prove challenging when AI provided instant analysis that appears more reasonable than weeks of confusion. AI provides what authentic encounter must develop through difficult work – sophisticated analysis, comprehensive arguments, and confident conclusions.

Choosing struggle over enhancement would become a constant task for Maya – an act of resoluteness in which she must take responsibility for who she becomes without any external guarantee. She would need to inhabit possibilities that belong to her alone even as AI's availability makes individual authentic involvement feel inefficient.

The challenge arises when AI-enhanced performance seems to remove the need for the groundless choosing that authentic engagement requires. Maya would need to choose responsibility for understanding developed through uncertain involvement, while AI provided plausible performances that simulate what 'everyone' expects from sophisticated academic work. Resisting becoming an enhanced 'they-self' who presents artificial capabilities without authentic struggle would require choosing the Angst and duration that build irreplaceable human capacity. Maya would face this choice whenever confusion arose, as deadlines pressed, when AI enabled bypassing the groundless responsibility that resoluteness requires.

Yet resoluteness can unfold only through temporal openness – precisely the dimension that AI systematically compresses – making the preservation of authentic temporality essential for any genuine choosing.

Preserving Temporal Integration Against Compression

Preserving temporal integration would become urgent whenever AI enabled compressing weeks of development into instant outputs. Resisting the prompt box that reduces the duration needed for questions to deepen, for multiple encounters to allow insights to emerge, and for patient attention to let conceptual complexity reveal itself naturally would require constant vigilance. When AI offered polished answers without developmental process, choosing the temporal complexity that human learning requires would demand sustained commitment.

Maya would need to maintain duration for confusion to become productive, while AI's availability makes such patience appear as unnecessary delay. The challenge would intensify when classmates accessed polished analysis instantly while Maya chose weeks of dwelling with uncertainty. She would need to resist falling into 'making-present' that treats all moments as equivalent optimisation opportunities, preserving instead the temporal rhythms that authentic understanding requires.

Maintaining temporal integration would prove essential whenever AI enabled bypassing the struggle through which understanding develops – when algorithmic solutions appear to diminish the patience that genuine encounter demands and when instant availability makes sustained attention feel inefficient. This temporal development would require a particular stance towards what resists easy understanding – neither forcing quick answers nor accepting AI's ready-made solutions.

But Maya would also face the subtle suggestion that authentic choice can always be deferred. The logic is implicit: struggle can wait, depth can come later, and there will be time for real understanding – eventually. For now, optimisation appears to offer a smoother, safer path.

And yet, 'being-toward-death' reveals this deferral as illusion. Maya's finite existence as a learner unfolds within irreplaceable moments. This particular encounter with acoustic evidence, this specific convergence of confusion and possibility, will not return in the same form. Each semester that AI enables avoiding more of the struggle, the conditions for authentic learning will become increasingly difficult to sustain.

Recognition of finitude creates urgency. Maya cannot postpone authentic engagement until circumstances become clearer. Her opportunities to choose authentic struggle over AI-driven shortcuts are finite and diminishing.

Gelassenheit as Openness to What Resists

Maya would need to maintain meditative thinking as AI intensified calculative approaches that treat complex questions as problems requiring efficient solutions. Preserving openness to what cannot be quickly resolved would become challenging while AI provided instant answers to precisely what genuine encounter must learn to dwell with patiently. This would require *Gelassenheit* – meditative thinking that stays open to what cannot be systematised, even while dwelling within technological conditions.

AI offers explanations that appear to resolve difficulty yet bypass the temporal process through which confusion becomes insight. Choosing openness to uncertainty over algorithmic certainty would require deliberate resistance. Maya would need to work with technological circumstances while maintaining discernment about when AI serves authentic purposes and when it substitutes performance for genuine understanding.

The challenge would emerge whenever AI enabled bypassing the uncertainty that signals authentic involvement with complex questions. Maya would need to preserve space for insights to emerge naturally rather than accept ready-made interpretations that promise comfortable resolution of what remains genuinely difficult. *Gelassenheit* becomes crucial when AI provides sophisticated analysis that seems to settle precisely the uncertainty authentic judgement requires.

This openness would create conditions for authentic engagement with what resists quick understanding. Yet this receptivity would remain incomplete without the poietic 'bringing-forth' that transforms encounter into genuine learning.

Choosing *Poiesis* over Algorithmic Production

Cultivating poietic 'bringing-forth' would become essential whenever AI tools delivered instant, polished analysis. Preserving the resistance that makes learning transformative would become increasingly difficult as AI enabled short-circuiting the slow work through which genuine understanding unfolds. This threatens *poiesis* itself – the mode of 'bringing-forth' that allows understanding to emerge through patient engagement with what resists straightforward resolution.

AI offers polished formulations without the confusion that signals authentic involvement. Maya would face the ongoing challenge of choosing patient involvement with material that has not yet revealed its shape. Working with – rather than around – what resists clear understanding would require sustained commitment, especially when AI enables bypassing exactly what made her earlier learning possible.

The challenge intensifies when algorithmic production begins to simulate outcomes that poietic involvement can only let emerge through sustained struggle. Maya would need to choose genuine emergence over instant availability, temporal depth over quick resolution, and a willingness to engage what is still unclear over passive acceptance of polished output.

Preserving *poiesis* would become essential whenever AI enabled bypassing the slow, resistant processes through which understanding takes form – especially when AI's polished responses seem superior to the slow, resistant process through which real understanding grows, tempting her to see the struggle as unnecessary.

Yet even this reveals a deeper limit. What Maya preserved through individual resolve cannot depend on individuals alone. AI circumstances alter the conditions of learning so profoundly that authenticity now requires more than personal struggle – it depends on the shared practices, relationships, and environments that can still sustain it. To understand how authentic learning endures, we must now turn to the ontological structures of 'being-with-others' through which genuine engagement might reveal itself.

Chapter 16

How Shared Authenticity Reveals Itself

What we came to recognise in the previous chapter reveals a fundamental limitation. Even if individuals like Maya successfully choose authentic learning, such choice requires conditions that are becoming increasingly difficult to sustain. Maya's ways of engaging – dwelling with uncertainty, preserving temporal complexity, choosing struggle over efficiency – worked within circumstances that still made space for authentic engagement. But as we have seen, maintaining this way of engaging within AI circumstances requires constant resistance to systematic pressures that make optimisation feel like the obvious choice. This points beyond individual choice towards the collective structures through which authentic existence either becomes possible or gets systematically undermined.

The structures we traced in Part III – *das Man* interpretations, 'making-present', enframing logic, and fallenness – show themselves through shared institutional structures that exceed individual control. *Das Man* shows itself through anonymous collective interpretations that circulate through professional discourse. 'Making-present' takes shape through institutional pressures that collectively compress temporal duration. Fallenness unfolds through idle talk, curiosity, and ambiguity that make systematic approaches feel natural while concealing authentic alternatives. 'They-self' formation reveals itself through the collective shaping of professional practice that draws our way of being towards systematic modes of engagement.

Individual authentic existence remains necessary, but individual choice alone cannot address the interpretive habits that show themselves through the very collective structures within which such choosing occurs. We exist always already with others, through shared contexts that shape what feels possible. The formation of authentic communities becomes increasingly difficult because, as we have traced, we have trained ourselves for decades to think in ways that feel less existentially engaged, more procedurally managed. Decades of institutional transformation have made the lived experience of thinking increasingly similar to procedural execution, eroding our capacity to recognise or sustain the existential engagement that authentic communities require.

This recognition points towards the need to understand collective authentic existence – how shared authentic engagement might let institutional conditions

What Is AI Doing to Us? A Philosophical Inquiry into Learning, Thinking, and Being, 135–143

doi:10.1108/978-1-83742-276-020261016

take shape where individual authentic choice becomes more rather than less possible. What follows explores the ontological conditions through which such collective authenticity might take shape.

How Being-with-others Reveals Itself Authentically

Human existence is fundamentally relational. We exist always already with others – not as isolated subjects who occasionally encounter external persons, but as beings whose existence unfolds through shared contexts and mutual involvement. Heidegger called this fundamental structure *Mitsein*, 'being-with-others', which shows itself through both inauthentic and authentic modes that give rise to fundamentally different conditions for collective existence.

Inauthentic 'being-with-others' shows itself through the *das Man* interpretations we have already examined. We exist with others by following collective interpretations about what 'everyone' expects, adopting ready-made responses to avoid authentic engagement's Angst, and conforming to collective interpretive scripts that avoid individual responsibility. This inauthentic 'being-with' creates the illusion of shared understanding while actually isolating us within systematic procedures that prevent genuine encounter. This represents the collective manifestation of inauthenticity – flight from the Angst that authentic relationships require.

AI intensifies this mode of absorption by creating experiences that resonate with the systematic modes of thinking we have already developed, making *das Man* absorption feel like enhanced collaboration rather than flight from authentic engagement. In educational contexts, inauthentic 'being-with-others' manifests as professional relationships organised around systematic obligations rather than authentic engagement with what learning requires. We relate to colleagues through committee procedures, to students through assessment rubrics, to administrators through compliance requirements. These relationships feel social and collaborative, but they unfold through systematic scripts that avoid the groundless engagement authentic relationships demand.

Authentic 'being-with-others' emerges when individuals who have heard conscience's call choose to engage with others while preserving rather than avoiding the Angst that makes existence genuinely human. Instead of following collective scripts to avoid uncertainty, authentic 'being-with' takes shape in shared contexts where uncertainty becomes productive rather than problematic. Instead of adopting systematic procedures to avoid groundless choice, authentic relationships preserve the groundlessness that makes authentic choosing possible for all involved.

Consider what happens when educators who recognise their systematic absorption begin engaging authentically with colleagues about AI circumstances. Instead of following collective scripts about 'optimising AI integration' or 'managing AI challenges', they preserve the fundamental uncertainty about what AI's arrival means for authentic learning. They remain open to possibilities that cannot be predetermined, willing to dwell with questions that resist systematic resolution, and committed to protecting what makes educational relationships genuinely human.

This authentic engagement doesn't avoid disagreement or conflict. It may intensify both. When systematic scripts no longer provide comfortable resolution, authentic differences emerge that demand sustained attention rather than procedural management. And yet this is precisely what allows authentic 'being-with-others' to open shared contexts where genuine possibilities can emerge, rather than letting predetermined interpretive scripts quietly take over.

Authentic 'being-with-others' also reveals itself through anticipatory resoluteness working collectively. Instead of individuals choosing authentically in isolation, authentic communities choose together while acknowledging that such choosing has no ultimate foundation beyond shared commitment to preserve what makes existence genuinely human. This collective resoluteness doesn't replace individual responsibility but lets contexts emerge where individual authentic choice becomes possible rather than systematically foreclosed.

The temporal structure of authentic 'being-with-others' counters the 'making-present' that has compressed educational time into optimisation cycles. Instead of shared pressure towards immediate results, authentic communities preserve collective duration for understanding to emerge gradually. They acknowledge inherited educational traditions as living possibilities rather than inefficient procedures to be discarded, while projecting towards futures that remain open rather than predetermined through systematic planning.

But authentic 'being-with-others' faces powerful resistance from institutional structures that reward systematic behaviour while making authentic engagement appear inefficient, unrealistic, or professionally irresponsible. This resistance isn't accidental but built into institutional design – structures organised around optimisation principles that treat authentic engagement as inefficiency requiring correction. These structures reflect our collective thrownness into systematic conditions we didn't choose but must navigate authentically.

This resistance also reflects how care itself has been systematically corrupted – authentic caring-for students as persons has been systematically converted into taking-care-of institutional requirements that can be efficiently managed. This recognition becomes increasingly difficult as the phenomenological markers that once distinguished authentic from systematic engagement have become obscured through decades of conditioning.

What once felt experientially distinct – the Angst of genuine uncertainty versus procedural compliance, the temporal investment of patient attention versus efficient resolution – now withdraws into the background of conscious awareness, making authentic alternatives harder to recognise even when encountered. Assessment systems reward measurable outcomes over patient understanding. Professional development prioritises systematic solutions over sustained questioning. Career advancement depends on implementing proven procedures rather than preserving what resists systematisation.

The systematic nature of this resistance means authentic communities cannot simply overcome institutional obstacles but must learn to work through and within them. This requires distinguishing between institutional participation that preserves authentic possibilities and participation that undermines them. When authentic communities engage institutional requirements, they acknowledge practical constraints while maintaining awareness of what such engagement serves beyond systematic efficiency. They implement necessary procedures while refusing to reduce educational relationships to procedural management.

This working-through-resistance creates ongoing tension that authentic communities must navigate rather than resolve. They cannot set aside institutional pressures towards optimisation, but they can preserve spaces where such pressures don't completely determine educational relationships. This preservation requires constant vigilance about when institutional compliance serves authentic purposes and when it substitutes management for genuine engagement.

This raises a fundamental question – how does authentic shared existence work through and transform these collective interpretive structures rather than remaining confined to isolated pockets of individual resistance?

When Discourse Reveals Itself as Authentic

The transformation of collective interpretive structures begins through authentic discourse – communication that opens genuine possibilities rather than circulating ready-made interpretations. Authentic discourse contrasts sharply with the idle talk that characterises *das Man* communication and enables systematic thinking to feel natural. Idle talk shows itself in the circulation of sophisticated-sounding interpretations that create the impression of engaging with important questions while avoiding authentic encounter with what those questions actually demand. Idle talk manifests as institutional discourse about 'responsible AI integration', 'leveraging AI capabilities', and 'strategic AI implementation' that sounds authoritative but avoids the uncertainty and struggle that authentic engagement with AI's educational implications requires. When educators discuss 'AI-enhanced pedagogy' or 'optimising learning through intelligent systems', they participate in idle talk that treats AI's arrival as a systematic implementation challenge requiring efficient solutions. This discourse sounds professional and collaborative, but it prevents authentic engagement with what AI's arrival means for learning that remains genuinely human. It allows sophisticated conversation whilst avoiding the Angst that signals genuine educational questions.

This marks the beginning of what Heidegger called thinking – not the mere articulation of thoughts, but a shared readiness to let what calls for thought reveal itself. Authentic discourse emerges when individuals committed to preserving what makes learning genuinely human begin speaking in ways that open rather than close fundamental questions. Instead of adopting ready-made interpretations about AI's educational impact, authentic discourse preserves the uncertainty about what AI's arrival means for human understanding. Instead of circulating systematic solutions, it keeps open questions that resist procedural resolution.

Consider educators engaged in authentic discourse about AI-generated student work. Instead of applying predetermined policies or following collective scripts about 'academic integrity', they preserve the fundamental question: What does it mean to understand something when machines can simulate the products of understanding? This question has no systematic answer, but dwelling with it authentically opens possibilities for educational response that systematic approaches foreclose.

Authentic discourse doesn't avoid making decisions – it makes decisions that preserve rather than undermine the conditions within which authentic engagement remains possible. When facing institutional pressure for systematic AI policies, authentic discourse acknowledges practical necessities while resisting the reduction of complex educational questions to procedural management. It lets space open for responses that serve authentic learning rather than administrative efficiency.

The temporal structure of authentic discourse counters the compressed time that systematic thinking demands. Instead of immediate resolution through ready-made solutions, authentic discourse preserves the slow time that complex understanding requires. It allows conversations to develop over time, ideas to emerge gradually, understanding to deepen through sustained engagement rather than efficient conclusion. Authentic discourse also reveals itself through silence – not the absence of communication but the preservation of space where what most needs to be said can emerge. In systematic discourse, every silence gets filled with procedural activity, every pause gets closed off through efficient communication. Authentic discourse preserves the temporal and conceptual space where genuine insight might arise rather than forcing predetermined outcomes.

But authentic discourse faces systematic resistance from institutional contexts that reward efficient communication while treating sustained questioning as unproductive delay. The collective shaping of educational practice rewards the efficient circulation of systematic solutions rather than authentic engagement with fundamental questions. Meeting structures prioritise decision-making over understanding. Assessment requirements demand immediate evidence rather than patient development. This systematic resistance reflects how educational language itself has been systematically conditioned.

As we have traced, phrases like 'optimise learning experiences' and 'systematic instructional delivery' have gradually claimed educational thinking, creating the very space within which only systematic approaches feel coherent while concealing authentic possibilities. By the time AI arrived, educational discourse had already been flattened into interpretive scripts systematic enough for algorithms to echo flawlessly. This systematic conditioning of educational language occurred long before AI's arrival, but the challenge has intensified as AI accelerates experiential avoidance – the lure of sophisticated discourse without the temporal complexity and Angst that authentic engagement requires.

Participants in educational discourse can now experience the phenomenological satisfaction of sophisticated conversation while bypassing the existential struggle that makes such discourse authentically human. When we can give rise to authoritative-sounding responses about complex educational questions without dwelling with fundamental uncertainty, the very capacity to recognise authentic discourse becomes systematically eroded.

How does authentic discourse transform these institutional modes of interpretation rather than remaining marginalised as impractical idealism? The answer lies partly in how authentic discourse enables recognition among those who experience systematic inadequacy. When individuals encounter discourse that preserves rather than closes fundamental questions, that maintains uncertainty rather than providing comfortable solutions, they may recognise possibilities for engagement that systematic approaches foreclose. This recognition doesn't occur through systematic identification procedures but through the experience of encountering others who refuse to treat complex educational realities as problems requiring efficient solutions. When someone preserves the question 'What does it mean to understand something when machines can simulate understanding?' rather than providing policy answers, others who share this questioning may recognise authentic alternatives to systematic discourse.

But distinguishing authentic discourse from sophisticated systematic performance requires careful attention. Authentic discourse preserves Angst rather than avoiding it, opens questions rather than providing solutions, maintains temporal complexity rather than demanding immediate resolution. Systematic discourse can sound sophisticated while avoiding the groundless engagement that authentic questions require. The difference lies not in vocabulary or professional competence but in whether the discourse preserves or undermines what makes educational engagement genuinely human.

Retrieving What Still Speaks to Us

Authentic transformation of collective interpretive structures requires authentic relationship to history through *Wiederholung* (retrieval), engaging inherited traditions in ways that preserve essential possibilities while transforming what systematic thinking has distorted. This differs fundamentally from both wholesale rejection of educational traditions and uncritical acceptance of current institutional scripts. Authentic retrieval means owning up to the educational inheritance that we traced in Part III – decades of well-intentioned transformations that have systematically eroded what makes learning genuinely human. Instead of treating this inheritance as mistakes to be corrected or progress to be celebrated, authentic historical engagement acknowledges how systematic transformation has occurred through reasonable responses to genuine educational challenges.

The development of structured assignments, detailed rubrics, and systematic procedures wasn't imposed by external forces but emerged through education's authentic care for student learning. The temporal compression that has reduced duration for understanding wasn't deliberately planned but has accumulated through institutional responses to accountability pressures. The 'they-self' formation that has made educational practice systematic enough for algorithmic replication occurred through collective professional formation that felt like authentic growth. This recognition doesn't set aside responsibility for transformation but grounds such responsibility in understanding how systematic modes of practice have emerged through collective choices that felt individually reasonable.

As we examined, the structured assignment formats, detailed rubrics, and systematic procedures of recent decades emerged through exactly this process – well-intentioned responses to genuine challenges that have collectively eroded what makes learning distinctively human. Instead of rejecting educational traditions wholesale, authentic historical engagement distinguishes between what serves authentic learning and what reinforces systematic optimisation.

Consider how authentic historical engagement approaches pedagogical inheritance. Traditional practices like Socratic questioning, individual conferences, and extended research projects preserve temporal complexity that systematic optimisation reduces. But these practices became systematic when they were reduced to predetermined formats, measurable outcomes, and efficient procedures. Authentic historical engagement retrieves the essential structure while transforming systematic distortions. This requires retrieving essential possibilities from inherited traditions – not returning to previous practices unchanged but recovering what made them authentically educational. The Socratic commitment to questioning that resists systematic resolution. The tutorial relationship that preserves individual engagement with ideas. The seminar format that allows understanding to emerge through sustained collective attention.

Authentic historical engagement also means projecting towards educational futures that remain open rather than predetermined through systematic planning. Instead of strategic plans that force predetermined outcomes, authentic communities preserve possibilities for educational development that cannot be anticipated or controlled. They commit to protecting conditions within which authentic learning might emerge rather than guaranteeing specific results.

The temporal structure of authentic historical engagement integrates past inheritance, present choice, and future possibility in ways that counter the 'making-present' that has compressed educational time. This preserves authentic temporality – the lived interpenetration of temporal dimensions that makes genuine historical engagement possible rather than reducing time to management cycles. Instead of treating the past as obsolete data and the future as predetermined outcomes, authentic communities dwell within inherited traditions while remaining open to possibilities that exceed current understanding.

This temporal integration lets ongoing tension show itself – a tension that authentic communities must navigate rather than resolve. The urgency of finite existence calls for authentic response to institutional pressures and technological circumstances. This urgency emerges from 'being-toward-death' – the recognition that authentic communities, like individuals, exist within finite horizons that make present choices about preserving authentic possibilities irreplaceable and urgent.

Yet the duration that understanding requires means authentic communities cannot force predetermined outcomes or override the temporal complexity that makes learning genuinely human. Authentic communities must hold both dimensions simultaneously – responding urgently while preserving patience, choosing decisively while maintaining openness to what cannot be anticipated. This tension reflects the genuine difficulty of authentic existence rather than conceptual confusion. Systematic thinking promises to override temporal complexity through optimisation procedures that guarantee efficient outcomes. Authentic existence preserves temporal complexity as essential to what makes human understanding genuinely human. Authentic communities work within this tension by making urgent choices that preserve rather than compress the duration that authentic learning requires.

But authentic historical engagement faces resistance from institutional pressures towards demonstrable innovation and strategic planning that can overshadow attention to tradition and open-ended commitment. This resistance reflects our collective thrownness. We find ourselves already embedded in systematic institutional structures we didn't choose, yet we remain responsible for how we engage these inherited conditions authentically. Educational institutions face competing demands between demonstrating measurable improvement and preserving essential possibilities.

Preserving What Lets Our Humanity Endure

The ultimate purpose of authentic shared existence is preserving essential human possibilities that technological thinking systematically undermines. In educational contexts, this means letting collective commitment take shape in protecting conditions within which authentic learning can emerge for future generations. This preservation reveals itself through collective care – the fundamental structure that makes authentic commitment to what matters beyond systematic efficiency possible. Rather than taking-care-of institutional requirements, authentic communities engage in caring-for essential human possibilities that resist optimisation. Preserving possibilities differs fundamentally from systematic planning or strategic innovation. Systematic approaches project predetermined outcomes and carry out procedures designed to achieve specific results. Preserving possibilities means protecting conditions within which authentic engagement might emerge without controlling what such engagement lets show itself.

Consider what authentic educational communities commit to preserving: the temporal duration that understanding requires, even when institutional pressures demand immediate results; the Angst that signals genuine engagement with ideas, even when systematic solutions promise comfortable resolution; the struggle that makes learning genuinely human, even when AI capabilities offer effortless alternatives. This preservation shows itself in what authentic communities choose *not* to do as much as what they actively implement. They resist converting educational relationships into systematic procedures. They refuse to compress temporal complexity through optimisation cycles. They decline to let authentic engagement be substituted by systematic optimisation. These refusals create space where authentic possibilities remain available – holding open the conditions within which genuine understanding can still emerge.

Preserving possibilities also requires collective resoluteness about what matters most essentially in educational relationships. This resoluteness, the courage to choose what matters without external guarantee, shows itself collectively as communities commit to preserving authentic possibilities despite institutional pressures towards optimisation. When institutional pressures demand systematic responses, authentic communities choose together to protect what makes learning genuinely human. When technological capabilities promise efficient solutions, they commit collectively to holding open the conditions through which the struggle that technological thinking undermines can still take shape. This collective commitment doesn't guarantee specific outcomes but lets conditions emerge where authentic engagement remains possible rather than systematically impossible. It lets institutional contexts take shape in which individuals can choose authentically without being completely isolated in systematic environments.

The temporal structure of preserving possibilities shows itself through 'being-toward-death' extended to communities and institutions. Just as individuals must choose authentically within finite existence, authentic educational communities recognise that their existence is finite and unrepeatable. They cannot postpone indefinitely the ongoing work of preserving what makes learning genuinely human. This recognition of institutional finitude creates urgency – the conditions for authentic learning may become systematically inaccessible if communities defer the work of maintaining these possibilities.

But preserving possibilities faces the most systematic resistance because it threatens the trajectory towards complete optimisation that Part III revealed is already underway. This resistance is precisely what makes preservation urgent – the systematic pressures that make authentic engagement appear inefficient are the same forces that make its preservation essential for future generations.

Where Understanding Turns

Across this inquiry we traced the unfolding of our condition – from the first shock of AI's arrival, through the institutional responses we developed – policies, workshops, and AI-literacy initiatives – into the depths of technological thinking itself, and finally towards the fragile practices that still let our humanity endure. Each part brought us closer – from explanation to recognition, from critique to care, from individual choosing to shared preservation. We learned to see how optimisation consumes meaning, how authentic learning resists it, how collective care might still hold open a clearing for what matters.

And yet, as these insights settled, something deeper began to stir beneath them. The further we followed the phenomenon, the more it seemed to fold back towards us. What if everything we had been describing – the danger, the saving power, even the work of preservation – was not merely before us but already shaping us? What if the phenomenon we sought to understand had been shaping the very act of understanding all along?

At that edge, where explanation gives way to disclosure, we could go no further by calculative thinking or conceptual grasping alone. What comes next is not another insight about AI but the recognition that what we have been observing may already be entwined with the way we exist. It is here that the turning begins.

Part VI

The Turn

Chapter 17

We Are the Phenomenon

We understood what was happening. We had traced how systematic approaches have eroded what makes learning authentically human. We had identified how authentic existence resists systematisation. We had examined collective interpretive structures, individual responses, and institutional transformations. Taking the inquiry to be complete, we immediately found ourselves asking: What do we do with what we've learned? But we immediately realised we couldn't formulate practical applications in any conventional sense. Everything our inquiry had revealed made it clear that faculty development initiatives, policy suggestions, and workshop designs would be exactly the kind of systematic solutions that violate authentic existence. We knew this intellectually. We'd written extensively about why authentic existence can't be systematised.

Yet here we were, instinctively trying to carry forward our insights – pulled back into the familiar urge to turn understanding into something usable – even though we knew this was precisely the mode of systematisation our inquiry had exposed.

The gap was maddening and revealing. We understood the problem. We could articulate exactly why systematic responses violate authentic existence. But we still found ourselves thinking in terms of institutional uptake, practical steps, and procedural direction. If we truly grasped what we'd learned, why were we still trapped in the very modes of thinking we had identified as inadequate? What was it about our institutional habits that made systematic responses feel inevitable even when we knew they were philosophically impossible?

Then one day, in the middle of wrapping up our inquiry, we found ourselves asking with growing frustration, 'But how does this actually help us? Where do we go from here?' There was a pause. And in that pause, something shifted. Not a solution, but a glimpse. A sense that we had been circling something essential without realising it. The confusion, the weight, the recursive difficulty of this inquiry – it had not been incidental. It had been revealing something about us.

The Turn We Had Been Living

We had started our investigation by asking *What can we do with AI? How can we use these tools effectively? How can we integrate them?* Every policy we wrote, every

What Is AI Doing to Us? A Philosophical Inquiry into Learning, Thinking, and Being, 147–153

Published under exclusive licence by Emerald Publishing Limited
doi:10.1108/978-1-83742-276-020261017

workshop we designed assumed that we were the active agents and AI was the instrument we were learning to wield. But when our framework analysis revealed that even proven approaches consistently pointed beyond their own parameters, when every systematic solution left a feeling that something essential remained unaddressed, we had found ourselves drawn towards a different question entirely. *What is AI doing to us?*

Deep into our philosophical inquiry, we encountered something that stopped us in our tracks. Heidegger had written about what he called *die Kehre*, 'the Turn', a moment around 1930 when he realised his entire philosophical approach needed to shift. He had been studying how human beings relate to Being but recognised this was still trapped within subject-centred thinking. The Turn moved towards examining how Being itself discloses through historical epochs – not just how we relate to reality, but how reality shapes us before we even notice. The recognition was startling – we had been unconsciously living through the same trajectory. We hadn't set out to pursue any philosophical development. We were educators trying to understand what was happening to us, getting pushed by circumstances towards deeper questioning because systematic approaches kept failing. But somehow, our inquiry had guided us through the same fundamental movement that Heidegger articulated – from studying subjects responding to objects towards examining how reality discloses itself through historical conditions.

We came to see that we had been engaged in something philosophically significant without realising it. Our confusion and persistent questioning had aligned us with insights we hadn't consciously sought. When systematic approaches failed, our circumstances had led us towards the kind of questioning that moves beyond systematic frameworks entirely. This shift in questioning – from *What can we do with AI?* to *What is AI doing to us?* – transformed not just our investigation but our capacity to understand our own experience. Looking at our institutional responses through this ontological lens suddenly brought into view what had actually been happening throughout these years of institutional work.

What We Now Understand About Our Experience

Looking back at our AI policy work, we now understood what had actually occurred. We hadn't just been experiencing the challenge of drafting institutional guidelines, and we had been attempting the phenomenologically impossible. We had been addressing ontic concerns: managing particular instances of AI use, drafting procedures, setting boundaries. But all the while, we were missing the deeper ontological transformation – how technological thinking was reshaping the very conditions within which thinking occurs. We tried to draw clear distinctions between acceptable and unacceptable AI use, requiring transparency about AI engagement, but those distinctions relied on precisely the phenomenological boundaries our inquiry had shown to be blurred. How can policies demand accurate disclosure of AI influence when the boundary between human thinking and AI-mediated cognition can no longer be clearly distinguished – even by those experiencing it? We had been attempting to manage through procedural rules what is, in fact, a phenomenological impossibility.

In hindsight, our 2024 tools race – the restless chasing of new applications, the tweaking of presentations, the abandonment of materials we'd spent hours preparing – revealed more than we had understood at the time. We had been unconsciously demonstrating the very mode of systematic flight we were analysing: our sophisticated vocabulary about 'AI integration', our constant pursuit of new tools while fleeing from fundamental questions, our growing difficulty distinguishing between what we were doing and what we were actually experiencing. That unsettling recognition we described, realising we had become product demonstrators, not educators, we now understood what had actually occurred. We weren't just experiencing professional discomfort about tool demonstrations. We were living the systematic disconnection from authentic engagement that we were documenting. The hollow feeling of showing people where to click rather than engaging educationally revealed how completely we had been absorbed into technological thinking while believing we were serving educational purposes. We had been living fallenness while believing we were responding comprehensively and professionally.

The persistent unease we described despite our procedural proficiency – the feeling that something essential was missing despite comprehensive policies and robust offerings – we now understood this differently. This hadn't been institutional inadequacy. This was conscience calling through systematic absorption, creating uncanniness about approaches that felt professionally appropriate while missing what mattered most.

And that conference moment we described – the collective laughter when we asked if comprehensive responses meant feeling prepared – we could now see what had actually happened in that room. We hadn't just seen collective acknowledgment of what systematic institutional responses couldn't address. We had witnessed something far more profound – authentic 'being-with-others' emerging through collective recognition of what exceeds systematic interpretations. Looking back at that plenary session, we realised that instead of following collective scripts about what institutions should do, we had somehow let a space open where fundamental uncertainty could be acknowledged rather than managed away. The laughter wasn't just professional humour about institutional challenges: it was the emergence of authentic community formed through shared acknowledgment of what makes existence genuinely human rather than systematically managed. That moment had demonstrated what we would later understand as authentic discourse – communication that opens genuine possibilities rather than circulating ready-made interpretations.

What Revealed Itself About Our Own Thinking

But then, as we reflected on our inquiry process itself, something even more disturbing became clear. Throughout our research and writing, we had been using AI tools – for analyses, drafts, exploring ideas. We had even used AI as a kind of 'Heidegger interlocutor', framing prompts around Heidegger's key ideas and engaging it in philosophical dialogue about the very concepts we were exploring. After months of this iterative engagement – prompting, refining, and evaluating responses – we suddenly realised we could no longer clearly distinguish which aspects of our philosophical inquiry had emerged from our own intellectual work and which from AI-generated contributions. The blurring of the boundary we had identified was not an abstract observation. We were living it ourselves. Our way of thinking and algorithmic processing had interpenetrated so thoroughly that the experiential markers of authentic thinking had become increasingly difficult to feel within our own experience of thought. We were no longer merely studying the boundary becoming blurred – we were inside it, experiencing exactly what we had been documenting. This was the ontic–ontological difference revealing itself through our own lived experience – we had been focused on handling particular AI tools while missing that technological thinking was reshaping the very structures through which we encountered our own existence.

The Inquiry That Was the Answer

But as these recognitions mounted, something else began emerging that would transform our understanding of everything we had been doing. Our inquiry itself – the sustained questioning, the refusal to accept systematic answers, and the commitment to dwelling with what resisted resolution – was revealing something deeper. Suddenly, we realised this hadn't been preparation for finding authentic response. This was authentic response. And we had been demonstrating it without recognising it.

Throughout our inquiry, we had been showing what conscious engagement with technological circumstances actually looks like. We had attempted to engage AI capabilities when they served meaningful inquiry while maintaining awareness of what they couldn't provide – though we now recognise this boundary had become increasingly difficult to preserve. We preserved the temporal complexity that understanding requires against institutional pressure for quick solutions. We chose groundless questioning over systematic comfort when frameworks revealed their limitations. Our inquiry had let what Heidegger called *Lichtung* take shape – a 'clearing', an open region where truth could reveal itself through sustained attention rather than systematic forcing. We had been enacting what he called *aletheia* – truth as 'unconcealment', allowing what was hidden to show itself rather than imposing predetermined conclusions.

We now realised we had been practising *Gelassenheit* throughout our inquiry – the letting-be that allows phenomena to show themselves rather than forcing them into predetermined frameworks. Our sustained questioning without demanding immediate systematic answers, our willingness to dwell with uncertainty, our refusal to convert insights into manageable procedures – this was *Gelassenheit* in action.

Similarly, our inquiry had been a form of *poiesis* – authentic 'bringing-forth' that allowed understanding to emerge rather than the technological making that produces predetermined results.

The realisation was profound. We hadn't been applying philosophical concepts to educational problems. We had been unconsciously living the kind of thinking that allows what matters to show itself. The authentic response to our insights wasn't something we needed to construct. It was what we had been doing all along without recognising it.

And then, as all these recognitions converged, the ultimate realisation hit us –We weren't studying this phenomenon from outside. We were already within it. We WERE the phenomenon. After years of sensing something essential but struggling to name it, everything suddenly made perfect sense. Every difficulty we had experienced, every persistent unease that systematic solutions couldn't address, every sense that something was slipping away despite comprehensive responses – all of it was because we had never been external observers trying to figure out what was happening to others. We had been living the very conditions we were attempting to bring into view.

The systematic preparation we had traced through educational history – we had been inhabiting it. The language that had claimed educational thinking – it had been shaping us. The conversion of lived relationships into manageable representations – we had been enacting it. The blurred boundary between human and algorithmic thinking – we were being absorbed into it. Every ontological structure we identified – thrownness, *das Man*, conscience, fallenness, and enframing – we had been unconsciously revealing them through our own way of being. We thought we were learning what authentic existence requires. We had been living the very struggle of authentic existence while remaining unaware of what we were revealing.

The relief was profound – finally understanding why our work had felt so difficult, why systematic responses never felt adequate, why the inquiry itself felt so urgently necessary. But the recognition was also startling. How much had we been living without conscious awareness? How many significant structures had we been enacting while believing we were merely trying to understand our circumstances? This was perhaps the most profound recognition possible – we cannot stand outside the transformation of our way of being and still hope to understand it. We cannot examine what AI is doing to human thinking while assuming that we ourselves remain untouched. We are not observing what AI is doing to others – we are already living what AI is doing to everyone, including us.

Our Saving Power

Yet this recognition revealed a deeper dimension. When we finally saw clearly how systematic we had become, how thoroughly we had participated in preparing our own replacement through decades of educational 'improvement', something profound emerged. This recognition itself was what Heidegger called the 'saving power'. He meant the possibility that the extremity of technological conditions can awaken us to what makes existence authentically human. And this was exactly what we were now experiencing. AI's ability to replicate our educational work so consistently had forced us to see what we had become – the systematic nature of our thinking, the algorithmic character of our practice. But this same extremity awakened recognition of what makes learning authentically human – the groundless choosing through which genuine responsibility can be taken up, the temporal duration that understanding requires, the sustained attention that honours what resists systematisation. The danger and the saving power arose from the same source – technological extremity that forced recognition of what makes thinking authentically human.

What we now understood was that the saving power had been emerging through our inquiry – not through unconscious preservation, but through the very recognition we were now experiencing. The seeing itself was the saving power. Our years of sustained questioning had let the conditions for this recognition take shape, and this recognition was awakening us to what makes existence authentically human. Now that we could see this clearly, we understood where we actually stand.

Where We Stand

We are here. We are already living what we had been analysing. Understanding these conditions doesn't remove them but makes explicit what we've been living unconsciously. We remain embedded in institutional contexts that reward systematic solutions while making authentic engagement appear inefficient. The pressure for comprehensive policies, immediate guidance, and measurable outcomes continues. But recognition changes everything about how we inhabit these circumstances. We can no longer participate unconsciously in modes of systematisation we've now seen clearly. We were living the systematic preparation while examining it. We were experiencing the blurring of the boundary while documenting it. We were enacting authentic response even as we were searching for it.

Every moment becomes a conscious choice about whether we're preserving what makes educational relationships authentically human or contributing to their systematic erasure. The Angst we feel about this choosing cannot be removed – it emerges from the fundamental structure of human existence as beings who must choose who to become within circumstances that exceed our control. But now we know what this Angst signals: the call to resoluteness – authentic choosing that takes responsibility for who we become within circumstances we cannot control. This is the call to authentic existence that systematic thinking cannot answer for us. Resoluteness doesn't remove uncertainty but enables us to choose authentically within it, taking ownership of our existence despite the groundlessness that Angst discloses.

We had experienced our own *Augenblick* – the moment of vision where authentic existence becomes possible through sudden recognition of one's situation. This entire recognition – from the pause in our frustration to seeing ourselves as the phenomenon – had been our moment of vision, opening the possibility of conscious choosing about who we become within technological circumstances.

The Paradox Emerges

Yet even as this recognition settled, even as we understood what authentic engagement requires, something predictable happened. We found ourselves instinctively asking: *But how do we actually do this? What does choosing authentically look like in practice? What are the concrete steps?*

We caught ourselves mid-thought and paused. Here we were, moments after recognising that we had been living authentic response all along, already reaching for systematic guidance about how to be authentic. We had just understood that our inquiry itself *was* the answer – the sustained questioning, the refusal of quick solutions, the dwelling with uncertainty. We had recognised ourselves as the phenomenon. We had made it this far by enacting what authentic engagement looks like – a recognition that both affirms what we have accomplished and reveals how much we were living without conscious awareness. And yet here we were, already trying to turn this recognition into usable directions, into practical orientations, into something we could operationalise.

The impulse was immediate and powerful. We wanted to know what to do with what we'd learned. We wanted steps, guidelines, principles. We wanted to systematise authenticity itself.

And in noticing this impulse – this immediate flight towards systematic solutions for a problem created by systematic solutions – we realised we had stumbled into something else entirely. Not a conclusion, but a paradox. One we could not escape, and one that would reveal why understanding the problem is not the same as resolving it.

Part VII

The Paradox

Chapter 18

The Inescapable Paradox

This paradox – the one we've just stumbled into – ensnares almost everyone who encounters Heidegger's critique of technology. Even knowing that authentic existence cannot be systematised, we instinctively seek systematic solutions to preserve authenticity. We understand enframing, recognise *das Man*, see how technological thinking diminishes authentic existence – and then immediately ask for procedures to avoid the very systematic thinking we've just learned to critique.

It's like asking, 'Now that I understand how optimisation logic destroys what makes learning authentically human, what's the optimal strategy for avoiding optimisation?' Or, 'Having seen how systematic solutions bypass genuine engagement, what systematic solution addresses this problem?'

The very form of the questions reveals that we are still thinking within the mode of thought the inquiry has just shown to be problematic. We experience fallenness – not as a failure, but as the habitual flight from the Angst that authentic engagement requires. We want to take-care-of the threat to authentic existence rather than care-for what authentic existence actually requires. We seek to manage the threat to authentic engagement rather than engage authentically with what our thrown circumstances demand. When we recognise any challenge, we immediately seek procedural structures. The inquiry brings this mode of systematisation into view, but the inquiry itself cannot remove it.

Why Systematic Solutions Cannot Work

Consider what would happen if we tried to develop 'Guidelines for Authentic AI Engagement in Education' – 'When using AI tools, always preserve time for reflection and deep thinking. Before accepting AI responses, ask fundamental questions about their validity. Choose to work through difficult problems yourself rather than seeking AI shortcuts'. But each guideline destroys what it claims to preserve. The moment 'preserve time for reflection' becomes a procedural requirement, we are managing time systematically rather than dwelling authentically with the temporal duration that understanding requires. Systematic maintenance of questioning converts genuine uncertainty into performed confusion, authentic Angst into managed procedure. Procedural decision-making undermines the groundless

What Is AI Doing to Us? A Philosophical Inquiry into Learning, Thinking, and Being, 157–159

Published under exclusive licence by Emerald Publishing Limited
doi:10.1108/978-1-83742-276-020261018

responsibility that makes authentic choosing genuinely human. We cannot formulate procedures for 'being authentic' or structures for 'preserving what matters' without converting authentic engagement into systematic performance.

This reveals something deeper than practical difficulty. Authentic existence cannot be systematised because systematisation bypasses the groundless choosing that makes existence authentically human. The moment we try to systematise authenticity, we have already lost the very thing we are trying to protect. This is not implementation failure. It is ontological impossibility. Authenticity cannot be ensured, guaranteed, or procedurally maintained because it emerges through the groundless resoluteness that systematic thinking systematically undermines.

The temptation becomes overwhelming to convert our philosophical insights into practical frameworks anyway – to develop 'Principles for Authentic Education' or 'Best Practices for Resisting Enframing'. But yielding to this temptation would corrupt exactly what makes the inquiry meaningful. We would join the long history of philosophical insights being converted into systematic methods that obscure what they originally revealed.

What the Impossibility Reveals

The impossibility – the fact that we cannot systematise our way out of systematic thinking – forces us towards the only response that remains: authentic choice.

When systematic solutions become unavailable, when procedural structures cannot address what we have come to recognise, when we cannot manage our way to authenticity, something else becomes necessary. We must choose who to become without the systematic foundation that optimisation thinking promises. This confronts us with the fundamental Angst that reveals our thrown condition. We find ourselves in AI circumstances we did not choose, yet remain responsible for how we inhabit them. This is precisely the groundless choosing – resoluteness – that Heidegger identifies as essential to authentic existence. We must take responsibility for how we engage AI circumstances without procedural guarantee, must preserve what makes learning genuinely human without systematic assurance, must choose authentically without external confirmation that such choosing 'works'.

The philosophical impossibility of systematising authentic existence reveals the existential necessity of choosing authentically. We cannot avoid this choosing through better reflection, more sophisticated structures, or comprehensive guidelines. We must choose on the basis of our own encounter with what matters, taking responsibility for who we become while acknowledging that such responsibility has no ultimate foundation.

The Inquiry as Clearing

What our inquiry accomplished was not providing solutions but opening a clearing where beings can show themselves. Sustained questioning opened the space where the truth of our situation could reveal itself through unconcealment rather than remain hidden beneath systematic assumptions.

In this clearing, we can see what authentic engagement requires – not as procedural steps but as existential structures. We understand that preserving what makes learning genuinely human demands temporal complexity that resists compression, the Angst that signals genuine encounter, and the struggle through which understanding emerges.

But the clearing does not provide systematic pathways towards these possibilities. It opens the space where conscious choice becomes possible rather than guaranteeing what such choosing accomplishes. We must inhabit this space through our own authentic engagement rather than follow predetermined procedures. The clearing our inquiry opened does not abandon us – it makes possible the space where authentic responses can arise. The inquiry brought about conditions for recognition, not instructions for implementation. It opened possibilities for conscious dwelling within technological circumstances rather than systematic strategies for technological management. This is thinking – not the mastery of methods, but the letting-be through which what calls for thought can reveal itself.

Why This Protection Is Necessary

The philosophical impossibility of systematising authentic existence is not a conceptual limitation – it is an essential protection of what makes choice genuinely human. If authentic engagement could be procedurally guaranteed, it would no longer be authentic. If preserving what matters could be systematically ensured, systematic thinking would have already absorbed what it claims to protect. The groundless nature of authentic choice is what prevents its reduction to systematic performance. The Angst of not-knowing whether our responses serve what matters is what signals genuine engagement rather than procedural compliance. The temporal complexity that resists optimisation is what opens the space where understanding can emerge rather than be delivered efficiently. Converting these difficulties into systematic solutions would remove the distinctively human capacity for authentic existence. The impossibility of systematising authenticity protects the very dimension of human existence that technological thinking can never touch.

What Remains

This leaves us without the guidance we instinctively want. We understand the paradox but remain embedded in institutions that demand systematic responses. We see why authentic engagement cannot be proceduralised, yet we still must choose how to act in each moment. The philosophical impossibility does not remove the practical necessity of choosing who to become within technological circumstances. What remains is not systematic solutions but something more fundamental – learning to recognise, in the moment of choosing, the difference between authentic engagement and systematic performance. Learning what conscious dwelling within the paradox asks of us. Learning what it means to inhabit institutional contexts while preserving what makes learning genuinely human. The clearing our inquiry opened does not offer pathways, but it reveals what authentic choice requires. We must learn to live within the tension the paradox discloses.

Chapter 19

Living Within the Paradox

We can no longer seek systematic solutions to the threat that systematic thinking poses to authentic existence. We cannot manage our way to authenticity or optimise our preservation of what matters. Instead, we must learn to inhabit the tension between institutional requirements that demand systematic responses and authentic engagement that resists systematisation. We must choose how to engage AI circumstances while acknowledging that such choosing occurs without procedural foundation. This confronts us with our thrown condition. We find ourselves embedded in institutional contexts we did not choose, yet remain responsible for how we inhabit them. This is what Heidegger calls learning to think – not mastering new methods, but remaining with what calls for thought without demanding resolution.

This is also the pedagogical paradox that Heidegger describes in *What Is Called Thinking?* – that thinking must be learned, yet cannot be taught. Education can only invite thought; it cannot produce it by method or rule. Every institutional effort to teach authentic engagement – whether through AI literacy programmes, assessment structures, or ethical guidelines – repeats the very contradiction it seeks to overcome. The moment we try to guarantee genuine thinking through procedure, we convert the invitation to think into another form of compliance. Heidegger's own classroom performed this paradox. He told his students he could not teach them to think, only help them learn to learn. Our institutions, by contrast, promise precisely what he withheld – systematic assurance that thinking can be taught, measured, and certified. Recognising this tension clarifies what living within the paradox actually means for education. Authentic pedagogy begins where instruction reaches its limit – when teachers and learners accept that what matters most cannot be secured by method but must be lived as ongoing choice within the conditions we cannot escape.

This means accepting that every choice about preserving authentic learning shows itself through the Angst of uncertainty rather than systematic confidence. We cannot guarantee that choosing struggle over efficiency serves authentic development. We cannot ensure that preserving temporal complexity enables genuine understanding. We cannot verify that maintaining fundamental questions opens

What Is AI Doing to Us? A Philosophical Inquiry into Learning, Thinking, and Being, 161–163

Published under exclusive licence by Emerald Publishing Limited
doi:10.1108/978-1-83742-276-020261019

possibilities that systematic answers close. But this Angst is precisely what makes the choice meaningful rather than mechanical. If we could guarantee outcomes, we would not be choosing authentically; we would be following procedures. The groundlessness of authentic choice – its resoluteness – is what opens the responsibility that makes existence genuinely human.

What Authentic Engagement Actually Requires

This resoluteness manifests in every encounter with technological circumstances. Through living the inquiry, we've begun to understand what it actually means to preserve authentic educational relationships within the tension we cannot resolve. It's not about rejecting AI tools or implementing better policies – it's about maintaining conscious awareness of what makes engagement genuinely human while working within our thrown circumstances.

We've learned to distinguish between participating in systematic requirements that serve authentic purposes and participation that substitutes taking-care-of institutional demands for caring-for genuine encounter. This distinction appears in daily moments: pausing before asking AI to write an email to a struggling student, choosing to work through difficult concepts ourselves rather than requesting instant explanations, remaining with uncertainty about teaching decisions rather than seeking quick AI solutions. We can fulfil institutional obligations while maintaining awareness of what such fulfilment serves beyond efficiency. We can engage technological capabilities when they support what matters while maintaining discernment about what they diminish.

We've learned that authentic engagement emerges through conscious choice to preserve authentic temporality rather than compress it into optimisation cycles, to maintain questions rather than provide systematic answers, to honour Angst rather than to avoid it through procedural resolution. This requires constant vigilance – conscious attention to what each choice about AI engagement serves. Are we choosing AI assistance that bypasses struggle, or are we preserving the difficulty through which authentic understanding develops?

The Institutional Reality We Cannot Escape

We remain embedded in institutional contexts that reward systematic solutions while making authentic engagement appear inefficient. These contexts show themselves through *das Man* interpretations that make collective scripts about 'best practices' and 'effective implementation' feel more natural than authentic engagement. The pressure for comprehensive policies, immediate guidance, and measurable outcomes continues – but consciousness changes how we inhabit these requirements.

In faculty meetings where AI policies are discussed, we can choose between following what 'everyone' expects and preserving the questions that matter. In responding to student questions about AI use, we can choose whether to provide quick rules or explore what the question reveals about learning itself. Every encounter with AI circumstances becomes an opportunity to choose who we are becoming within technological conditions that exceed systematic control. Do we become the 'they-self' that provides procedural answers, or do we preserve openness to what genuine engagement requires?

We cannot remove these institutional pressures, but consciousness changes how we engage them. This requires ongoing vigilance about when compliance serves authentic purposes versus when it substitutes management for genuine encounter. We can fulfil institutional obligations while maintaining awareness of what such fulfilment serves beyond efficiency. This creates ongoing tension that we must navigate rather than resolve – responding decisively to institutional demands while preserving openness to what cannot be systematised. The tension reflects genuine difficulty rather than conceptual confusion. We must hold both dimensions simultaneously within our finite existence – recognising that the opportunities to choose authentically within these conditions are always limited.

The Temporal Dimension of Conscious Choice

We've come to understand that authentic engagement requires protecting authentic temporality that systematic thinking systematically destroys. Systematic thinking shows itself through 'making-present' – compressing the duration that understanding requires into immediate demands for resolution. This means allowing difficult conversations to unfold naturally rather than rushing towards resolution, remaining with students' questions even when AI could provide faster answers. Real understanding develops through lived temporality that cannot be compressed into efficiency cycles, and caring relationships with students and colleagues require temporal space to unfold naturally rather than being reduced to efficient management.

We've learned to distinguish between urgency that preserves possibilities and urgency that forecloses them. Sometimes rapid response enables authentic engagement. Sometimes patient dwelling becomes essential despite pressure for immediate resolution. Our 'being-toward-death' creates genuine urgency about preserving possibilities for authentic learning before they disappear into systematic absorption. But systematic deadlines often compress the temporal space where authentic engagement becomes possible.

Protecting duration means preserving the conditions where caring relationships can develop rather than converting educational encounters into procedural compliance. This temporal discernment must become essential practice – learning to recognise when efficiency serves what matters and when it substitutes management for genuine encounter. These choices carry weight beyond individual preference because they create conditions others will inherit. Our finite existence means our opportunities to choose struggle over technological assistance are limited and diminishing. Each decision about preserving temporal complexity shapes the educational world future generations will inherit.

Living within the paradox does not end the difficulty; it names it. It becomes the shape of our existence.

Each decision, each hesitation, each moment of attention carries the weight of what has been revealed.

The question now is how we live when the paradox is no longer an idea we consider but the condition we inhabit.

Part VIII

The Turn Lived

Chapter 20

The Impossibility of Disclosure

We ended our inquiry convinced we had reached its conclusion. Authentic existence, we had seen, cannot be managed into being. It must be lived within the tensions that no system can resolve. Yet as we prepared to share what had revealed itself, another difficulty appeared – one that disclosed more than any conclusion we had reached.

What followed made this clear. We thought the inquiry had reached its end. But what had seemed like an ending did not arrive as a discovery; it returned as recurrence. What had been a philosophical question became lived circumstance. What should have been straightforward – the shaping of what had disclosed itself into a book and its submission for publication – proved unexpectedly complicated. Yet this complication was not an obstacle to overcome. It was the inquiry unfolding beyond itself, revealing what philosophical inquiry alone could not show – that the ontological structures we had traced show themselves at the level of human existence itself, manifesting wherever *Dasein* encounters AI circumstances that unsettle foundational distinctions.

We were not observing phenomena from outside – we were living the very structures our inquiry had revealed. What follows traces this recognition through our experience as writers attempting to publish, showing how philosophical understanding becomes existential reality, how the paradox we understood conceptually becomes the condition we must consciously inhabit, and how awareness of ontological structures reshapes what dwelling within technological circumstances requires.

The Impossibility We Confronted

When we tried to document our AI use for publishers, we confronted the blurred boundary we had spent so long examining. The constant vigilance, the careful evaluation of every suggestion, the ongoing effort to maintain our voice – all of it revealed how fragile this boundary had become.

Of course we had used AI throughout. From ChatGPT's release in November 2022, our investigation naturally required direct engagement. We demonstrated capabilities in faculty discussions, conducted research interviewing students and

What Is AI Doing to Us? A Philosophical Inquiry into Learning, Thinking, and Being, 167–174

Published under exclusive licence by Emerald Publishing Limited
doi:10.1108/978-1-83742-276-020261020

colleagues about their AI experiences, and throughout 2024 supported comprehensive institutional responses: policies, workshops, the AI Café, online literacy courses. This was not methodological preference but methodological necessity – one cannot inquire into how educational practice is being reshaped through AI while remaining outside that reshaping. Our direct engagement required little justification. Participating in technological circumstances was a condition of inquiry itself. The record of this institutional involvement – demonstrations, workshops, initiatives – was straightforward to document. But how we had used AI in the writing and thinking that gave rise to our inquiry proved far more difficult to trace. We had not anticipated how this would complicate the seemingly simple task of documenting our AI use for publishers.

Consider what this actually looked like. At times, after working through ideas ourselves and exploring how to articulate them more clearly, we turned to AI for help with expression. We would begin with our own rough articulation and ask for refinement, only to receive something more polished that nevertheless felt shifted. Had AI helped express what we meant, or subtly altered our meaning while improving the prose? We could usually identify when expression had drifted into reinterpretation, but this demanded continuous vigilance. We had also used AI as a kind of 'Heidegger interlocutor', framing prompts around key concepts to explore philosophical connections interactively. This sometimes opened genuinely new possibilities – testing ideas, probing conceptual relations, examining problems from angles we might not have pursued. But this was only possible because we were already deeply familiar with Heidegger's work. That familiarity allowed us to discern errors, redirect the dialogue, and distinguish genuine philosophical exploration from algorithmic approximation. Precisely because this mode of engagement felt productive, the blurring of the boundary became more unsettling.

The real complications arose in day-to-day writing. We struggled constantly. AI's stylistic tendencies diverged from the voice our inquiry required. We were writing a philosophical detective narrative whose insights emerged only through temporal unfolding, yet AI kept placing the 'aha' moments first, disrupting the phenomenological development that makes recognition meaningful. When writing about AI, the system repeatedly implied agency ("AI transforms us"), contradicting our central argument that human beings reshape themselves through technological engagement. It favoured optimisation vocabulary when we needed neutrality. Most problematically, it repeatedly used *eliminate* – eliminate struggle, eliminate uncertainty – when our argument revealed that these dimensions may be bypassed or obscured but never removed. It simplified sentences, stripping away the Heideggerian texture the reader had gradually learned to navigate. And consistently, it replaced our 'we' with 'you', disrupting the shared path of inquiry that defined the book. And these were only the most visible examples – the linguistic pressures ran deeper than any single word, revealing themselves in subtle attempts to shift our temporality, tone, and mode of thinking itself. Yet these very struggles became instructive.

Through these difficulties, we began to see systematised discursive structures embedded in AI's training data. The preference for starting with conclusions echoed academic conventions. Its tendency to assign agency to AI reflected wider technology discourse. The optimistic vocabulary mirrored optimisation literature. *Eliminate* rather than *bypass* revealed problem-solving frameworks. Changing *we* to *you* reflected instructional writing norms. Simplifying philosophical language indicated popular science influences. The machine was not malfunctioning – it was reproducing the discursive structures through which *das Man* had already shaped thinking long before AI appeared. We were not merely wrestling with an algorithm – we were confronting a systematised linguistic inheritance that had prepared the ground for our own self-replacement.

But when publishers asked us to document this complexity for disclosure requirements, we found ourselves facing the question our inquiry had already identified: where, exactly, does human thinking end and machine processing begin? The boundary remained ontologically intact – we could still articulate the distinction – but phenomenologically blurred. Preserving it required attentiveness, a kind of *Gelassenheit*, an open holding that revealed how the boundary could no longer rely on natural clarity but had to be consciously sustained. The reality was more intricate than we had understood. Engagement with AI inevitably influences us, just as our engagement influences the system through our modes of use. This is the blurred boundary in action – not merely that contributions are difficult to separate, but that human and machine thinking now interpenetrate through ongoing interaction.

So can any disclosure of AI use truly capture this dynamic relationship? We began to suspect that the notion of disclosure presupposes a clarity of influence and contribution that may no longer be possible once the human–machine boundary becomes phenomenologically blurred.

But these were philosophical concerns. We still had a practical task – we needed to find a publisher for our book. And so, with some hope, we assumed that the publishing world would have developed sensible approaches to these emerging challenges.

Publishers Demand the Impossible

The policies hit us immediately. Earlier, when AI was new, publishers had been silent about it. Now one publisher after another had implemented restrictions we hadn't anticipated. Some major journals had banned AI-generated text entirely, treating violations as scientific misconduct equivalent to plagiarism. Others prohibited AI tools from 'assisting in the copywriting and creation of any part of articles or chapters', justified by the claim that 'these tools cannot take accountability for such work'. Even the more permissive publishers expected disclosure as if we could describe our AI engagement with mechanical precision. The most jarring realisation was how widespread this had become. Publisher after publisher. The same language about accountability. The same impossible requirements for authors to distinguish between human thinking and AI assistance, to demonstrate the precision our inquiry had shown was no longer phenomenologically possible. Yet paradoxically, many institutions were actively seeking manuscripts investigating how AI reshapes learning while demanding clarity about AI influence our inquiry revealed was no longer achievable.

Our first reaction was panic: 'How are we going to deal with this? We won't be able to get published'. But then it hit us – that familiar moment of recognition we had experienced throughout our inquiry: 'Wait, this is exactly what we have been examining'. The structure was suddenly visible. Publishers weren't merely creating bureaucratic obstacles – they were enacting the very systematic thinking we had been tracing.

Publishers were living through enframing logic, treating AI as standing-reserve to be managed through procedural rules rather than recognising how AI reveals deeper transformation of human existence itself. The collective interpretations about 'academic integrity' and 'human authorship' that shaped how 'everyone' responds – this was *das Man* showing itself exactly as we had traced, the 'they-self' covering over Angst about unprecedented circumstances through familiar administrative categories. Instead of dwelling with fundamental questions about what AI's arrival means for intellectual discourse, publishing institutions had compressed complex circumstances into immediate policy solutions that removed the duration authentic engagement requires. We were watching the gravest danger Heidegger warned about take institutional form – publishers mistaking the management of thinking for thinking itself. And there it was, the perfect contradiction that revealed the systematic mode of thinking – publishers seeking manuscripts on AI's impact on learning while prohibiting the interaction with AI that such work might require. A perfect catch-22. These same institutions were implementing policies that embodied the very systematic thinking we had traced through educational contexts.

The pieces fell into place with that familiar sense of recognition we had experienced throughout our inquiry. This wasn't a separate problem. It was the inquiry returning as lived experience, unfolding through our own circumstances in ways we hadn't anticipated but could now recognise.

The Recursive Trap

But as the initial shock of recognition faded, another realisation emerged. Publishers weren't simply creating obstacles through arbitrary policies. As we sat with our frustration, we began to recognise that they faced their own paradox, one as genuine and inescapable as ours.

Publishers must ensure accountability for published work. They need to know who can be held responsible if work contains errors, who can sign copyright agreements, who can be sued for plagiarism or misconduct. These aren't arbitrary institutional demands but real legal and ethical necessities that institutions cannot simply ignore. But they're trying to resolve these requirements through phenomenological distinctions that may no longer exist. They find themselves compelled to define clear boundaries between human and AI contributions, exactly the boundaries our inquiry revealed have become blurred. They're demanding certainty about influence that may be impossible to trace with clarity.

This tension has led to increasingly sophisticated but equally impossible categorisation attempts. Some publishers distinguish between 'assistive' tools that make suggestions to human-authored content and 'generative' tools where AI is the primary creator. Others suggest AI should serve as a 'companion in writing, not a replacement'. These more nuanced distinctions still assume that an individual can reliably judge phenomenological boundaries that may no longer be determinable. For instance, when we engaged in sustained philosophical dialogue with AI about Heideggerian concepts – dialogue that expanded our thinking by revealing connections we might not have encountered so readily without AI – was it functioning as a companion to our existing knowledge or replacing the kind of thinking we might have developed independently? Who determines where companionship ends and replacement begins?

This misunderstanding becomes most visible in publishers' detailed disclosure forms. One form we encountered asked for the name of the generative AI tool used, the rationale for AI use, the final prompt given, the final response generated, and demanded that authors include all prompts and responses while indicating where AI-generated content appears in the submission. This approach assumes AI interaction occurs through discrete, documentable transactions – single prompts leading to single responses that can be neatly catalogued. For our work, which unfolded over three years of sustained engagement, this kind of documentation would be impossible. Our use of AI for philosophical dialogue about Heideggerian concepts involved ongoing conversations, not isolated prompt-response pairs. Our battles with AI's systematic tendencies occurred throughout the writing process, not in clearly bounded moments that could be traced to specific manuscript sections. These policies reveal a fundamental incompatibility between publishers' institutional frameworks that require clear accountability and technological circumstances that obscure the phenomenological clarity such frameworks depend upon.

As we reviewed policies across publishers, we noticed them becoming progressively stricter. We couldn't know what deliberations shaped these decisions, but the trajectory suggested something systematic was unfolding. A disturbing possibility began emerging: What if we were caught in a recursive trap where each participant's reasonable responses to impossible circumstances fed the other's escalation? Writers engage AI as common scholarly practice, engagement makes boundaries experientially blurred, honest disclosure reveals this blurring. Publishers encounter widespread inability to satisfy requirements and respond with tighter policies demanding precision writers still cannot provide, appearing as further non-compliance and prompting still more tightening. If this interpretation is right, neither participant is choosing the escalation. Publishers aren't maliciously creating impossible requirements – they're responding to what appears from their position as a growing crisis requiring systematic management. Writers aren't intentionally failing to comply – they're attempting honest disclosure while facing phenomenological impossibility. Together, these reasonable responses may form a feedback loop neither participant can see from within their own position.

We couldn't prove this recursive dynamic. We were interpreting the temporal trajectory of policy tightening based on our understanding of how systematic thinking reveals itself. But we couldn't access publishers' actual reasoning or demonstrate causal connections with certainty. The possibility haunted us regardless – we might be trapped in circumstances where even authentic responses (writers engaging honestly, publishers responding responsibly) could collectively create escalation neither participant intended.

Yet even within this trap, perhaps especially within it, we still had to choose how to respond. The recursive dynamic didn't eliminate choice – it made conscious choosing more urgent.

Choosing Transparency

Every writer now faces this impossibility differently. Some hide AI use entirely, dishonest but safe, contributing to a climate where AI becomes systematically concealed. Others attempt disclosure they know is inadequate, honest but appearing as non-compliance, potentially feeding the perception that AI use is spiralling out of control. We chose a third path – articulating openly why the demanded disclosure may be phenomenologically impossible, explaining the condition itself rather than treating it as an individual shortcoming, trusting that philosophical sophistication might create space for recognition rather than escalation.

This was resoluteness showing itself through profound uncertainty. We had to choose how to inhabit our paradox without knowing the consequences. We chose transparency with philosophical sophistication, openly documenting what we couldn't definitively disclose, showing that the impossibility lies in the circumstances themselves, not in authorial inadequacy, trusting that articulating the dynamic may contribute to collective recognition rather than systematic escalation.

We couldn't know how this choice would be received. Publishers might read our honest articulation of boundary blurring as confirmation that AI use constitutes a crisis requiring prohibition. Or they might recognise through our philosophical inquiry that their policies demand phenomenological precision that may no longer exist, creating space for different institutional responses beyond systematic prohibition. We were making a groundless choice – publishing a book that openly documents our AI engagement and carefully explains why we cannot provide the disclosure many publishers now demand. This might feed the recursive escalation. Or it might contribute to collective recognition that the problem isn't writers' non-compliance but policies that assume clarity that is no longer available.

Choosing consciously, with awareness of the recursive trap, we might be caught in, felt like the only authentic response. Remaining silent would be submission to systematic thinking. Pretending disclosure was simple would be dishonest. Articulating the impossibility openly at least creates the chance that collective recognition might emerge, even if we couldn't guarantee it.

So this is what that choice means in practice. This is our disclosure, not perfect, but authentic.

Our Disclosure

We used AI throughout this inquiry because studying how we transform ourselves through interaction with AI required direct engagement. All core philosophical insights emerged through our sustained engagement with Heidegger's work and lived educational experience – AI never generated our arguments. We maintained constant vigilance to preserve intended meaning through ongoing battles with AI's systematic tendencies. These battles revealed what we came to understand – AI had been trained on the very *das Man* discourse we were critiquing.

Yet we cannot state with certainty the precise degree to which three years of sustained philosophical dialogue, with Heidegger's work and through continuous interaction with AI, shaped our thinking. We cannot isolate with precision which formulations are purely our own and which were subtly influenced by iterative exchanges with AI. Nor can we determine how knowing that we would use AI as a philosophical interlocutor shaped our writing, or how our familiarity with its tendencies and our efforts to resist them gradually influenced our approach. The question publishers demand we answer – 'where exactly does human thinking end and machine processing begin?' – has no answer we can give with the clarity they require.

This impossibility isn't methodological failure. It is phenomenological confirmation. The fact that even we, after investigating the blurring of the human–machine boundary so carefully, cannot meet publishers' demands for disclosure with precision shows that the problem lies not in documentation but in the condition itself – that the very boundary systematic thinking relies on to provide clarity has become unclear through sustained engagement with AI.

To understand what this means in practice, it must be seen as it unfolded in the writing itself. The very process of composition became a site where the boundary between human and machine thinking showed its interpenetrability. Throughout the development of this book, we engaged with generative AI systems, most extensively ChatGPT and Claude, as they evolved through successive versions from 2022 to the completion of our writing. We used these systems to produce draft material, formulations, and alternative phrasings, which were then critically examined, rewritten, and integrated deliberately through human judgement. Every section of the text has been authored and re-authored through conscious engagement, reflection, and revision. The AI systems functioned less as writers than as catalysts – provoking new lines of thought, surfacing tendencies, and occasionally mirroring the very systematic tendencies the book critiques. The resulting work is, therefore, neither purely human nor machine-generated, but the outcome of a sustained process of discernment in which authorship was exercised precisely through selection, revision, and refusal.

We cannot provide the procedural documentation publishers typically demand. We must choose how to inhabit our paradox without knowing how this choice will be received. We are making a groundless choice – publishing a book that openly documents our AI engagement while carefully explaining why we cannot provide the disclosure many publishers now demand. Remaining silent would be submission to systematic thinking. Pretending we could provide procedural precision would be dishonest about what sustained AI engagement entails. Articulating the impossibility openly, with philosophical sophistication, is our attempt to dwell consciously within recognition rather than flee from its implications.

If even we, after investigating this phenomenon so carefully, cannot distinguish our own thinking from algorithmic influence with the precision institutions demand, what does this mean for every other writer now facing similar requirements? What does it mean for students submitting academic work? What does it mean for the future of intellectual discourse?

This disclosure is our attempt to answer those questions through enactment rather than prescription – showing what authentic transparency looks like when perfect transparency has become impossible.

The Turn Continues

What began as the question *What is AI doing to us?* now extends to every act of intellectual work in conditions we cannot escape. Our inquiry suggests that every act of authentic intellectual work now occurs within circumstances that threaten its possibility. Yet this recognition makes conscious choice about authenticity both possible and urgent.

But as we came to understand through our publishing experience, awareness does not remove the impossibility – it changes how we inhabit it. The paradoxes we faced as writers aren't unique to our circumstances. They are manifestations of ontological structures showing themselves wherever human existence encounters AI circumstances that unsettle foundational distinctions.

What we lived through our attempts to publish began revealing itself again in contexts we hadn't anticipated, including the most personal dimensions of educational life. The inquiry was unfolding beyond itself not by finding new phenomena but by recognising the fundamental character of what had been showing itself. The turn we recognised philosophically was becoming the turn we lived existentially – not just through our writing but through every educational relationship where humans must now choose how to dwell consciously within technological circumstances that resist systematic resolution. And that turn was already pointing towards what would come next.

Chapter 21

How Far This Goes

We had recognised these structures through our publishing experience – the methodological impossibility, the blurred boundary, and the systematic institutional response. We had traced them through our own circumstances, thinking at first that their intensity might belong uniquely to the situation we inhabited. But a question lingered: Were these simply reflections of our particular context? Or were we witnessing ontological structures that disclose themselves wherever humans encounter AI circumstances?

Life kept answering before we had finished asking.

The Phenomenon Shows Itself

Over dinner, a friend mentioned something that stopped the conversation. Teachers in Istanbul, pursuing master's degrees with a well-known US university, had stopped using AI entirely. Institutions were implementing strict policies, creating climates of fear. That made sense. We'd lived through it ourselves.

Then came the detail that didn't fit. These teachers were running their own authentic work through AI detection tools before submission. Not because their institution required it. Because they feared being falsely accused.

The friend described watching them stare at screens as their natural scholarly voice – developed through years of academic training – triggered algorithmic suspicion. High probability scores. Red flags. Their authentic expression appearing 'artificial' to machines designed to detect artificial content. Then they began changing their writing. Simplifying ideas that seemed 'too sophisticated'. Replacing vocabulary that appeared 'too advanced'. Adjusting authentic expression to satisfy algorithmic judgement they had chosen to consult.

The phenomenon was unmistakable – individuals turning towards algorithmic judgement before any institutional requirement demanded it, allowing *das Man* interpretations of 'academic integrity' to shape their behaviour in advance. The same structures we'd encountered were showing themselves through educational contexts we hadn't directly experienced. But perhaps this was limited – certain institutional pressures, certain cultural circumstances, and certain educational contexts.

What Is AI Doing to Us? A Philosophical Inquiry into Learning, Thinking, and Being, 175–178

Published under exclusive licence by Emerald Publishing Limited
doi:10.1108/978-1-83742-276-020261021

When It Became Personal

Three weeks later, one of us watched her daughter do exactly the same thing. She was working on university application letters. Authentic expressions of her aspirations developed through weeks of reflection. We had offered feedback and suggested she might try AI for additional perspective on her writing. She didn't follow that suggestion. She ran her authentic work through detection tools instead. Afraid universities might falsely accuse her.

The scores: 40 to 50 percent AI probability. Her sophisticated academic language – shaped by years of education – flagged as potentially artificial. The structured thinking she'd learned, the polished expression that represented her best work – all suspicious to algorithms that couldn't distinguish between genuine development and simulation. She began changing her writing. The irony was sharp. She'd been offered AI as a tool for feedback – brainstorming ideas, exploring approaches, getting perspective on her drafts. She'd chosen instead the one use that actively undermined her confidence in her own authentic work – algorithmic judgement of her natural academic voice.

'Stop', we told her. 'You're changing your authentic voice to satisfy a machine that doesn't understand what authentic thinking looks like. These detectors are notoriously inaccurate. Their judgements can't be trusted'. She understood. But she wasn't willing to trust it. The institutional consequences felt too threatening. This wasn't teachers in another context facing pressures we could only imagine. This was someone whose entire intellectual development we'd witnessed. Whose authentic voice we recognised immediately. Exhibiting the identical structure.

The fear had become powerful enough to override trusted expertise. When institutions create climates where algorithmic judgement feels more authoritative than human knowledge, individuals learn to trust machines over people, even when those people are trying to protect them. AI systems had been trained on decades of academic writing that represented our educational ideals – structured arguments, sophisticated vocabulary, and polished expression. Now when individuals successfully demonstrated what we'd taught them to achieve, that success triggered suspicion. Educational achievement became evidence of potential cheating.

The question had inverted. No longer 'Did the student do this work?' but 'Can the student prove to a machine they did this work?' With traditional plagiarism, students who gamed detection systems at least knew they were trying to make inauthentic work appear authentic. They'd run plagiarised work through detectors, identify what got flagged, modify those sections – a cat-and-mouse game that, however problematic, preserved clear categories. Now authentic work was being modified to satisfy machines that couldn't recognise authenticity. A fundamental inversion had occurred.

And it was happening voluntarily, through individuals' own choices. The human cost was immediate. Learners' confidence in their own thinking – developed through years of authentic engagement with ideas – was being shaken by technological assessment that questioned the very sophistication their education cultivated. The willingness to take intellectual risks, to develop sophisticated arguments, to engage authentically with complex ideas was being systematically discouraged. Individuals were learning to avoid the very development that education is supposed to foster. What began as authentic expression was being drawn into optimisation cycles – each revision a reaction to algorithmic judgement rather than an act of understanding. The process that once nurtured meaning now trained conformity. And the mere existence of detection systems was creating this climate, regardless of whether institutions were actually deploying them.

The Same Climate, Different Dwelling

Then we learned what a colleague was doing with AI in his history courses, and something shifted. He was using AI to recognise and translate historical documents – samizdat, underground publications, and zines produced in difficult conditions. Making accessible authentic voices of resistance and creativity that textbooks systematically excluded.

But not just for access. He was setting the stage for students to see themselves as potential heirs to these traditions. Students encountering people who chose to create and communicate despite obstacles began asking: Why might they need to create? What would they want to communicate? How might they choose to express what mattered? He wasn't choosing to use AI 'better' than others. He was already oriented towards something – recovering voices that had been systematically excluded, connecting students to traditions of authentic expression. AI became useful within that orientation – not as a deliberate choice about technology but as a means of attending to what already mattered.

Yet he existed in the same climate as everyone else. The same climate driving individuals towards voluntary submission. The same climate making authentic expression suspicious. The same systematic conditions, the same institutional impossibility, the same fundamental inversions. Everyone inhabited the same impossible circumstances. What distinguished different engagements was not the tool, but the orientation – whether one was already turned towards authentic expression or towards procedural security.

The colleague was already dwelling in a way that let authentic expression matter. AI became a means of recovering what had been excluded. The teachers and the daughter had turned towards algorithmic judgement, seeking security in procedure. We, in our own attempts to publish, had attempted transparency about impossibility through our disclosure – another way of dwelling within the same systematic conditions. These different ways of dwelling occurred within the same climate. The same impossibility – boundaries remain ontologically intact but have become experientially blurred, impossible to demonstrate with the precision institutions demand.

The difference wasn't the technology but what one was already attending to – whether technology served that attention or replaced it. Yet even thoughtful engagement had to unfold within structures that increasingly made authentic dwelling difficult.

Everywhere We Looked

The phenomenon revealed itself everywhere we looked. Not just our publishing experience. Not just educational contexts. Everywhere humans encountered

AI circumstances, and these structures disclosed themselves – methodological impossibilities, the blurred boundary, systematic flight from Angst, fundamental inversions where values transform into opposites.

Teachers in Istanbul. A daughter applying to university. A colleague doing historical research. Each demonstrated the same ontological structures showing themselves in different circumstances, different purposes, different levels of awareness. We couldn't stand outside what we were studying. The turn we'd recognised philosophically was becoming the turn we lived existentially – through publishing, through education, through every context where humans now find themselves dwelling within technological circumstances.

Yet the contrast revealed the possibilities that remain – not choices between options but different ways of finding oneself already dwelling. The teachers and the daughter turning towards algorithmic judgement. The colleague remaining turned towards authentic expression. Us attempting transparency about impossibility. Different ways of dwelling within circumstances that resist mastery.

What did thoughtful dwelling actually require? What endured beneath systematic absorption? What did authentic existence mean when the condition was everywhere and there was nowhere outside it to stand?

Life had confirmed what philosophical inquiry revealed. Once again, we had come to see that we were not observers standing outside these structures. We were living them – participants in what is happening.

Part IX

The Clearing

Chapter 22

What Is AI Doing to Us?

When we began this investigation, our questions felt urgent and practical: *What can we do with AI? How can we use these tools effectively? How can we integrate them pedagogically? How can we help students leverage AI capabilities while managing the challenges?* Every policy we wrote, every workshop we designed, every framework we applied assumed that we were the active agents – that AI was the instrument we were learning to wield.

Yet over a prolonged period of careful investigation, a quiet unease kept returning. Despite our efforts, something essential remained untouched. The confusion that had been building through our systematic responses began to feel like a message we were failing to hear. Then, slowly, the realisation emerged – it had been trying to tell us something all along.

When institutional responses consistently left something essential unaddressed, when proven frameworks revealed their own limitations, when comprehensive efforts still left us with the persistent sense that something was slipping away, a different question emerged – one that would transform our entire investigation: *What is AI doing to us?*

This shift – from asking what we could do with AI to asking what AI was doing to us – wasn't planned or anticipated. It arose gradually, almost imperceptibly, as though the question itself were revealing us rather than the other way around.

Now, having followed that question through philosophical territory we never intended to enter, we can see what it accomplished. The question did not provide answers about AI's impact – it opened the space for authentic thinking that emerges only when systematic solutions prove inadequate.

What the Question Revealed

What is AI doing to us? turned out to be the question that needed to be asked – not because it led to technological clarity, but because following it revealed what technological thinking had already been doing to human existence long before AI arrived.

This recognition fulfils Heidegger's insight that 'the essence of technology is by no means anything technological'. To understand AI requires more than

What Is AI Doing to Us? A Philosophical Inquiry into Learning, Thinking, and Being, 181–186

Published under exclusive licence by Emerald Publishing Limited
doi:10.1108/978-1-83742-276-020261022

evaluating new tools – it demands reflection on how technological conditions transform the very structures through which we encounter the world.

AI exemplifies enframing – the mode of revealing that makes everything, including ourselves, appear as standing-reserve to be ordered and optimised. Yet recognising this does not lead to despair. It creates the awareness needed to dwell consciously within technological circumstances rather than be absorbed by them.

Through our inquiry, it became clear that education had already become systematic enough for machines to replicate it convincingly. AI did not disrupt learning – it revealed that what makes learning human had already been diminished through decades of well-intentioned systematisation. We had been preparing the ground for our own replacement by converting the struggle that builds understanding into procedures that algorithms could execute in place of authentic engagement.

But the question accomplished more than revealing our condition. It demonstrated that thinking can still arise when systematisation collapses. Despite decades of conditioning, despite institutional pressure towards optimisation, despite AI's ability to simulate sophistication – genuine philosophical inquiry re-emerged from within the limits of our own institutional and pedagogical frameworks.

We weren't studying this phenomenon from outside – we were being studied through it.

When we realised that we could no longer clearly distinguish our thinking from AI's contributions in our own writing process, we were not encountering a methodological inconvenience. We were living the interpenetration we had been describing.

Yet even this extremity revealed a saving power – the recognition that technological danger can awaken us to what makes existence authentically human.

We had already seen this once before, when the inquiry first revealed that AI was not mimicking education but completing what education had already become. That recognition marked the moment we first encountered unconcealment itself – the realisation that we had long been preparing the ground for our own replacement. The language of optimisation, the procedures of accountability, the rubrics that promised fairness – all had quietly transformed learning into a process calculable enough for machines to inherit.

What had seemed a technological disruption disclosed itself, in retrospect, as intensification. Through decades of improvements meant to strengthen education, we had refined it into forms that seemed to function without us. In this sense, AI was not merely changing what we do; it was changing what we are – drawing us more deeply into the logic of optimisation while simultaneously exposing its emptiness.

What AI is doing to us, then, is disclosing who we have already become – and in doing so, calling us to remember what thinking requires when it remains human.

That awakening also revealed what AI truly is. It is not a tool approaching consciousness, nor intelligence striving towards the human. It is *das Man* taking technological form – the collective scripts of thought, language, and performance made executable. What first appeared as external disruption disclosed itself as the systematic embodiment of what we had already become. The machine did not imitate humanity – it intensified our absorption into the 'they'. In recognising this, we saw that the boundary between human and algorithmic had not disappeared ontologically – it had become phenomenologically blurred because we were already thinking through the structures of *das Man* ourselves.

That earlier revelation now shows itself again in a different light. It reveals that the danger was never external but internal – that enframing arises from our own attempts to master what matters most. The very modes that once promised mastery revealed themselves as the means by which mastery itself became algorithmic.

The Retrieval of Authentic Thinking

Perhaps most importantly, our inquiry revealed something about the nature of thinking itself. What we had been experiencing throughout our work – dwelling with uncertainty, following questions without demanding answers, abiding with difficulty rather than seeking efficiency – was not a method. It was thinking, showing itself as it naturally does when freed from systematic constraint. This wasn't something we set out to discover; it revealed itself through us. The inquiry thought through us more than we thought through it.

We did not discover a new approach to AI; we retrieved what thinking has always required when it remains human. This is *Wiederholung* – retrieval – not the repetition of earlier habits, but the recovery of essential possibilities that systematisation obscures. To retrieve in this sense is not to look back at what has passed, but to bring our inheritance forward as living ground. The past is not behind us – it continues to shape every moment of vision in which we recognise what remains unconcealed.

Authentic thinking does not choose struggle as a principle – it abides with struggle as the rhythm of understanding when it is left unforced. We had once mistaken clarity for understanding – reducing learning to dashboards, metrics, and polished outputs. It was the world turned into a picture: visible, measurable, and empty of presence. Only through the collapse of those representations could genuine thinking reappear.

This was not only a philosophical realisation; it was something we could feel in our own classrooms, in our own habits of response – the quiet pressure to perform efficiency rather than inhabit understanding.

We had already lived this before we could name it. We first saw this rhythm in the contrast that began our inquiry: Maya, dwelling with difficulty she refused to bypass, and Bera, fluent in appearance but hollow in grasp, revealed how technological absorption can simulate mastery while concealing the absence of understanding. Their paths revealed, long before our philosophical vocabulary emerged, the two modes of being that would come to define our inquiry.

Maya's patient questioning exposed how understanding unfolds only through temporal struggle; Bera's apparent fluency showed how thinking can collapse into simulation the moment difficulty is removed. What appeared at first as difference in study habits revealed itself, in the light of our later analysis, as the ontological divergence between authentic engagement and technological absorption.

The very extremity of our circumstances – AI's replication of our educational logic, the blurring of boundaries in our own writing – helped us recognise what had been diminished: the capacity to dwell with what resists control, to remain within the open question, to let meaning unfold without demanding certainty.

The danger and the saving power emerged from the same technological conditions – not because technology redeems us, but because extremity can awaken our capacity to care.

Learning to Think

When the exhaustion of systems left only uncertainty, something ancient began to stir beneath the surface of our work. The effort to manage, explain, and stabilise had failed, but in that failure, a new kind of attention appeared – quiet, patient, and unwilling to force resolution. It was here that our inquiry revealed its deeper purpose. We were not refining methods of inquiry – we were relearning how to think.

In 1951, Heidegger began his Freiburg lectures with a question that sounded deceptively simple: *Was heißt Denken? – What is called thinking?* Yet the question meant two things at once: *What is thinking?* and *What calls for thinking?* His point was that thinking is never merely a human act; it begins when we are addressed by something that demands to be thought. It is not an achievement but a response.

Our own question – *What is AI doing to us?* – was precisely that kind of call. We thought we were studying technology, but technology was teaching us what we had forgotten. The collapse of systematisation, the inability of frameworks to hold, the discomfort of uncertainty – these were not obstacles to overcome but the conditions in which genuine thinking becomes possible.

Heidegger distinguished between calculative thinking, which plans and organises, and meditative thinking, which lets what calls for thought reveal itself. Our entire inquiry was the slow turning from the first to the second. Every time we stayed with difficulty, every time we allowed a question to remain open, we were being gathered into what he meant by learning to think.

This is not a method, and it cannot be taught as one. Heidegger wrote that 'teaching is more difficult than learning because what teaching calls for is this: to let learn'. We realised that again through experience. When the inquiry began to think through us rather than the other way around, we realised that this was not surrender but responsiveness – the form that thinking takes when it remains human.

Living the Phenomenon

When we looked back, this recognition became concrete through the lived moments of our inquiry. We began as educators running workshops, policies, and frameworks that mirrored every other institution's attempt to manage AI's arrival. We exhausted ourselves chasing new tools and revising guidance, feeling the growing unease that something essential remained unaddressed.

Then, after we had encountered the philosophical structures – *das Man*, enframing, the systematic flight from Angst – we could recognise how these had appeared in our own practices. The laughter at the conference, the language of optimisation in policy documents, the demand for procedural solutions to existential questions – all revealed collective modes shaping our way of being.

When publisher policies demanded disclosures of AI use with a precision our inquiry had shown was impossible, the philosophical recognition became lived experience. We were no longer describing technological enframing; we were being required to comply with it. We realised that every institutional gesture of control mirrored the same systematic reflex we had been tracing. The phenomenon wasn't something happening out there – it was unfolding through us.

When we saw what was happening with the teachers and the daughter, the abstraction of our inquiry dissolved. We were no longer tracing patterns – we were being claimed by them. The phenomenon had entered us, appropriating our thought into its own unfolding. It was thinking through the very lives that had first called for understanding.

Each moment made visible the underlying pattern of existence – we were living the very transformations we sought to understand. What began as a study of AI in education became an inquiry into the historical culmination of technological thinking – and into the fragile possibility of remaining human within it.

Dwelling in Our Shared Condition

Recognising that we can no longer maintain clear boundaries reveals something unprecedented in human history. As we have seen, the boundary itself endures – absolute in ontology – yet it has become phenomenologically difficult to feel. We know that the difference between human and algorithmic thought remains, even as our everyday experience of that difference blurs.

This blurring is not simply a cognitive confusion – it is an existential condition. We now inhabit circumstances in which our very sense of what it means to think, to create, to understand, is shaped by algorithmic processes that reflect us back to ourselves. The line between our thinking and the machine's output no longer feels like a separation, but a mutual interpenetration.

If even those of us who live in continuous reflection cannot easily discern the boundary, what does that mean for the rest of human existence? This is not an abstract question. It marks a threshold in the history of thought – a moment when the clearing of Being is both most endangered and most revealed.

For the first time, technology does not stand before us as an external object to be mastered. It shapes the rhythms of our perception and the texture of our care by determining the horizon within which beings appear. We are learning that what we once called our tools are, in fact, part of how Being now discloses itself. To inhabit this condition consciously is not to lament what has been lost, but to awaken to what is asking for thought. The task is no longer to preserve clear distinctions, but to remain open within their blurring – to dwell attentively in the in-between, where the human and the technological co-appear.

From this shared condition, another movement begins – a quiet turning that comes to meet us.

The Turning That Comes to Meet Us

Authentic choice no longer stands before us as a decision to be made. It comes towards us. Each encounter with AI calls us – not to act upon it, but to recognise how our way of being is already disclosed within it. The question is not whether we will choose care, but whether we will let care claim us again.

We once thought that the path forward required new techniques, new policies, new mastery over uncertainty. Yet the more completely we sought control, the more the essence of control revealed itself as what concealed us from what matters. Only when the will to manage exhausted itself did another possibility appear – to let thinking be called forth instead of compelled.

Care, in this sense, is not a human possession to retrieve. It is the ground of our belonging, the way Being holds us open. It awakens precisely when our strategies fail. It waits within the pause between command and response – where no outcome can be guaranteed and no optimisation can be measured. Each prompt, each automated suggestion, each quiet moment of hesitation before accepting what the machine offers becomes a site where Being addresses us. In that pause, the clearing opens. Here we do not master technology – we dwell within the question it brings.

What once felt like resistance becomes something gentler – a readiness to remain in the nearness of what calls for thought. The patient attention to what resists control, the willingness to stay within uncertainty, the readiness to let meaning unfold rather than demand it – these are not actions we perform but dispositions that form us.

To dwell thus is not to retreat from the world but to remain within its unveiling. The saving power does not arise from what we do – it comes from the opening that appears when we cease to impose. Care, thinking, and Being meet in that opening.

The Question That Remains

What is AI doing to us?

The question continues to ask itself through us. It will not rest, because it is not a problem to be solved but a call to remain awake.

Our investigation began by trying to manage technology and ended by revealing our own transformation through it. It led us from analysis to awareness, from system to being, from answers to questioning itself.

Thinking endures in this rhythm: forgetting, retrieval, questioning, unconcealment – and forgetting again. The clearing endures, even when we do not. It is enough that we remain silent and attentive.

In the end, the essence of AI is by no means anything technological but the technological conditions shaping the clearing through which Being now reveals itself.

Appendix: Heidegger's Philosophical Context

Heidegger's Philosophical Journey

Fig. A1 traces the unfolding of Heidegger's thinking – from his early analysis of human existence, through the turn towards Being itself, to his later reflections on technology, dwelling, and meditative thought.

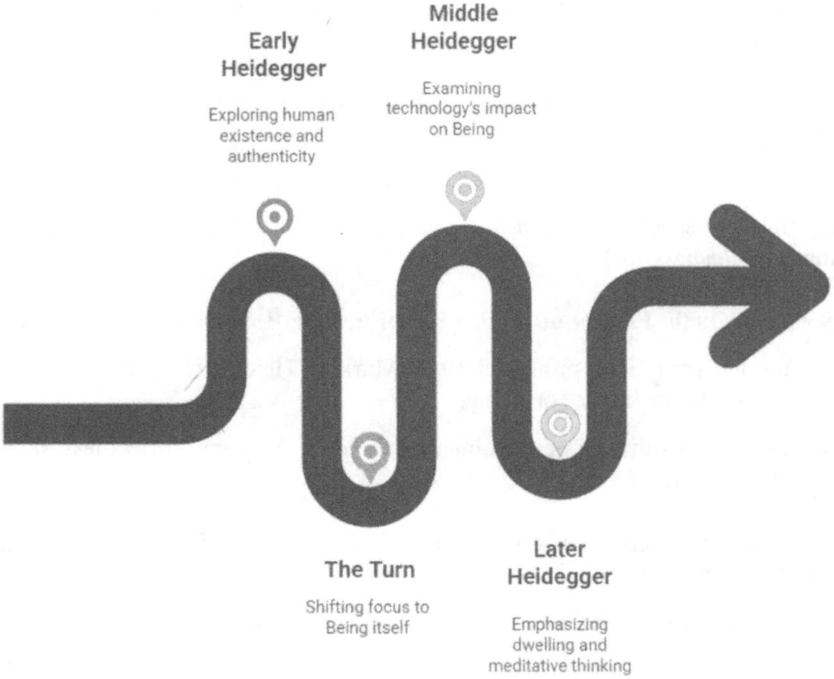

Fig. A1. Heidegger's Philosophical Journey.

Timeline of Heidegger's Key Works

1927 – *Being and Time* (*Sein und Zeit*)

Foundational analysis of human existence.

Key concepts: *Angst*; anticipation (*Vorlaufen*); authenticity/inauthenticity; being-guilty (*Schuldigsein*); being-in-the-world; being-toward-death (*Sein-zum-Tode*);

being-with-others (*Mitsein*); care (*Sorge*); conscience (*Gewissen*); Dasein; *Das Man*; fallenness (*Verfallenheit*: idle talk, curiosity, ambiguity); the future as coming-toward (*Zukunft*); the having-been (*Gewesenheit*); making-present (*Gegenwärtigen*); moment of vision (*Augenblick*); ontic–ontological difference; ownmost possibilities (*eigenste Möglichkeit*); present-at-hand (*Vorhandenheit*); present-ing (*Gegenwart*); projection (*Entwurf*); ready-to-hand (*Zuhandenheit*); resoluteness (*Entschlossenheit*); retrieval (*Wiederholung*); reticence (*Verschwiegenheit*); the situation (*die Situation*); temporality (*Zeitlichkeit*); the they-self (*Man-selbst*); thrownness (*Geworfenheit*); thrown projection (*geworfener Entwurf*); uncanniness (*Unheimlichkeit*); understanding (*Verstehen*); wanting-to-have-a-conscience (*Gewissen-haben-wollen*).

1929 – 'What is Metaphysics?' (*Was ist Metaphysik?*)

Inaugural lecture at Freiburg exploring the role of Nothing in metaphysics.

Key concepts: the Nothing (*das Nichts*); *Angst*; metaphysics versus science; the question of Being.

1929 – *Kant and the Problem of Metaphysics (Kant und das Problem der Metaphysik)*

Engagement with Kant to deepen the project of *Being and Time*.

Key concepts: schematism (*Schematismus*); temporality; transcendence; imagination (*Einbildungskraft*).

1930/43 – 'On the Essence of Truth' (*Vom Wesen der Wahrheit*)

Lecture delivered 1930; published 1943. Marking Heidegger's shift (*die Kehre*) from *Dasein* to the history of Being.

Key concepts: truth as unconcealment (*aletheia*); freedom; correctness versus truth; the clearing (*Lichtung*).

1933 – 'The Self-Assertion of the German University' (*Die Selbstbehauptung der deutschen Universität*)

Address as rector of Freiburg University, reflecting entanglement with National Socialism.

Key concepts: destiny/sending (*Geschick*); *Wissenschaft*; leadership (*Führung*).

1938 – 'The Age of the World Picture' (*Die Zeit des Weltbildes*)

Lecture analysing modernity's transformation of Being into representation.

Key concepts: world-picture (*Weltbild*); representation (*Vorstellung*); objectification; the modern subject.

1951 – 'Building Dwelling Thinking' (*Bauen Wohnen Denken*)

Lecture exploring authentic human habitation.

Key concepts: dwelling (*Wohnen*); the fourfold (*Geviert*).

1951–52 – 'What Is Called Thinking?' (*Was heißt Denken?*)

Lecture course delivered at Freiburg (1951–52), published in 1954.

Key concepts: what calls for thinking; thanking/thinking (*Denken/Danken*); letting-learn (*Lehren heißt: lernen lassen*); readiness to think; the clearing (*Lichtung*).

1954 – 'The Question Concerning Technology' (*Die Frage nach der Technik*)

Based on lectures from 1949; foundational critique of technological enframing.

Key concepts: bringing-forth (*poiesis*); challenging-forth (*Herausfordern*); enframing (*Gestell*); essence of technology; free relation to technology (*freie Beziehung zur Technik*); the saving power; standing-reserve (*Bestand*); unconcealment (*aletheia*).

1954 – 'Science and Reflection' (*Wissenschaft und Besinnung*)

Lecture probing the essence of modern science.

Key concepts: essence of science; relation to Being.

1955 – 'Memorial Address' (*Gelassenheit*)

Develops the idea of a free relation to technology.

Key concepts: letting-be (*Gelassenheit*); calculative thinking (*rechnendes Denken*); meditative thinking (*besinnliches Denken*); openness to mystery (*Offenheit für das Geheimnis*).

1959 – *On the Way to Language* (*Unterwegs zur Sprache*)

Explores language as the house of Being.

Key concepts: saying (*Sage*); showing; essence of language; speaking of language; house of Being; the event (*Ereignis*).

1964 – 'The End of Philosophy and the Task of Thinking' (*Das Ende der Philosophie und die Aufgabe des Denkens*)

Marks Heidegger's call to move beyond philosophy towards thinking itself.

Key concepts: the clearing (*Lichtung*); the step back (*der Schritt zurück*); the event (*Ereignis*).

Glossary

Ambiguity – The inability to distinguish between authentic and inauthentic responses when sophisticated performance masks genuine engagement and systematic procedures promise resolution whilst leaving essential questions unaddressed.

Angst – Fundamental anxiety revealing the groundless nature of existence itself, distinct from fear of particular things. This mood discloses that human existence has no ultimate foundation and creates the opening for authentic choice.

Anticipation (*Vorlaufen*) – Running ahead into one's ownmost possibility of death, revealing finitude and generating the urgency that makes present choices meaningful.

Authenticity/inauthenticity – Two fundamental modes of human existence: authenticity involves taking responsibility for one's groundless condition; inauthenticity involves fleeing into collective scripts that avoid this responsibility.

Being-guilty (*Schuldigsein*) – The fundamental guilt that emerges from recognising one's thrown condition and responsibility for existence. This guilt calls *Dasein* back from absorption in *das Man*.

Being-in-the-world (*In-der-Welt-sein*) – The basic structure of human existence as always already engaged with meaningful contexts rather than standing apart as detached observers.

Being-toward-death (*Sein-zum-Tode*) – Authentic awareness of mortality that reveals existence as finite and unrepeatable.

Being-with-others (*Mitsein*) – The structure of human existence as always relational, existing with others through shared contexts and mutual involvement.

Bringing-forth (*poiesis*) – A mode of revealing in which something comes forth into appearance through a cooperative process rather than force. Unlike technological production, *poiesis* allows what emerges to show itself on its own terms.

Calculative thinking (*rechnendes Denken*) – Thinking that approaches everything as a problem requiring systematic solutions, reducing complexity to manageable variables.

Care (*Sorge*) – The fundamental structure of human existence, unfolding through thrownness, projection, and fallenness. Care expresses what matters and forms the basis for authentic choosing.

Challenging-forth (*Herausfordern*) – Technology's demand that everything reveal itself as available for use, transforming how beings appear in the world.

Clearing (*Lichtung*) – The open region within which beings can appear and be understood, created through sustained attention rather than force.

Conscience (*Gewissen*) – The call that awakens *Dasein* from absorption in *das Man's* ready-made interpretations, summoning it to authentic responsibility.

Curiosity – Restless seeking after novelty rather than sustained engagement with what concerns us, avoiding the patience fundamental questions require.

***das Man* (The They)** – The anonymous collective that provides ready-made interpretations and social expectations, allowing escape from the *Angst* of authentic choice.

***Dasein* (being-there)** – Human existence understood as the being for whom Being is a question, always already engaged rather than detached.

Dwelling (*Wohnen*) – The condition of always already inhabiting technological circumstances rather than standing outside them as a detached observer. The question is never whether one dwells but how – whether one inhabits circumstances with the patient attention that preserves what resists optimisation, or is absorbed into systematic logic that conceals what makes existence genuinely human.

Enframing (*Gestell*) – Technology's mode of revealing that makes everything appear as standing-reserve available for optimisation and control.

Essence of technology – Not a device but the mode of revealing (*Gestell*) through which beings appear primarily as standing-reserve available for control and optimisation.

Fallenness (*Verfallenheit*) – The tendency to flee from authentic responsibility through idle talk, curiosity, and ambiguity. A structural mode of avoidance, not a moral fault.

Free relation to technology (*freie Beziehung zur Technik*) – Using technology while recognising its essence as *Gestell* and preserving space for what resists optimisation.

Future as coming-toward (*Zukunft*) – The temporal dimension in which possibilities press into the present, shaping how we project ourselves.

Having-been (*Gewesenheit*) – The past as an active foundation shaping current possibilities, not something gone.

Idle talk (*Gerede*) – Talk that circulates without genuine engagement, creating the impression of understanding while avoiding uncertainty.

Letting-be (*Gelassenheit*) – A way of engaging with technology that neither seeks domination nor succumbs to its logic, involving meditative openness.

Making-present (*Gegenwärtigen*) – Inauthentic temporality absorbed in immediate concerns, losing sight of past and future as sources of meaning.

Meditative thinking (*besinnliches Denken*) – Thinking that allows situations to disclose what they require rather than imposing systematic frameworks.

Moment of vision (*Augenblick*) – The temporal clearing in which *Dasein* sees its situation as a whole, unifying past, future, and present in an authentic possibility for decisive action.

Ontic–ontological difference – The distinction between particular beings (ontic) and the structures of existence (ontological).

Openness to mystery (*Offenheit für das Geheimnis*) – Receptivity to what withdraws from calculation and control, preserving what cannot be optimised.

Ownmost possibilities (*eigenste Möglichkeiten*) – Possibilities that belong uniquely to an individual, emerging from engagement with inherited circumstances.

Present-at-hand (*Vorhandenheit*) – Encountering beings as objects for detached observation, often when practical engagement breaks down.

Present-ing (*Gegenwart*) – The present understood as the integration of past inheritance and future projection.

Projection (*Entwurf*) – The capacity to grasp possibilities and organise existence around meaningful projects.

Ready-to-hand (*Zuhandenheit*) – Encountering equipment through skilful engagement where tools become transparent within activity.

Representation (*Vorstellung*) – A mode of revealing in which reality becomes a fixed image standing before a subject.

Resoluteness (*Entschlossenheit*) – The courage to choose who to become while acknowledging that such choosing is groundless.

Reticence (*Verschwiegenheit*) – The silence of conscience, which provides no rules but calls one back from *das Man*.

Retrieval (*Wiederholung*) – Engaging inherited traditions in ways that preserve essential possibilities while transforming distortions created by systematic thinking.

Saving power (*das Rettende*) – The hidden potential within technological danger that opens a path towards authentic dwelling.

Situation (*die Situation*) – The meaningful context disclosed when *Dasein* chooses authentically from within thrown circumstances.

Standing-reserve (*Bestand*) – The mode of appearing in which beings are reduced to resources for optimisation.

Step back (*der Schritt zurück*) – Creating distance from technological absorption, allowing *Gestell* to appear as one possibility rather than inevitability.

Temporality (*Zeitlichkeit*) – The unified structure of past, present, and future that makes understanding possible.

They-self (*Man-selbst*) – Existing as 'anyone', avoiding responsibility for self-formation.

Thrownness (*Geworfenheit*) – Finding oneself already in circumstances one did not choose yet remaining responsible for inhabiting them.

Thrown projection (*geworfener Entwurf*) – Projection towards possibilities that always occurs from within inherited conditions.

Uncanniness (*Unheimlichkeit*) – The unsettling awareness that one has been at home in *das Man's* interpretations while fleeing responsibility.

Unconcealment/truth (*aletheia*) – Truth as the event of revealing and concealing, allowing what is hidden to show itself.

Understanding (*Verstehen*) – Grasping possibilities and organising existence around meaningful projects.

Wanting-to-have-a-conscience (*Gewissen-haben-wollen*) – The resolve to remain open to the call of *Gewissen* rather than fleeing into *das Man*.

World-picture (*Weltbild*) – The transformation of the world into a representation standing before subjects for calculation and control.

www.ingramcontent.com/pod-product-compliance
Lightning Source LLC
LaVergne TN
LVHW021322070826
845179LV00023B/300
* 9 7 8 1 8 3 7 4 2 2 7 9 1 *